D0622739

TIME AND POWER

The Lawrence Stone Lectures

Sponsored by:
The Shelby Cullom Davis Center for Historical Studies and Princeton
University Press

A list of titles in this series appears at the back of the book.

Time and Power

VISIONS OF HISTORY IN
GERMAN POLITICS, FROM
THE THIRTY YEARS' WAR
TO THE THIRD REICH

Christopher Clark

PRINCETON UNIVERSITY PRESS

PRINCETON & OXFORD

T 134452

VISTA GRANDE
PUBLIC LIBRARY

Copyright © 2019 by Christopher Clark

Published by Princeton University Press
41 William Street, Princeton, New Jersey 08540
6 Oxford Street, Woodstock, Oxfordshire OX20 1TR

press.princeton.edu

All Rights Reserved

LCCN 2018960827
ISBN 978-0-691-18165-3

British Library Cataloging-in-Publication Data is available

Editorial: Brigitta van Rheinberg, Amanda Peery, and Eric Crahan
Production Editorial: Brigitte Pelner
Jacket Design: C. Alvarez-Gaffin
Jacket/Cover Credit: Jacket Images (left to right): 1) Frederick William, Elector
    of Brandenburg, 2) Frederick William II of Prussia, 3) Otto von Bismarck,
    4) Adolf Hitler
Production: Erin Suydam
Publicity: James Schneider
Copyeditor: Joseph Dahm

This book has been composed in Miller

Printed on acid-free paper ∞

Printed in the United States of America

10 9 8 7 6 5 4 3 2 1

To Kate and Justin Clark, siblings for all seasons

CONTENTS

ACKNOWLEDGEMENTS

IN THEORY, the pool of intellectual debt ought to shrink with each new book, as one grows older and more independent. In my experience, the opposite has been the case. As you get older, you get less shy about asking for help and you venture further into terrain where you depend on the guidance of others. This book could not have been written without the encouragement, conversation, and advice of many friends and colleagues. Special thanks go to the following, who read all or part of the manuscript and offered detailed comments and stimulating suggestions: Deborah Baker, David Barclay, Peter Burke, Marcus Colla, Amitav Ghosh, Oliver Haardt, Charlotte Johann, Duncan Kelly, Jürgen Luh, Annika Seemann, John Thompson, Adam Tooze, Alexandra Walsham, and Waseem Yaqoob. As then-anonymous reviewers for Princeton University Press, François Hartog, Jürgen Osterhammel, and Andy Rabinbach made enormously helpful comments on the manuscript. Nora Berend, Francisco de Bethencourt, Tim Blanning, Annabel Brett, Matthew Champion, Kate Clark, Allegra Fryxell, Alexander Geppert, Beatrice de Graaf, Paul Hartle, Ulrich Herbert, Shruti Kapila, Hans-Christof Kraus, Jonathan Lamb, Rose Melikan, Bridget Orr, Anna Ross, Kevin Rudd, Magnus Ryan, Martin Sabrow, and Quentin Skinner all offered precious advice on specific issues or passages of text. Nina Lübbren's writing and thinking about time and narrative in art have shaped the book in many ways. Josef and Alexander, once happy distractions from the work of writing, have grown into thoughtful conversation partners whose insights nudged me through various bottlenecks. Kristina Spohr read and commented on the text at many stages in its evolution and sustained its author with criticism, advice, and companionship.

The History Department of Princeton University gave me the opportunity to develop the ideas explored in this book by inviting me to present the Lawrence Stone Lectures in April 2015, and my thanks go to Brigitta van Rheinberg of Princeton University Press for her encouragement of this project from its inception and Brigitte Pelner, Amanda Peery, and Joseph Dahm for help with the preparation of the text for publication. I am grateful to my colleagues at the History Faculty of the University of Cambridge and at St Catharine's College, and to one in particular, Sir Christopher Bayly, who died in April 2015. Even now, whenever I walk into the main court of St Catharine's of an afternoon, I look across to the window of C3, on the off chance that Chris might be leaning in his shirt sleeves on the window sill and invite me up for a drink. The conversations that followed always led to unexpected places.

Time is an elusive but also an inescapable subject matter, especially now that the relationship between past, present, and future has become such a central preoccupation of politics and public discourse. In times of flux, the most lasting things acquire heightened value, which is why I dedicate this book to my sister Kate and my brother Justin, who were there (almost) from the start.

TIME AND POWER

FIGURE 1.1. Frederick William, the Great Elector,
engraving by Pieter de Jode from a portrait by Anselmus van Hulle.
Source: Anselmus van Hulle, *Les hommes illustres qui ont
vécu dans le XVII. siècle...* (Amsterdam, 1717).

Introduction

AS GRAVITY BENDS LIGHT, so power bends time. This book is about what happens when temporal awareness is lensed through a structure of power. It is interested in the forms of historicity appropriated and articulated by those who wield political power. By 'historicity' I do not mean a doctrine or theory about the meaning of history, nor a mode of historiographical practice. Rather, I use the term in the sense elaborated by François Hartog to denote a set of assumptions about how the past, the present, and the future are connected.[1] These assumptions may find explicit rhetorical expression or may articulate themselves through cultural choices, public rituals, or the deployment of arguments or of metaphors and other figurative language that imply a 'temporally structured form of perception', without overtly employing temporal categories.[2] They may be implicit in the forms of argument deployed to justify political action, or to argue against it.[3] Whatever forms they take, the historicities characteristic of cultures or regimes are marked by 'specific interpretations of what is temporally relevant'.[4] From this it follows that the configuration of this relationship in turn gives rise to a sense of time that possesses an intuited shape or timescape, depending upon which parts of the past are felt to be near and related intimately with the present and which are perceived as alien and remote.[5]

The book focuses on four moments. It opens with the struggle between Friedrich Wilhelm of Brandenburg-Prussia (1620–88), known as the Great Elector, and his provincial estates after the end of the Thirty Years' War, examining how these disputes invoked starkly opposed temporalities and tracing their impact on the emergent historiography of Brandenburg-Prussia. The Elector's reign was marked, I argue, by an awareness of the present as a precarious threshold between a catastrophic past and an uncertain future, in which one of the chief concerns of the sovereign was to free the state from the entanglements of tradition in order to choose freely between different possible futures.

The second chapter focuses on the historical writings of Frederick II, the only Prussian monarch ever to have written a history of his own lands. It argues that this king consciously retreated from the conflictual view of the state expounded at the court of his great-grandfather, the Great Elector, and that this departure reflected both the changed constellation of social power sustaining the Prussian throne and Frederick's idiosyncratic understanding of his own place in history. In place of the forwards-leaning historicity of the Great Elector, I suggest, Frederick imagined a post-Westphalian condition of stasis, embracing a neoclassical, steady-state temporality in which motifs of timelessness and cyclical repetition predominated and the state was no longer an engine of historical change but a historically nonspecific fact and a logical necessity.

Chapter 3 is a study of Bismarck's historicity, as articulated in his political arguments, rhetoric, and techniques. For Bismarck, the statesman was a decision maker, carried forwards on the torrent of history, whose task was to manage the interplay between the forces unleashed by the revolutions of 1848 while at the same time upholding and protecting the privileged structures and prerogatives of the monarchical state, without which history threatened to degenerate into mere tumult. It argues that Bismarck's historicity was riven by a tension between his commitment to the timeless permanence of the state and the churn and change of politics and public life. The collapse in 1918 of the system Bismarck created brought in its wake a crisis in historical awareness, since it destroyed a form of state power that had become the focal point and guarantor of historical thinking and awareness.

Among the inheritors of this crisis, the fourth chapter argues, were the National Socialists, who initiated a radical break with the very idea of history as a ceaseless 'iteration of the new'. Whereas Bismarck's historicity had been founded on the assumption that history was a complexly structured, forwards-rushing sequence of ever new and non-foreordained situations, the Nazis plinthed the most radical aspirations of their regime on a deep identity between the present, a remote past, and a remote future. The result was a form of regime historicity that was unprecedented in Prussia-Germany, but also quite distinct from the totalitarian temporal experiments of the Italian fascist and Soviet communist systems.

The objective of this book is thus to invert the project pursued in François Hartog's *Regimes of Historicity* and explore instead the historicity of (a small selection of) regimes. One could do this by examining the ways in which formal state structures—ministries, military commands, electoral and royal courts, and bureaucracies—managed time, situated themselves in history, and imagined the future, though this would beg questions about whether the term 'state' can be taken to denote something that was continually present in the same sense over the period covered by this book. I have chosen a different approach. I am interested in how those who wielded power justified their comportment with arguments and behaviours that bore a specific temporal signature. How these shapers of power related to the formal structures of government varied from case to case. The Great Elector wielded power from within an executive structure that he gradually and in a largely improvised way assembled around himself during his long reign. Frederick II's reign was marked by a drastic personalisation of power and by the semi-detachment of the monarch from many of the structures in which state authority formally resided. Bismarck situated himself in the turbulent space between the Prusso-German monarchical executive and the unpredictable forces at work in a post-revolutionary public sphere. And the National Socialist leadership cohort was the nemesis of the bureaucratic state structure—a vehement disavowal of the state as the vehicle and goal of history's striving was at the heart of Nazi historicity.

History's Temporal Turn

Time—or more precisely the variety of orders of time—is not a new theme in historical studies. Today it is a commonplace that time is not a neutral, universal substance in whose emptiness something called 'history' unfolds, but a contingent cultural construction whose shape, structure, and texture have varied. This insight has given rise over the last fifteen years to such a lively and diverse field of research that we can speak of a 'temporal turn' in historical studies, a shift in sensibilities comparable with the linguistic and cultural turns of the 1980s and 1990s, one of those re-patternings of attention by which the discipline of history periodically refreshes itself.[6]

The temporal turn in present-day historical studies can cite distinguished philosophical and theoretical antecedents. In his

1889 doctoral dissertation, the French philosopher Henri Bergson argued that time as a dimension of human consciousness was non-homogeneous and 'qualitatively multiple'; Durkheim's *Elementary Forms of the Religious Life* (1912) laid the foundations of a sociology of time as something collectively experienced and socially constructed; in *The Social Framework of Memory* (1925), Maurice Halbwachs applied Durkheim's insights to the social production of memory; two years later, Martin Heidegger's *Being and Time* proposed that the 'existential and ontological constitution of the totality of human consciousness [*Dasein*]' was 'grounded in temporality'; and since the Second World War, literary theorists and especially narratologists have subjected the temporal structures of texts to intensive study.[7]

Among the first historians to reflect on the implications of these theoretical currents for historical writing was Marc Bloch, who dedicated a short sub-chapter of his wartime classic *The Historian's Craft* to the problem of 'historical time'. By contrast with the 'artificially homogeneous' and abstract time of the natural sciences, Bloch wrote, 'the time of history is a concrete and living reality with an irreversible onward rush. It is the very plasma in which events are immersed, and the field that renders them intelligible'. At its heart is an unresolvable tension between continuity and 'perpetual change'.[8] Bloch's reflections on the temporality of history remained fragmentary, but the work of Braudel, Jacques Le Goff, and other historians in the *Annales* tradition deepened and expanded these intuitions, developing a sharp awareness of the diversity of temporal scales and textures. For Braudel, the relationship between the short-term disruptions known as 'events' and the longer-term continuities that define epochs became a central problem of the historian's practice. Le Goff explored the diverse temporal textures of occupational, liturgical, and devotional practices.[9]

As these reflections make clear, historicity and temporality are connected but not identical categories. In this book, I use the latter term to denote a political actor's intuitive sense of the texture of experienced time. If historicity is rooted in a set of assumptions about the relationships between past, present, and future, temporality captures something less reflected and more immediate: a feeling for the motion of time. Is the future moving towards the present or receding away from it? Does the past threaten to encroach on the present, or does it fall away towards the edges of awareness? How accommodating is the temporal frame for political action, and how does the imagined flow of time relate to the propensity of decision makers to perceive it as portioned out in 'moments'? Is the present experienced as movement or as stasis? What is permanent and what is not in the minds of those who wield power?

The Modernisation of Time

If the *Annales* school temporalised history, it was a German historian, Reinhart Koselleck, who historicised temporality. In *Futures Past*, a collection of sparkling essays on the 'semantics of historical time', Koselleck explored the history of time awareness, creating a subtle array of analytical tools. At the heart of his project was the transition from premodern to modern ways of experiencing and apprehending time. He discussed changes in time awareness from the Renaissance onwards, especially processes of cultural secularisation that had undermined the hold of biblical prophecy on Christian visions of the future. But his central claim was that the period he called the 'transitional era' (*Sattelzeit*)—spanning the years from around 1750 to around 1850—witnessed a profound alteration in Western European temporal awareness. This transformation was composed of many strands: as the flow of time, manifested in events, appeared to accelerate, the felt distance from the past increased; universal principles gave way to contingency; the authority of the past as a storehouse of wisdom and instruction for the present waned; key concepts—'revolution', 'class', 'progress', 'state'—were saturated with the momentum of historical change; stories, chronicles, and anecdotes about the past merged into something processual, singular, and all-encompassing, a single totality, the 'History' theorised by Hegel and taught in the humanities departments of modern universities. The consequence was a profound shift in the felt texture and shape of time: the recursive timescapes of premodern societies made way for something called History, now understood as a sequence of transformative and irreversible events that came to be experienced as 'the relentless iteration of the new'. The disruption, violence, and discontinuity of the Revolutionary and Napoleonic eras generated dissonances between the 'space of experience' and the 'horizon of expectation' that were to be emblematic for the modern era.[10]

In the opening essay of *Futures Past*, Koselleck interrogated Albrecht Altdorfer's *The Battle of Issus*, an image painted in 1529 depicting the victory of Alexander the Great over the Persians at the Battle of Issus in 333 BCE.[11] Why was it, Koselleck asked, that Altdorfer depicted the Greeks as present-day Germans and the Persians as present-day Turks? Why did the image show crowds of men and horses swarming across a Germanic, alpine landscape decorated with recognisably European buildings, even though the original encounter had taken place in Asia Minor? Why did the details in his painting so closely resemble contemporary representations of the Ottoman siege of Vienna, still under way in 1529 when Altdorfer painted his image? The answer, Koselleck proposed, was that for Altdorfer the relationship between the Battle of Issus and the Ottoman siege was prophetic and allegorical. The first battle had ushered in the end of the Persian Empire, as foreseen in the prophetic dream recorded in the Book of Daniel. The second seemed to herald the end of the Roman Empire (i.e., the Holy Roman Empire), seen as the next step in the timetable adumbrated by Daniel's prophecy. Both events existed within the same envelope of prophetic time. Only this made it possible to pleat time as Altdorfer did, superimposing sixteenth-century Turks onto ancient Persians.

To sharpen the contrast with modern temporal awareness, Koselleck brought in as witness the German poet, critic, and scholar Friedrich Schlegel, who, it so happens, viewed the Battle of Issus in the 1820s and wrote an enthusiastic essay on it. Schlegel praised Altdorfer's painting as 'the greatest feat of the age of chivalry'. Koselleck zeroed in on this observation—for Schlegel, it seemed, there was a distancing expanse of time between himself and the painting. More than that, Schlegel felt that the painting belonged to a different age—*Zeitalter*—from his own. So it was a question not just of the quantity of time elapsed, but of a break in the fabric of time, a tectonic fault between this time and a previous one. Something, Koselleck reasoned, had intervened between the time of Altdorfer and the time of Schlegel, with the paradoxical result that a greater expanse of time seemed to separate Schlegel from Altdorfer than appeared to separate Altdorfer from the deeds of Alexander. The Battle of Issus, in other words, exemplified a premodern, *untemporalised* sense of time and with it the lack of what we would call historical consciousness. Schlegel, by contrast, stood proxy for a modern temporal awareness that apprehended the past as distant, superseded, and ontologically separate.[12]

It would be difficult to overstate the influence of Koselleck's work on the historical study of temporality. He asked bold and original questions, unfolding their implications with impressive subtlety, lucidity, and depth of reasoning. His use of semantic change to track epochal mutations of awareness was foundational. He borrowed analytical categories from philosophy and literary theory and developed them as tools for calibrating processes of change—the 'horizon of expectation' (*Erwartungshorizont*) came from the reception theory of Gadamer and Jauss; *Zeitlichkeit*, a term denoting both the quality of time (its ceaseless motion, its texture) and the condition of existing in time, was drawn from Heidegger; 'temporalisation' (*Verzeitlichung*), meaning the historicisation of past and present time in the modern era, derived from Arthur O. Lovejoy's *Great Chain of Being*; the concept of acceleration as a hallmark of modern sensibility was already associated with Nietzsche. But if Koselleck did not invent these categories, he 'occupied, filled and popularised them', assembling them as tools for charting the mutation of temporal orders over time. All of them have entered the repertoire of the temporal turn.[13]

Even more influential was Koselleck's preoccupation with the transition from premodern to modern temporal orders.[14] The literature of the temporal turn has been predominantly concerned with mapping this threshold. There have been studies of the acceleration of travel in the railway era; the rising salience of punctuality and lateness; the scandal of 'wasted' time as a symptom of modern time regimes; the commodification of ever smaller amounts of time in the era of telegraphy; the shrinking of space through the advent of high-speed mass transit; the rise of nostalgia as a signature malady of modernity.[15] In studies of this kind, the advent of modernity and the attendant modernisation of temporal awareness have been the focus of attention.

Yet uncertainties remain about the qualitative nature of the transition from 'traditional' to 'modern' temporality. Rather than producing a stable toolkit of widely used hermeneutical categories, recent writing on modern temporalities has generated a thicket of heterogeneous metaphors. The transition from traditional to modern temporalities is variously conceptualised as a process of acceleration, expansion, narrowing, regeneration, compression, distanciation, splitting, fracturing, emptying, annihilation, intensification, and liquefaction.[16] And the category 'temporality' has itself been used in a variety of senses. In some studies, the term denotes an experiential domain, a tendency on the part of individuals or communities to orient themselves towards cyclical markers such as the seasons or liturgical celebrations, the perceived texture of time as it unfolds, fluctuations in the experienced duration of specific events, the relationship between experience and expectation, a divergence in the rhythms of private and public life, or patterns of time-management practices associated with certain occupational cultures.[17] Other studies focus on 'chronosophical' questions, or philosophical reflections on time and its relationship with history or with human existence more generally.[18]

Power and Time

Agentless processes of change, whose narratives have often been anchored in the systemic and processual arguments of modernisation theory, have tended to dominate the temporality literature.[19] But there have also been excellent studies of how regimes of power intervened in the temporal order. These have explored the use of calendars, for example, as an instrument of political power. The transition from the Julian to the Gregorian calendar in Western Europe, a process that took over three centuries, was always intertwined with power struggles.[20] In Habsburg Austria, the accession to the throne of the enlightened Jansenist reformer Joseph II broke the traditional dominance of the liturgical cycle at court, while the drastic reduction of feast days alienated elements of the population attached to their traditional devotions and the sociable rhythms of the old Catholic year.[21] On 24 October 1793, the Jacobin-controlled National Convention adopted a new 'republican calendar' intended to mark a radical break with the past and the inauguration of a new era. Had it succeeded in establishing itself over the longer term, the ten-day week (*décade*) would have transformed the living and work cycles of the French, alienating them from the cycles of the Christian liturgical year and setting them apart from the rest of the European continent.[22]

Historians of empire, too, have examined the 'intimate connection' between time and imperial power—especially as manifested in the imposition of standardised regimes of clock discipline on labour and production processes.[23] Here, the emphasis has been on the partially coerced transition from pre- or nonmodern (aboriginal) to modern (imperial or Western) temporalities, though many studies have also drawn attention to the survival of indigenous temporalities in the face of pressure from colonial authorities.[24] Vanessa Ogle's magisterial study of the global standardisation of clock time revealed an 'additive and unintended process' in which the uncoordinated efforts of numerous actors converged with global disruption (the Second World War) and the requirements imposed by new infrastructure (military and commercial aviation) to bring about the introduction of uniform time zones.[25] Sebastian Conrad has illuminated how the extension and intensification of imperial power interacted with nineteenth-century semantic and cultural shifts to produce 'global transformations of the time regime'.[26]

The disruption of systems of power from below can also generate shifts in time sense, as studies of late Qing China have shown.[27] The period of violent upheaval comprising the

Taiping, Nian, Gelao, and Hui rebellions of the 1850s to 1870s and the incursions by the Western powers that followed gave rise to such profound ruptures with the remembered past, Luke S. K. Kwong has argued, that they transformed historical awareness, at least within the cultural elite. In traditional China, history was upheld as a treasury of good examples reflecting a state of cosmic interconnectedness and the harmonious management of human affairs. Events in the present were interpreted in the light of analogies drawn from the past. This did not mean that Chinese scholars and administrators were incapable of constructing 'specific kinds of linear progression', but these, Kwong argued, were embedded in a cyclical, strongly recursive, and nonlinear timescape.

The hold of this traditional temporality was broken only when immense waves of social turbulence and political violence undermined the authority of the imperial government, severing the thread of continuity with the past, placing the survival of the country in question and with it the authority of a history that had been counted out in imperial reigns. The time-honoured practice of seeking instruction from the historical record broke down, just as, for Koselleck, the topos of history as the teacher of life had waned in Western Europe. The notion that the current era of destruction would make way, as in the past, for an age of restoration and redemption no longer seemed trustworthy. Faced with what they saw as the radical unprecedentedness of contemporary conditions, late Qing Chinese intellectuals reached for more linear and developmental, Western- and Meiji-inspired narratives in order to capture a sense of the accumulation and acceleration of events that were 'gathering momentum in a forward thrust towards the future'.[28]

Among the most ambitious modern interventions in the temporal order were those of the totalitarian regimes of twentieth-century Europe. In January 1918, the Soviet Union abandoned the Julian calendar adopted by Peter the Great in 1699 and replaced it with the Gregorian calendar commonly in use in the West, pulling the country thirteen days forward. The rise of Stalin to unchallenged dominance brought further initiatives. In 1930, Stalin proclaimed a new five-day week. There was to be no Saturday or Sunday, just a sequence of five days identified by numbers and colours—yellow, orange, red, purple, and green.[29] This particular project was eventually abandoned as impracticable, but the Soviet Union launched a revolutionary experiment in reordering the human relationship with time; it aspired to inaugurate a temporality in which the vanguard party overcame the constraints of conventional 'bourgeois' linear time through the infinite intensification of work.[30]

Recent studies of Italian fascism have focused on the efforts of fascist intellectuals and propaganda to establish a new temporality centred around the party itself as the ultimate historical agent.[31] And the historian of transnational fascism Roger Griffin has characterised the advent of National Socialist government in Germany as a 'temporal revolution'.[32] Eric Michaud's exploration of the 'Nazi myth' focused on the paradoxical relationship between 'motion' and 'motionlessness' in Nazi visual imagery and related this to the logic of Christian eschatology, in which the subject is suspended between the memory of a past redemption (in the form of Christ's incarnation) and the anticipation of a future collective salvation.[33] Emilio Gentile has spoken of a fascist 'sacralisation of politics' through which the rites and usages of the Christian tradition were adapted to the purposes of the Mussolini regime, creating an 'internal symbolic universe' in which timeless universality of liturgical performance was transferred to the collective experience of politics.[34] All three totalitarian dictatorships, Charles Maier and Martin Sabrow have suggested, represented far-reaching interventions, not only in the social and political, but also in the temporal order.[35]

Framing temporality as an effect or epiphenomenon of power shifts the focus of attention from diffused processes of change towards 'chronopolitics', the study of how 'certain views toward time and toward the nature of change' become implicated in processes of decision making.[36] And this in turn means enquiring after 'the imagination of time and history' that has, in various countries and epochs, given 'meaning and legitimacy' to the actions and arguments of the sovereign authority.[37] It means, to borrow the words of Charles Maier, addressing the 'question of how politics is about time' and of what kind of time is 'presupposed by politics'.[38]

None of the regimes discussed in this book attempted formally to restructure the collective experience of time in the manner of the French National Convention, through the imposition of a new calendar. But all of them captured and selectively intensified ambient temporalities, weaving them into the arguments and representations with which they justified themselves and their actions. One of the distinctive features of this book is that it offers a longitudinal survey, following the same ancestral territorial entity (Brandenburg-Prussia) through successive political incarnations. An advantage of this approach is that it allows us to pick up the reflexive, self-historicising dimension of chronopolitical change. States have deep memories, and there is a cumulative logic to their self-awareness, even when one regime abjures the claims or practices of its predecessor. Joining the dots diachronically might thus enable us to plot the outlines of a 'time-history', at least within one rather narrow domain of human activity.[39] The German (Prussian) focus of this study arises above all from a pragmatic decision to focus on what I know best. But Germany is an especially interesting case study for an enquiry into the relationship between temporality, historicity, and power. The frequency and depth of political rupture in German Europe over the last four centuries allows us to observe again and again the impact of political change on temporal and historical awareness. I return in the conclusion to the question of whether there was anything specifically Prussian or German in the trajectory that emerges from this exercise.

A further advantage of the longitudinal approach is that it allows us to probe the relationship between 'modernisation' and temporality. Several recent studies have suggested that the transformations associated by Koselleck with the *Sattelzeit* can in fact be discerned in earlier regimes—the city-state courts of Renaissance Italy and early modern Germany, for example, or even medieval Europe and the Middle East.[40] Merely moving the threshold backwards leaves the teleology of the paradigm intact, of course, if this is achieved simply by retrofitting the analytical categories of modernisation to an earlier era. But it is also worth asking whether we need to read Koselleck's typology of temporalities in chronological sequence; an alternative view would understand him as a theorist of multiple parallel temporalities.[41]

In this book, I have tried to attend closely to the specific temporal textures of each regime. The sequence that results is more oscillating, recursive, and nonlinear than a strongly sequential and modernisation-based theory would allow. This need not mean that modernisation was not taking place; it might simply reflect the obliqueness and contingent quality of the relationships between the wielders of power and the kinds of processes that have tended to interest modernisation theorists. The Great Elector aligned himself with an activist understanding of history that pitted him against the contemporary defenders of privilege and tradition. Frederick II attempted to counter the processes of social change that were transforming his kingdom from within, articulating a highly aestheticised political vision marked by stasis and equilibrium. Otto von Bismarck adapted his politics to the political and social forces driving the turbulent movement of history, but also remained committed to an idea of the monarchical state as unchanging and transcendent that he believed he had inherited from the age of Frederick. And the National Socialist regime broke with all of these precedents, rejecting the very idea of a history composed of disruptions and contingency and embedding its political vision in a millennial timescape, in which the distant future was merely the fulfilled promise of the past.

In none of the four eras this book examines did the temporalities of power explored here crowd out other forms of time awareness, even if they were sometimes directed against them. Throughout the period under review in this book, political life was structured by a plurality of coexistent temporal orders.[42] Yet the temporality of political power as wielded by its most influential agents retained and retains a special importance. It was the place where the political rationalisations of power expressed themselves as claims about the past and expectations of the future.

The salience of regime chronopolitics has not waned, and the appeal to imagined timescapes remains one of the key tools of political communication. This book was written during the crescendo and triumph of the Brexit campaign in Britain, a campaign driven by the aspiration to 'take back control'. The Brexiteer Boris Johnson was the chief propagator of this slogan, but he was also the author of a biography of Winston Churchill (subtitle: *How One Man Made History*) in which the iconic statesman bore an uncanny resemblance to Johnson himself. And the Brexit campaign was animated by the appeal to an idealised past in which the 'English-speaking peoples' had effortlessly dominated the world. The prominence of such motifs among Brexiteer arguments was evidence, Duncan Bell suggested, 'of the mesmeric grip that the Empire retains over swathes of the British governing class'.[43]

The impact of the Brexit referendum was still reverberating in the United Kingdom when Donald Trump won the US presidential elections. Trump, whose trademarked campaign slogan was 'Make America Great Again®', brought to the most powerful elected office in the world a political vision founded on a trenchant disavowal both of the neoliberal future of globalisation and of the scientific anticipation of climate change, which he described as a hoax perpetrated upon the rest of humankind by the Chinese.[44] The most influential ideologue on his staff, Stephen Bannon, later dismissed from his post, subscribed to the esoteric historical theory expounded by William Strauss and Neil Howe in a book called *The Fourth Turning: What Cycles of History Tell Us about America's Next Rendezvous with Destiny* (New York, 1997), in which it was argued that the histories of nations unfold in eighty- to hundred-year cycles, divided by violent periods of 'turning' that can last a generation. Whether President Trump himself ever immersed himself in these ideas is unknown, but he too has mounted a challenge at least to conventional American historicity by becoming the first president of modern times overtly to reject the notion that America occupies an exceptional and paradigmatic place at the vanguard of history's forwards movement. On the contrary, he has suggested, today's America is a backwards country with a broken society and infrastructure, whose task is to reach back into a past where American values were still uncontaminated and American society was intact.[45] 'When we win', Trump told the working-class voters of Moon Township Pennsylvania in 2016, 'we are bringing steel back, we are going to bring steel back to Pennsylvania, like it used to be. We are putting our steel workers and our miners back to work.

We are. We will be bringing back our once-great steel companies'.[46] At the same time, his febrile communicative style has opened up a rift between the hyper-accelerated present of Twitter and the slow deliberative processes that are the daily fare of traditional democracies and administrations attuned to constitutional norms.

In the United States, Poland, Hungary, and other countries experiencing a populist revival, new pasts are being fabricated to displace old futures. Celebrating the success of Donald Trump, the French National Front leader Marine Le Pen observed that in the United States 'people [were] taking their future back'; the French, she predicted, would soon do the same.[47] Reflecting on how the wielders and shapers of political power temporalised their politics in one small province of the past will do little to diminish the contemporary allure of such manipulations, but it may at least help us to read them more attentively.

CHAPTER ONE

The History Machine

FREDERICK WILLIAM, the prince known as the Great Elector, was the first Brandenburg Elector of whom numerous portraits survive. Many of them were commissioned by the sitter himself. They document the changing appearance of a man who spent forty-eight years—longer than any other member of his dynasty— in sovereign office. Depictions from the early years of the reign show a commanding, upright figure with a long face framed by flowing dark hair; in the later images, the body has swollen, the face is bloated, and the hair has been replaced by cascades of artificial curls. And yet one thing is common to all the portraits painted from life: intelligent, dark eyes that fix the viewer in a sharp stare.[1] The engraving shown opposite page 1 (figure 1.1) was based on a sketch by Anselmus van Hulle, court painter to the Prince of Orange. In 1645 or 1646, van Hulle attended the negotiations for the Peace of Westphalia in Münster and Osnabrück in order to capture the likenesses of the sovereign and delegates taking part. The decision to frame the engraved portrait of each peacemaker in the manner of an epitaph suggests this was not merely a portrait. It was intended to serve as a memorial to a man of renown who had left a mark on the history of his times.[2]

Frederick William presided over the restoration—indeed the transformation—of the Brandenburg composite monarchy in the aftermath of the devastations of the Thirty Years' War. During his reign, which lasted from 1640 until 1688, Brandenburg acquired a small but respectable army, a land bridge across Eastern Pomerania to the Baltic coast, a modest Baltic fleet, and even a colony on the west coast of Africa. Brandenburg became a regional power, a sought-after ally, and a principal party to major peace settlements.[3]

In 1667, Frederick William, the Great Elector, composed a 'Fatherly Instruction' for his heir. The document began, in the manner of the traditional princely testament, with exhortations to lead a pious and god-fearing life, but it soon broadened into a politico-historical tract of a type without precedent in the history of the Hohenzollern dynasty. Sharp contrasts were drawn between the past and the present. The Duchy of Prussia, the prince reminded his heir, had once languished in the 'intolerable condition' of vassalage to the Crown of Poland; only the Elector's acquisition of sovereignty over the Duchy had annulled that oppressive state of affairs. 'All this cannot be described; the Archive and the accounts will bear witness to it'.[4] The future Elector was urged to develop what we would call a historical perspective on the problems that beset him in the present. Industrious consultation of the archive would reveal not only how important it was to maintain good relations with France, but also how these should be balanced with 'the respect that You, as an Elector, must have for the Reich and Emperor'. There was also a strong sense of the new order established by the Peace of Westphalia and the importance of defending it if necessary against any power or powers that should set out to overturn it.[5] In short, this was a document acutely sensitive to its own location in history and charged with an awareness of the tension between cultural and institutional continuity and the forces of change.

This chapter is about that tension. It is doubtful whether the Elector ever developed a coherent view of 'history', in the sense of a philosophical standpoint on its meaning or nature. He was a man oriented towards questions of power and security, not given to speculative reflections or to the discussion of issues of principle.[6] And 'history' in its present-day sense, an abstract, collective-singular noun denoting an all-encompassing, multi-layered process of transformation, did not yet exist. The word had not yet undergone that process of expansion and 'temporalisation' that would establish it as one of the matrix concepts of modernity.[7] Yet the Elector and his regime did possess, so this chapter will argue, something more intuitive, a highly distinctive and dynamic form of historicity, rooted in the sense that the monarchical state occupied an exposed location on the threshold between a catastrophic past and a threat-rich future.

In order to flesh out this claim and clarify its implications, I first examine the arguments deployed in the conflict between the electoral government and the noble-dominated provincial Estates, focusing in particular on the historicity implicit in the arguments offered by both sides, because when the prince invoked the idea of 'necessity' or 'emergency' against the entrenched claims of the traditional holders of provincial power, he was in effect playing the future against the past.[8] I then ask whether there was something Calvinist in the historicity of the Elector and of his government—confessional tensions, after all, were woven into the conflicts between the Elector's largely Calvinist administration and his Lutheran Estates. The Reformed faith was the most complex intellectual system to which the Elector made a conscious commitment. A final section examines the efforts of the Elector's government to secure the services of an official historian, focusing in particular on the writings of Samuel Pufendorf, who came to Berlin to take up his post as official historiographer in January 1688, a few months before the Elector's death. Here I suggest that Pufendorf first provided, as a theorist, powerful philosophical justifications for the consolidation of Electoral power and then fashioned, as a historian, an ambitious, archivally researched narrative that captured the dynamic historicity of the Elector and his officials. The chapter closes with a brief reflection on how the repudiation of traditional privilege that became a salient theme of the Elector's reign found expression in the elaborate ceremony that attended the coronation of the first Prussia king in 1701.

Composite Monarchy in an Age of War

The political entity whose throne Frederick William ascended in 1640 was no unitary state. It was a 'composite monarchy' comprising territories acquired by different means, subject to diverse laws and ruled under different titles. The heartland was the Electorate of Brandenburg, purchased by the Hohenzollerns in 1417 for four hundred thousand Hungarian gold guilders. Through strategic marital alliances, successive generations of Hohenzollern Electors had acquired territorial claims to a number of noncontiguous territories to the east and the west: Ducal Prussia on the Baltic and the Duchy of Jülich-Kleve, a complex of Rhenish territories comprising Jülich, Kleve (Cleves), Berg, and the Counties of Mark and Ravensberg. Thanks to a family connection dating back to 1530, the Hohenzollerns also claimed the right of succession to Pomerania, a strategically important territory between Brandenburg and the Baltic Sea.

Within their diverse possessions, the Electors of Brandenburg shared power with regional elites organised in representative bodies called Estates. In Brandenburg, the Estates approved (or not) taxes levied by the Elector and (from 1549) administered their collection. In return, they possessed far-reaching powers and concessions. The Elector was forbidden, for example, to enter into alliances without first seeking the approval of the Estates.[9] In a declaration published in 1540 and reiterated on various occasions until 1653, the Elector even promised that he would not 'decide or undertake any important things upon which the flourishing or decline of the lands may depend, without the foreknowledge and consultation of all our estates'.[10] The provincial nobilities owned the lion's share of the landed wealth in the Electorate; they were also the Elector's most important creditors. But their outlook was vehemently parochial; they had no interest in helping the Elector to secure faraway territories of which they knew little.

The estates inhabited a mental world of mixed and overlapping sovereignties. The Estates of Kleve maintained a diplomatic representative in The Hague and looked to the Dutch Republic, the Imperial Diet (the assembly of the Holy Roman Empire), and on occasions even to Vienna for support against illicit interventions from Berlin.[11] They envisaged establishing their own system of taxation and forming a corporate 'hereditary union' with the nearby territories of Mark, Jülich, and Berg and frequently conferred with the Estates of these lands on how best to respond to (and resist) demands from Berlin.[12] The estates of Ducal Prussia, for their part, were still subjects of the Polish crown; they saw neighbouring Poland as the guarantor of their ancient privileges. As one senior Electoral official irritably remarked, the leaders of the Prussian Estates were 'true neighbours of the Poles' and 'indifferent to the defence of [their own] country'.[13]

The turbulence and destruction of the Thirty Years' War (1618–48) placed these delicately balanced arrangements under pressure. In Brandenburg, the estates remained deeply sceptical of military expenditures and foreign combinations of any kind. Even after repeated incursions into Brandenburg territory by Protestant and Imperial troops, they remained impassive in the face of entreaties for financial assistance from the sovereign.[14] As they saw it, their function was to forestall unwarranted adventures and to preserve the fabric of provincial privilege against incursions from the centre.[15] But as the war dragged on, the fiscal privileges of the Brandenburg nobilities began to look fragile.[16] Foreign princes and generals had no compunction in extorting contributions from the provinces of Brandenburg; why should the Elector not take his share? This would involve rolling back the ancient 'liberties' of the Estates. For this task, the Elector turned to Count Adam Schwarzenberg, a Catholic and a foreigner with no ties to the provincial nobility. Schwarzenberg lost no time in imposing a new tax without any recourse to the usual provincial organs. He curtailed the power of the Estates to oversee state expenditures and suspended the Privy Council, transferring its responsibilities to the Council of War, whose members were chosen for their complete independence from the Estates. In short, Schwarzenberg installed a fiscal autocracy that broke decisively with corporate tradition.[17] The corporate nobility came to loathe him for his assault on their corporate liberties. In 1638–39, when Schwarzenberg's power was in its zenith, fly sheets circulated in Berlin decrying the 'Hispanic servitude' of his rule.[18]

The effects of the war on the Duchy of Kleve were less drastic. Here, as across Germany, heavy contributions and extortions were levied as various armies fought for control of the strategically important lower Rhine. But the occupation of the eastern areas on the right bank of the Rhine by Dutch troops brought money into the country, revived trade, and strengthened the political connection with The Hague. Whereas the interventions of Count Schwarzenberg, combined with widespread devastation, had weakened the Estates in Brandenburg, the Estates of Kleve remained as powerful as ever and continued to be confident in the political support of the nearby United Provinces, whose garrisons remained in many towns, even after the war had come to an end.[19]

Ducal Prussia lay outside the areas of the most intense conflict during the Thirty Years' War and thus managed to avoid the destruction visited upon Brandenburg. Here, the Estates had traditionally ruled the roost, meeting regularly in full session and keeping a tight grip on central and local government, the militia, and the territorial finances. The traditional Prussian right of appeal to the Polish crown, still formally sovereign in the territory, meant that they would not easily be pressed into cooperating.[20]

Prince versus Estates

In December 1640, when Frederick William acceded to the throne, Brandenburg was still under foreign occupation. A two-year truce was agreed with the Swedes in July 1641, but the looting, burning, and general misbehaviour continued.[21] Only in March 1643 did Frederick William return from the relative safety of Königsberg in Ducal Prussia to ruined Berlin, a city he scarcely recognised. Here he found a population depleted and malnourished and buildings destroyed by fire or in a parlous state of repair.[22] The predicament that had bedevilled his father's reign remained unsolved. Brandenburg had no military force with which to establish its independence. The small army created by Schwarzenberg was already falling apart and there was no money to pay for a replacement. In the Duchy of Kleve and the County of Mark, the new Elector was sovereign in name only; these were still occupied by Imperial, Spanish, Dutch, Hessian, and French troops.[23] As for Pomerania, it was likely to remain under Swedish occupation for the foreseeable future. Johann Friedrich von Leuchtmar, a privy councillor and the Elector's former tutor, summarised Brandenburg's predicament in a report of 1644: Poland, he predicted, would seize Prussia as soon as it was strong enough;

Kleve in the west was under the control of the Dutch Republic. Brandenburg stood 'on the edge of the abyss'.[24]

In order to restore the independence of his monarchy and press home his territorial claims, the Elector needed a flexible and disciplined territorial fighting force. The creation of such an instrument became one of the consuming preoccupations of his reign.[25] It also placed the Elector on a collision course with the Estates. In a letter of October 1645 to the Estates of Kleve, he explained that he needed to occupy the entire area of the Duchy with his own troops in order to avert the prospect of being driven out of his possessions by rivals in the region. And 'since a soldier cannot live on wind', this would mean the continuation of special financial contributions. These were necessary, the Elector explained, because the retention of cities was not possible without an occupying force:

> In these irregular times of war and this ruined state of affairs, in this state of extreme need (where a case cannot always be made for privilege [ubi privilegii ratio haberi semper non potest]) we sincerely hope that you will not view these measures, which are undertaken in the spirit of faithful and paternal princely care for the rescue and conservation of Our lands and indeed for the welfare of you and yours, as a deliberate and premeditated infraction of the privileges you have already invoked in this matter (of which, incidentally, We have to date received no thorough report), and that you will not insist on the disbanding of these troops, who have been raised at such heavy cost, or on the demolition of the fortifications (which could not happen without the greatest danger and ruin . . . to Our reputation and Our country).[26]

This was a rather loose bundle of arguments. 'I'm doing this for your own good' was one of them, though not one that the Estates were likely to find persuasive. In a later declaration to the delegates of the Kleve Estates in Königsberg, the Elector fleshed out this claim, noting that were the Estates to succeed in blocking supply, the result would be misery, as the collapse of the Elector's small armed forces opened the Duchy to further 'enemy attacks and sieges' and thus to 'utmost ruin and danger'.[27] More forceful was the reference to the broader state of emergency that had given rise to his demands for money— though it is interesting to note the softness of the Latin parenthesis, which stopped short of proposing a global suppression of privilege, even under extreme circumstances. The observation that the Elector had not as yet been fully apprised of what the privileges in question actually were implied scepticism about the precise scope and the legal foundation of the Estates' claims. Finally, there was the reminder that refusing to comply would have ruinous consequences for the prince himself and for his lands.

This was the case the Elector made to justify the contributions he intended to levy on his subjects in Kleve. At their core was the claim that the Elector had no choice but to act as he did. 'We remain graciously confident', he declared in a letter to his officials in the Duchy in November 1645, 'that they [the Estates] will duly take this to heart as an unavoidable necessity (unvermeidliche Nothwendigkeit)'; other letters spoke of 'a need that cannot be circumvented' (unumgängliche Noth) or of 'extreme need' (äusserste Noth).[28]

The standoff between the sovereign and the Kleve Estates came to a head during the Northern War of 1655–60.[29] In 1657, Frederick William demanded the raising of over four thousand armed men and the payment of eighty thousand Reichsthaler to finance the new troops and cover the expense of maintaining garrisons and fortresses. In presenting this request to the Estates, Moritz von Nassau-Siegen, the Elector's governor in the Duchy, observed that the Elector had tried as far as possible to avoid burdening the Estates with further demands. Now, however, he was in a position where he could pursue his 'project to achieve peace' (den vorhabenden friedens zweck) only with the support of his 'loyal Estates and subjects' (dero getrewen Staenden und Unterthanen). If these were to 'abandon' him, he warned, the Elector's 'need' (Noth)—emergency might be a better translation in this context—would become even more pressing and the desired peace even harder to achieve. 'And since the only true friend was a friend in need' (Und dan nun ein getrewer freund in der noth erkant wuerde), the Governor reasoned, in terms that recall the logic of a protection racket, the Elector did not doubt that the Estates would be his 'friends' and come to his aid.[30]

In response to this importuning, the Estates of Kleve, like those of the Elector's other lands, dug in their heels, insisting on their hereditary rights and privileges. In 1649, the Brandenburg Estates, too, refused to approve funds for a campaign against the Swedes in Pomerania, despite the Elector's earnest reminder that all his territories were now 'limbs of one head' (membra unius capitis) and that Pomerania ought thus to be supported as if it were 'part of the Electorate'.[31] In Kleve, where the wealthy urban patriciate still regarded the Elector as a foreign interloper, the Estates revived the traditional 'hereditary union' with Mark, Jülich, and Berg; leading spokesmen even drew parallels with the contemporary upheavals in England and threatened by implication to treat the Elector as the parliamentary party were treating King Charles. Frederick William's threats to apply 'military executive actions' were largely futile, since the Estates were supported by the Dutch garrisons still occupying the Duchy.[32] When the Elector stepped up the pressure during the Northern War, the Estates pointed out that their fundamental duty was to see to it that 'subsequent generations' (posteritet) were not robbed of their privileges.

In a classic exposition of the provincial perspective, the Estates explained that the subjects were in no condition to 'assist the Elector in this war that did not concern them'. They assured the Elector that they intended no disrespect; the fact was that the duty incumbent upon them 'pro conservatione Privilegiorum et boni publici' prevented them from acceding to the Elector's request, even if they had wished to. In the eyes of the Estates, the 'preservation of privileges' and 'the public good' appeared to be one and the same thing. Here as in other German lands, local elites responded to the demands and unilateral measures of the prince by invoking the rights of a 'fatherland' the protection of whose 'ancient constitution' was the duty of every noble 'patriot'.[33]

In Ducal Prussia, negotiations with the Estates were complicated by the residual sovereignty of the Polish Crown. Here, the Estates possessed the right of appeal to a jurisdiction completely outside the Elector's control. Their acquiescence in the Hohenzollern claim to their Duchy had been secured only on the condition that the transfer of custodianship over the Duchy to the Electoral House of Brandenburg would not incur any diminution of their corporate privileges. The half century before the succession of Frederick William had been marked by ambivalent trends: on the one hand an expansion of corporate rights that reinforced the preeminence of the Duchy's nobility, on the other hand signs in the 1620s and 1630s of a rapprochement between the Prussian Estates and the Brandenburg administration.[34] But in Prussia too, as in every other Hohenzollern land, the Estates baulked at the Elector's requests for money and protested at every initiative by the Electoral administration that injured the fabric of their traditional exemptions and rights.

In the Hohenzollern lands, as elsewhere in Germany and Europe, the conflict between the central executive and the holders of provincial power encompassed many issues—the right to be consulted on key questions of foreign policy, the right to oppose the introduction of new taxes, the power, known as the *Indigenatsrecht*, to appoint local officials, and the traditional mechanisms of corporate provincial control over the armed forces, for example. One should not cast this confrontation in absolute terms: there was no global abolition of privilege, and the Brandenburg Elector never rejected in principle the argument from 'ancient provenance', though his councillors did on occasion point up the ideological and manipulative character of such arguments.[35] The 'fabric of norms' linking the prince and the regional nobilities was stretched, but not broken.[36] Frederick William had no intention of transforming his state into a unitary centralised polity in the manner imputed to him by some early twentieth-century historians. Again and again, however, he had to make the case that the Estates and the regions they represented should see themselves as parts of a single whole, and thus as bound to collaborate in the maintenance and defence of all the sovereign's lands and the pursuit of his legitimate territorial claims.[37]

This way of seeing things was alien to the Estates, who viewed the respective territories as discrete constitutional parcels, bound vertically to the person of the Elector, but not horizontally to each other. The Estates of the Mark Brandenburg saw Kleve and Ducal Prussia as 'foreign provinces' with no claim on Brandenburg's resources. Frederick William's long wars for Pomerania, by the same token, were merely private princely 'feuds', for which he had—in their view—no right to sequester the hard-earned wealth of his subjects.[38] And these disputes unfolded against the background of a polarisation in political and legal theory: while some authorities endorsed the ambitions of princes, others insisted on the ancient rights of the estates and the illegitimacy of any tax levied without their consultation and consent.[39]

Forms of Historicity

The Estates argued their case on the grounds of continuity with the past. Confronted by the Elector and his officials with demands for money or other resources, the Estates insisted on the continuation and solemn observance of their 'especial and particular privileges, freedoms, treaties, princely exemptions, marital agreements, territorial contracts, ancient traditions, law and justice'. The Prince's interventions were illegitimate *because* they were innovations. They represented a break with past practice. The 'traditional' privileges, rights, liberties, and so on were legitimate precisely because they were old. The discourse of the Estates bore the imprint of a fundamental esteem for what was old: this was a world in which rights and law in general derived their value and respectability from their having existed for a long time.[40] What counted for the Estates was the regress of documents enshrining the privileges and liberties of their fathers, and their fathers' fathers, documents that had supposedly been confirmed and reconfirmed by generations of princes. This may have looked like an invocation of inherited property title, but it was something at once larger and more diffuse: it was a constructed corporate memory of ancient right and usage. In this sense, the Estates were exemplars of a 'culture of legal remembering' that was characteristic of the corporate regional elites of the German lands.[41] In a draft Electoral Letter of Assurance they proposed to the Electoral administration in Königsberg, representatives of the Estates of Ducal Prussia found expansive language for their own traditional liberties:

We undertake to protect unchanged in every point and clause all of the praiseworthy old orders, customs, traditions and usages, letters of lease and other licenses, contracts, goods and chattels, agreements, letters and seals, immunities, jurisdictions, possessions, personal obligations and pardons, which the Honourable Estates in general and specifically have received, used and possessed from the times of the [German] Order right down to this hour, whether through the Order, or his Royal Majesty and the Crown of Poland or from our estimable forebears of blessed memory, Margraves and Electors of Brandenburg, [and we undertake to do this] without exception, such that no action will be initiated or permitted against them, in any manner or form whatsoever, whether in times of peace or of war.[42]

By contrast, Elector Frederick William, as we have seen, founded his claim to intervene and modify these arrangements on the need of the state and its inhabitants. To the 'libertas' of the Estates, he opposed the 'necessitas' of the central executive, a necessity that might under certain circumstances justify the dissolution or suspension of long-standing traditional arrangements.

This was an argument that could be articulated in two modes: it might simply mean that in times of dire necessity, the central executive had the right *temporarily* to suspend certain customary arrangements. This was the sense of the rather tentative Latin formulation used by the Elector in his letter of 1646 to the Kleve Estates: here he suggested that in an emergency, a case 'cannot always be made for privilege' (privilegii ratio haberi semper non potest).[43] In a curious reformulation of the same argument, Daniel Weimann, one of the Elector's officials in Kleve, described a meeting of March 1657, at which he had confronted the recalcitrant Estates representatives with the lapidary observation that 'privileges presupposed the absence of emergency' (Die Privilegien präsupponirten Unnoth).[44] But in its more radical form, the argument from need or emergency could assert the priority in principle and at all times of the central executive and its 'needs' over the historic 'liberties' of the provincial elites. In an interesting passage from his diary dated 22 March 1657, Weimann described a conversation with a group of Electoral officials, in which he remarked that it would be better to ignore the assemblies and remonstrations of the Estates and simply continue indefinitely to raise troops and taxes without local approval, for 'necessity knows no law and dissolves all obligations' (die nodt lidte kein gesetz undt entbinde von allen banden).[45]

The provincial defenders of libertas looked to the past, and to its manifold continuities with the present. For them, 'posterity' (Posteritet) was the preservation of rights established in the past for the sake of future generations.[46] The Electoral authorities, by contrast, looked to the future—for what was 'necessity' but the anticipation of future harms and the planning of their prevention? The raising of new and unapproved taxes and troops was a measure oriented towards future danger, the risk of future incursions, the need to secure one's interests in future peace negotiations. And the Elector, who conducted correspondence with courts across Europe, was surely in a better position to recognise such harms and opportunities in advance than the Estates, whose horizons were provincial, or regional at best. As he himself made clear, warding off potential threats meant reading the present trends in European politics:

The Honourable Estates [he observed in a declaration to a delegation from Kleve in 1645] will also bear in mind that current developments [*die jetzigen Läufe*] in the Roman Empire are taking such a dangerous direction that for the moment there is little prospect of the peace and tranquillity we have so long desired, and if one thinks the matter through, then there is certainly no prince whose land and people are in great danger than the Klevisch, Pomeranian and other hereditary lands of His Electoral Highness; indeed His entire Electoral state stands right now in the balance, and it will depend [on the Estates] whether what follows is the ascendancy of H.E.H. or the utmost ruin and downfall of H.E.H. and His lands.[47]

This argument presumed that the Elector and his officials were in a better position than his subjects to judge which dangers were most pressing and how they might best be addressed. The Estates were of course under no obligation to accept this presumption. They could and often did question the prince's reasoning; so, on occasion, did groups of more humble subjects. In the summer of 1640, with the Elector newly installed in Königsberg (Berlin was still a no-go zone), a group of free smallholders, free peasants, and other 'privileged people' in the districts of Samland, Nathangen, and Oberland in Ducal Prussia added an appendix to the general remonstrance of the Estates protesting that far from increasing the security of the country, the calling up of young men for military service 'in foreign places' had precisely the opposite effect: 'bearing in mind that if a danger (which God forbid) should arise, the best manpower we have to perform our services would be out of the country and we poor old-timers ... have to mount our horses in person, though we would be of little use in a fight'.[48]

In 1651, the Estates of the County of Mark disputed whether the international situation justified the maintenance of an expensive Electoral military contingent in their small territory. The context here was that Spain, which was at war with France, was still occupying Frankenthal in the Palatinate. Charles IV of Lorraine, whose domains separated Alsace from the main territory of France, was also at war with Louis XIV, who was still struggling to gain control over the country. But the Estates of Mark doubted whether this posed a threat to their own country. The Lorrainers, they argued, were now depleted in numbers, and it appeared that the King of Spain intended to leave Frankenthal and return it to the Elector Palatine in Heidelberg: 'So that neither an enemy nor hostilities are to be feared in the Holy Empire and thus we, in common with other subjects and Estates of the Empire are entitled to enjoy the sweet and noble fruits of peace; for which reason it will no longer be necessary for Your Electoral Highness to maintain so many high and costly officers, Commissars and troops'.[49] Here, the priority of the central over the provincial perspective was being questioned: from their location in the Rhineland, the representatives of Mark implied, they were better placed to make sense of the shifting balance of power in their own region (though for tactical reasons they appeared to accept the logic of necessity and confined themselves to questioning whether it was applicable in this case).

Moreover, it was one thing for the prince to claim to be warding off imminent dangers and another for him to *create* threats through his own precipitate or preemptive initiatives. Responding to complaints along these lines from the Estates of Kleve in 1651, the Elector informed them that he intended to continue maintaining his troops in their provinces and wanted them to pay him twelve thousand thalers towards their support. But he also assured them that it was not his intention to use these troops 'for the continuation of any hostilities'; they were there to provide 'security against foreign invasion'.[50] When the Estates' representatives objected that there was no sign of an imminent threat, the

Elector responded with the sage observation that one must not be fooled by the mere *appearance* of peace: despite open declarations of ceasefire, the armies of his old Neuburg rival, for example, were still concentrating and continued to pose a threat to Brandenburg's territories. As soon as the Neuburger stood down his forces, the Elector would do the same.[51]

In theory, then, dangers could subside as fast as they arose, and in this lay a seed of hope for the estates. In his declaration to the Kleve delegates of December 1645, the Elector reassured his interlocutors that the current fiscal innovations would exist only for as long as the danger was imminent: 'His Electoral Highness assures the Estates and their delegates that all of these things, which had to be done out of unavoidable necessity, are not intended in the least to be prejudicial to their documented privileges and tradition (Herkommen), and they should trust in God that these burdens will not last for long, but rather hopefully be ameliorated soon if not cease altogether.'[52] The problem was that a discrepancy persisted between the localised security thinking of the individual territories and the administration's efforts both to protect the scattered territories of the prince's patrimony and to pursue his claims in adjacent territories. As the Elector's political horizons broadened and the growth and improvement of his armed forces enabled Brandenburg to begin playing the role of a significant regional power in Northern Europe, the discrepancy between the princely and the provincial perspective became more pronounced.[53] During the Northern War of 1655–60, the Elector's army grew to twenty-five thousand men. By fighting first on the Swedish and then on the Polish-Imperial side, the Elector was able to prevent the powers engaged in the conflict from shutting him out of Ducal Prussia. It was a sign of Frederick William's growing weight in regional politics that he was appointed commander of the Brandenburg-Polish-Imperial allied army raised to fight the Swedes in 1658–59. A chain of successful military assaults followed, first in Schleswig-Holstein and Jutland and later in Pomerania.

'[It is] in the nature of alliances', the Austrian military strategist Count Montecuccoli sagely observed, 'that they are dissolved at the slightest inconvenience'.[54] In order to pay for his growing army, Frederick William needed foreign subsidies. Frequent alliance switching forced would-be partners into a bidding war and thereby pushed up the going price for an alliance, allowing him to supplement money extracted through contributions and new taxes from the Estates with less politically irksome external funding. The rapid alternation of alliances also reflected the complexity of Brandenburg's security needs. The integrity of the western territories depended on good relations with France and the United Provinces. The integrity of Ducal Prussia depended on good relations with Poland. The safety of Brandenburg's entire Baltic littoral depended on holding the Swedes at bay. The maintenance of the Elector's status and the pursuit of his inheritance claims within the empire depended upon good (or at least functional) relations with the Emperor. These imperatives interacted to generate unpredictable and rapidly shifting outcomes. It was a predicament that placed considerable strain on the decision-making networks close to the throne. During the winter of 1655–56, for example, as the Elector pondered which side to back in the opening phase of the Northern War, 'Swedish' and 'Polish' factions formed among the ministers and advisors and even the Elector's own family. The resulting mood of uncertainty and indecision prompted one of the Elector's most powerful councillors to complain that the Elector and his advisors 'want what they didn't want and do what they didn't think they would do'.[55] In switching thus from partner to partner, the Elector followed the advice of the Pomeranian Calvinist Privy Councillor Paul von Fuchs, who urged the Elector not to commit himself permanently to any one partner but always to follow a 'pendulum policy' (*Schaukelpolitik*).[56]

The complexity and even opacity of a foreign policy marked by sudden changes of affiliation was a further burden on relations between the prince and the Estates. The latter were sometimes reluctant (though the problem was less pronounced in the Elector's Brandenburg heartland) to follow the twists and turns of the Elector's policy. In an exasperated letter of complaint despatched to the Elector on 24 May 1657, the Estates of Kleve expressed dismay at the prospect of being drawn into a war with Poland: 'We feel ourselves obliged, on account of our duties towards the conservation of privileges and the public good [to repeat our earlier protests] for fear that we should sin by omission in allowing ourselves to become entangled in this currently remote conflict and like other land and people of His Electoral Highness to come to ruin, be ravaged with fire and sword and plunged into misery and captivity'.[57] In fact, it was a war with Sweden, not a war with Poland, that followed. But this merely underlined the difficulty, for the Estates, of sustaining the claim to co-arbitrate in questions touching on the security of the Elector's lands. Where the prince acted preemptively, it might be impossible to establish whether the 'emergency' that justified the overriding of traditional privileges was genuinely external in character. On several occasions, the Estates cautioned the Elector against engineering situations of conflict on his own initiative.[58]

Who had the authority to determine when the state of threat no longer existed? Increasingly, it was the Elector who monopolised this power. And he expected his subjects to accept his explanations on trust. In 1659, when the Kleve Estates complained yet again of their burdens, imposed by the Elector's ongoing campaign against the Swedes for Pomerania, the prince replied that there was nothing he would better like than to abolish these impositions. 'But we are graciously confident that you will sensibly take to heart present developments (*gegenwärtigen Conjuncturen*) and thus come to see how impossible it has hitherto been for us to take care of the maintenance of our Military Establishment (*Militäretats*) and take appropriate measures for the security of our lands. [And so We expect that you will continue to help Us] so that we can pursue our just cause and bring our State into security and peace by decisively completing the military operations already entered upon'.[59]

But what if the Elector proved unwilling to dismantle the innovation whose introduction had been justified by dire need, even when the emergency he had invoked manifestly became less dire, or dissipated altogether? Why should we keep paying for your army, now that peace has returned? asked the Estates of Brandenburg in 1650. 'Your Electoral Highness will surely concede that the maintenance of troops becomes, once peace has been concluded, a voluntary rather than a necessary subsidy'.[60] The Elector himself had promised in his Proposition of 1655 to the Estates Assembly of Ducal Prussia to disband his troops and to remove the new excise tax 'as soon as the emergency came to an end', grumbled the Ducal Prussian Estates in 1661. But even six years later, when the threat was no longer imminent or evident, nothing had been done to reverse these arrangements.[61]

In the spring of 1683, by which time the Elector had been ruling Brandenburg-Prussia for forty-three years, the Brandenburg Estates renewed their old complaint. The Elector had not merely saddled them repeatedly with 'extraordinary burdens' but also failed to observe the traditional obligation to consult with the Estates on the introduction of new taxes and levies. In his reply, the Elector adopted the persona of a weary *Landesvater* scratching his head at the ingratitude of his children. After all these years working hard for his subjects, he wrote, he was irritated to receive this cavilling letter. His reply closed with a revealing passage justifying the burdens imposed. These, he said, had been introduced not for the purpose of oppressing or weakening the Estates, but rather on account of 'the uncircumventable and lawless emergency (Noth), which God visited on us as a well-deserved plague upon the country and before which the invidious *leges fundamentales* invoked by the Estates had to give way'. And when would the plague have passed? In this text, the restoration of a true and lasting peace threatened to recede beyond the horizons of the prince's own life on earth. 'We long before God on high for better times and for such peaceful neighbours as Our forebears resting in God once had, so that his goodness might crown Our old age with a complete and secure state of peace, and We might die in the satisfaction of having brought Our lands into the real enjoyment of a relief so long awaited'.[62] As the trope of 'necessitas' was radicalised, transformed from an ad hoc argument for provisional interventions to a universal justification for permanent instruments of central power (a new and more encompassing fiscal regime, a permanent standing army, and so on), it was also temporally stretched. It referred less and less to a clear and present danger and more and more to a permanent anticipatory posture, a security apparatus focused on future contingencies.

This anticipatory posture was not just gestural or discursive; its deepening purchase on the structure of the Electoral government can be traced in the institutions he built. The Brandenburg campaign army grew dramatically, if unsteadily, from 3,000 men in 1641–42 to 8,000 in 1643–46, 25,000 during the Northern War of 1655–60, and 38,000 during the Dutch Wars of the 1670s. During the final decade of the Elector's reign, its size fluctuated between 20,000 and 30,000.[63] The improvised forces assembled for specific campaigns during the early years of the reign gradually evolved into what one could call a standing army. In April 1655, a General War Commissioner (Generalkriegskommissar) was appointed to oversee the handling of financial and other resources for the army, on the model of the military administration recently introduced in France. This innovation was initially conceived as a temporary wartime measure and only later established as a permanent feature of the territorial administration. After 1679, under the direction of the Pomeranian nobleman Joachim von Grumbkow, the General War Commissariat extended its reach throughout the Hohenzollern territories, gradually usurping the function of the Estate officials who had traditionally overseen military taxation and discipline at a local level. This synergy between war-making and the development of state-like central organs was something new; it became possible only when the war-making apparatus was separated from its traditional, provincial-aristocratic foundations.

The Estates had structured their arguments around the opposition between a state of normality inherited from the past and the extraordinary concessions they were obliged from time to time to make to the Elector. And in a sense the Elector had encouraged or licensed this view of the matter by deploying the language of 'emergency'. But over time, he came to mean something else: a 'new normal' not fixed to a foundation of traditional rights at all, but responsive to a constantly shifting flux of demands, to the 'conjunctures' and 'current trends' (*jetzigen Läufe*) of a constantly changing present, in short: to what we would call 'history'.

A Confessional Dynamic?

Was there anything more to the futurity implicit in the Elector's arguments than the mechanical conversion of future threats into present imperatives? The claim that the harms implicit in a possible future impose duties upon the present articulates a historicity in which the authority of the past over the present is diminished. It favours instead a mode of reasoning hostile to tradition (or at least to tradition in its own right) and prepared to deploy the future as an argument against inherited rights and structures of power.

Whether this future-oriented historicity was embedded in something more reflexive, an awareness of the larger movement of history, is hard to discern, all the more so as this sovereign was not given to speculative or philosophical reflection. Yet he did consciously adhere to at least one complex contemporary philosophical structure, namely the theology of his Calvinist faith. Frederick William was the first Brandenburg Elector to be born of two Calvinist parents, and the composite name Frederick William, a novelty in the history of the house of Hohenzollern, was devised precisely in order to symbolise the bond between Berlin (William was his father's second name) and the Calvinist Palatinate of his uncle, Frederick V. Only with this generation of the Hohenzollern family did the reorientation launched by the conversion to Calvinism of his grandfather John Sigismund in 1613 come fully into effect.

The confessional divide between the ruling house and the population is one of the intriguing peculiarities of Brandenburg-Prussian history. John Sigismund's conversion had placed the house of Hohenzollern on a new trajectory. It reinforced the dynasty's association with the small but combative camp of the Calvinist states in early seventeenth-century Imperial politics. It augmented the status of the Calvinist officials who were beginning to play an influential role in the central government. But it also placed the Elector in a religious camp for which no provision had been made in the Peace of Augsburg of 1555. Not until the Peace of Westphalia in 1648 would the right of the Calvinists to tolerance within the confessional patchwork of the Holy Roman Empire be enshrined in a binding treaty. The conversion of the monarch also drove a deep confessional trench between dynasty and people. Inasmuch as there existed a sense of territorial 'identity' in late sixteenth-century Branden-burg, this was intimately bound up with the Lutheran church, whose clergy spanned the length and breadth of the country.

John Sigismund initially believed that his own conversion would give the signal for a generalised—and largely volun-tary—'second Reformation' in Brandenburg. The Elector and his advisors assumed that the inherent superiority and clarity of Calvinist doctrine, when cogently and accessibly presented, would suffice to recommend it to the great majority of sub-jects. In this they were mistaken. The Lutheran networks bit-terly resisted any measures that appeared likely to further the transformation of Brandenburg into a Calvinist territory.[64] The strength of Lutheran resistance eventually forced John Sigismund and his Calvinist advisors to abandon their hopes of a Second Brandenburg Reformation. They settled instead for a 'court reformation' (Hofreformation), whose religious en-ergies petered out on the fringes of the political elite.[65] But it took a long time for the emotion to drain out of the Lutheran-Calvinist confrontation. Tension levels fluctuated with the ebb and flow of confessional polemic.[66]

This was still the situation when Elector Frederick Wil-liam took power in 1640. Frederick William reinforced his house's affiliation with the Calvinist faith in 1646 by marry-ing Louise Henriette, nineteen-year-old daughter of Fred-erick Henry, sovereign Prince of Orange and Stadhouder of

Holland, Zeeland, Utrecht, Guelders, and Overijssel. At the international negotiations in Münster that prepared the way for the Peace of Westphalia in 1648, he successfully campaigned for the inclusion of the Calvinists among the official tolerated confessions of the Holy Roman Empire.[67] Yet within his territories, the problem of confessional tension remained, and Ducal Prussia in particular, in which he spent the early years of his reign, but over which he would not secure full sovereignty until 1657, was a staunchly Lutheran country, dominated by noble elites deeply attached to their Lutheran traditions.

In 1642, only two years into his reign, the Elector responded with anger to the news that Lutheran polemicists in Königsberg were accusing him of renewing the Hohenzollern project to effect a 'second Reformation'. This development was particularly unwelcome at a moment when the Brandenburg court was exploring the possibility of a dynastic alliance with the Lutheran Crown of Sweden.[68] In a letter to his councillors, he lamented the theological bickering and name-calling that threatened to poison public life in Ducal Prussia. The catastrophic consequences of religious division could be observed across the German lands—the Lutheran subjects of Prussia, which had managed to escape the worst turmoil of war, should study this example and learn from it. The best course of action, the Elector proposed, would be 'a friendly and peaceful discussion among the theologians in Our presence and that of Our councillors, Estates and senior servants'. In such a context, each point could be carefully examined, and where there was a need for further elucidation, this could be provided in an informed way by both sides.[69]

In rejecting this proposal, the Lutheran clergy of Königsberg developed an argument from continuity with tradition that was strongly analogous to the corporatist arguments for privilege offered by the Estates. It would be 'half-heathen', they argued, to enter into a discussion without a prior 'condemnation of the error and incorrect doctrine' of the Reformed interlocutors. Particularly revealing was the Biblical reference offered by the Estates in support of this claim, 2 Kings 17. This passage in the Book of Kings relates how several thousand Israelites of ancient Samaria were captured by the Assyrians and resettled in lands under Assyrian control. These captives assimilated to the new political leadership and abandoned their old religion, ignoring the injunction of God, uttered through the mouths of seers and prophets, to 'keep My commandments *and* My statutes, according to all the law which I commanded your fathers'. They 'rejected His statutes and His covenant that He had made with their fathers, and His testimonies which He had testified against them'.[70] In short, so the argument ran: if the Prussian Lutherans acquiesced in the Elector's proposal, they would resemble the faithless Israelites of Samaria, who had betrayed their time-honoured covenants. To this they added an argument from legal authority: the Political Testament of Duke Albrecht the Elder, Duke of Prussia from 1525 until 1568, had stipulated that the Lutheran supremacy in the Duchy must not be tampered with.[71] The conference project was abandoned. When a symposium of Lutheran and Calvinist theologians did eventually meet at the Electoral palace in Berlin in 1662–63, it merely sharpened the differences between the two camps and led to a new wave of mutual denunciations.[72]

Here, as in the Elector's disputes with his estates, we can discern two opposed temporalities. The invitations to take part in colloquies implied that an open-ended process of discussion might in future resolve all remaining differences. The Lutheran view, in contrast, argued that the past, invoked in the form of tradition, imposed obligations upon the present. The term 'tolerance' has often been used to characterise the

Elector's political management of the Calvinist-Lutheran divide in his own lands, and the suggestion that the minority status of the Elector's confession imposed religious tolerance as a permanent and structural feature of Prussian public life is a commonplace in the older literature.[73] And it is certainly true that some of the most influential Calvinists of this era used irenic language to characterise the relationship between the two faiths.[74] Yet what is lost from view if we apply the rubric 'tolerance' is the partisan character of the Elector's measures and his abiding determination to reinforce the position of his Reformed co-religionists across his territories.[75] Under the 'Edict of Tolerance' issued in September 1664, Calvinist and Lutheran clergymen were ordered to abstain from mutual disparagements; all preachers were required to signal their acceptance of this order by signing and returning a pre-circulated reply.[76] Yet the impact of the edict was highly asymmetrical, since the theological polemics stemmed almost exclusively from Lutheran functionaries alarmed at Calvinist incursions. Only Lutheran preachers objected to the terms of the edict, and those who refused to sign the pre-circulated reply were summarily dismissed from their livings.[77]

These measures were flanked by numerous other interventions. Whenever he could, the Elector appointed Calvinists to senior court and government posts, dismissing Lutheran protests as vexatious efforts to sow distrust between the Elector and his subjects. The jurisdiction of the Privy Council with its Calvinist majority was extended at the expense of the Lutheran consistory. Lutheran preachers were menaced with capricious application of the censorship law: in one case a preacher was banished from Brandenburg for daring to mention in a sermon, alongside the great deeds of the Elector, those of his Lutheran rival the Swedish king Charles X Gustav. There was a consistent effort to cut the Lutherans in Brandenburg off from the Lutheran hub at Wittenberg, by denying them the right to take an active part in trans-territorial networks. New Calvinist parishes and churches were founded at every opportunity, and the Elector's famed policy of offering refuge to Huguenots—also Calvinist—persecuted in the France of Louis XIV served the same objective, since it brought thousands of new co-religionists into his lands.[78] In case there were any doubt about the concerted and systematic character of these efforts, the Elector advised his successor in the Political Testament to see to it that 'if such subjects of the Reformed Religion existed in his lands, [these] were taken up and appointed above others to services and offices at court and across the country and if none could be found in the Electorate of Brandenburg, to take foreign ones and prefer them to the Lutherans'.[79]

Given that the Reformed never amounted to more than 4 percent of the total population of Brandenburg-Prussia, these measures were never going to transform the confessional character of the country as a whole, although they did mean that the administrative personnel in Brandenburg and Pomerania became steadily more Calvinist and less Lutheran. In Ducal Prussia by contrast, with its long-standing institutions and its confident Lutheran elites, the Elector's efforts had less impact. The point I am interested in pursuing here is simply that the dynamic of 'confessionalisation' was sustained. The Elector did not retire from the fray and oversee the religious peace between Calvinists and Lutherans from a standpoint of religious neutrality. He remained committed to the 'Calvinisation' of court and government. And he did this because he continued to believe that the Reformed faith, with its roots in revealed biblical truth alone, represented a fundamental salvific advance on Lutheranism.

How exactly this confessional engagement bore upon the Elector's historicity is hard to say. Was he making an absolute claim on behalf of his faith, or merely securing the political preeminence of his co-religionists in order to consolidate his authority? In the Political Testament, as we have seen, Frederick William affirmed the importance of defending the new order embodied in the Peace of Westphalia, the first international treaty to include the Calvinists among the confessions with a claim to be 'tolerated' in the Holy Roman Empire. But when he proposed symposia and conferences between the two Protestant confessions, he was not endorsing religious peace as such (however much he might value it for reasons of public order and political interest), but rather seeking to bring the Lutherans *forwards* towards an agreement with the Reformed. The Elector forbade the public use of the term 'second reformation', because it was used for scaremongering by Lutheran polemicists, but the logic of a supersession was implicit in his handling of the relationship between the two denominations.

It is true that the theological historicity of the Calvinists was also recursive in character, in the sense that it involved a 'return' to the supposedly unsullied condition of the early church. But for them, the early church was not a 'tradition', nor was it something inherited; it was merely the remembered instantiation of a communion with Christ (*koinonia*) that, for the Reformed, was as much at home in the future as in the past. The Calvinist notion of a supra-historical *koinonia* with Christ, guaranteed to the faithful, marked a definitive break both with medieval and with early reformation theology. It opened up a new time horizon, mapped out by the combination of a remote God with the promise of fellowship always ensured by faith, a horizon within which everything was possible and 'constructible' in the this-worldly world. The Reformed understanding of the possibility of Christ's kingdom on earth proposed an impulse to action that was absent from the Lutheran doctrine of the Two Kingdoms (heaven and earth) as ontologically separate domains. Calvinist theology did not in itself offer a philosophy of history, but it did provide a framework in which there was an abundance of room for the chaotic particularities of present and future contingencies to be perceived, evaluated, and managed.[80] As a theological temperament, Calvinism thus reinforced a broader shift in the character of early modern European political rationalisation. The propagation across the late sixteenth- and seventeenth-century German states of the '*discorso* method' popularised by Machiavelli tended to displace arguments from authority and universal principle in favour of the weighing up of political options in a future that was yet to be determined.[81]

These features of Reformed theology resonated with assumptions anchored in the Elector's own youthful experience. At the age of fourteen, as the military crisis deepened in his father's lands and a wave of epidemics spread across Brandenburg, he was sent to the safety of the Dutch Republic, where he would spend the next four years of his life. The prince received instruction from professors in law, history, and politics at the University of Leiden, a renowned centre of the then-fashionable neostoical state theory. The prince's lessons emphasised the majesty of the law, the venerability of the state as the guarantor of order, and the centrality of duty and obligation to the office of sovereign. A particular concern of the neostoics was the need to subordinate the military to the authority and discipline of the state.[82] But it was outside the classroom, in the streets, docks, markets, and parade squares of the Dutch towns that Frederick William learned his most important lessons.

In the early seventeenth century, the Dutch Republic was at the height of its power and prosperity. Over more than sixty years, this small Calvinist country had fought successfully to assert its independence against the military might of

Catholic Spain and to establish itself as the foremost European headquarters of global trade. 'Let us take as our example the brave Dutch, who after pushing back the Romans [i.e., the Habsburgs] have been called promoters of liberty', wrote the Calvinist clergyman, Johann Bergius, trusted advisor, and religious counsellor to the Great Elector.[83] In their prosperity, material culture, and the sophistication and maturity of their political life, the United Provinces were 'the first country in Europe'.[84] Their orderly, bustling cities were physical arguments for the superiority of a certain way of life. They possessed a robust fiscal regime and a distinctive military culture with recognisably modern features: the regular and systematic drilling of troops in battleground manoeuvres, a high level of functional differentiation, and a disciplined professional officer corps. Frederick William had ample opportunity to observe the military prowess of the Republic at close hand—he visited his host and relative, Viceroy Prince Frederick Henry of Orange, in the Dutch encampment at Breda in 1637, where the Dutch recaptured a stronghold that had been lost to the Spaniards twelve years before.

Throughout his reign Frederick William strove to remodel his own patrimony in the image of what he had observed in the Netherlands. The training regime adopted by his army in 1654 was based on the drill book of Prince Maurice of Orange.[85] Dutch immigrants were encouraged to settle in Brandenburg on privileged terms. Frederick William remained convinced that 'navigation and trade are the principal pillars of a state, through which subjects, by sea and by manufactures on land, earn their food and keep'.[86] Hence his repeated efforts to secure, at great cost and against bitter Swedish resistance, control over Pomerania.[87] He became preoccupied with the idea that the link to the Baltic would enliven and commercialise Brandenburg, bringing the wealth and power that were so conspicuously on display in Amsterdam. In the 1650s and

1660s, he even negotiated international commercial treaties to secure privileged terms of trade for a merchant marine he did not yet possess.[88] In short, Frederick William knew Calvinism not just as a faith community, but as the animating ethos of a country he acknowledged as culturally and materially superior and worthy of emulation. And, as Peter Burke has observed, 'the emulation by sovereigns and governments of foreign models implied that action in the present might make their country prosperous in the future.'[89]

The Elector Becomes History

At the Battle of Warsaw in the summer of 1656, eighty-five hundred Brandenburg troops joined forces with the army of the King of Sweden to defeat a massive Polish-Tartar force. Elector Frederick William wrote a short account of the event and ordered it published in The Hague. He hoped by this means to counter the effect of contemporary Swedish reports that understated Brandenburg's—and specifically the Elector's—contribution to the victory.[90] His own account made it clear that the Allied success was due to a two-pronged attack, in which the Elector of Brandenburg had personally commanded and led the left wing, come under direct fire from the enemy batteries, and played a key role in wresting from the Poles control of a stretch of high ground that allowed the allies to subject the enemy to intensive bombardment.[91]

This modest effort to situate himself in the chronicle of his times made sense in a world that was becoming increasingly aware of the relationship between the news of contemporary events and the record that 'history' would bequeath to future generations. The most sensational embodiment of this nexus between news and history was the *Theatrum Europaeum*, a publishing project launched by the Frankfurt printer,

engraver, and entrepreneur Matthäus Merian. In a sequence
of opulently illustrated volumes running to between four
hundred and fifteen hundred pages, Merian and his collaborators and successors compiled an all-encompassing history
of recent times. The first volume, published in 1633, covered
the years between 1629 and the year of publication. The second, published two years later, backdated the story to 1618
and the outbreak of the Thirty Years' War that was still dev-
astating Central Europe when the volume appeared. Thereafter, the project advanced in steps of between two and eight
years over nineteen further volumes composed by at least ten
different writers until 1738. From the outset, the publishers
and the writers who worked with them aspired to capture the
larger panorama of history in a narrative that avoided partisan viewpoints damaging to the interests of any particular
party or individual, and sought 'simply to bring the historical
story [*historische Geschichte*] to light'.[92]

The *Theatrum* was and is remarkable for its technical ambition, especially the quality and profusion of the illustrations. In
the 'theatre' portrayed on its pages, sovereigns and statesmen
occupied a prominent place. They were the moving parts in a
story that was European in scope. But the most striking feature
of the *Theatrum* was its vision of European history as a connected system whose 'commotions' and realignments bound the
states of the continent together in one community of destiny.[93]
The need for such a history was urgent, the editor declared, not
just because prudent societies had always benefited from an understanding of their own times, but also because the violence
and devastations of *recent* European history confronted contemporaries with the duty of describing 'the course of our
World-Actions [*Welt-Actionen*] / in order to see thereby why we
began [the commotion of war], how we managed it and to
know approximately on account of which causes and by means

of which occasions we so lamentably spoiled, destroyed, ruined and devastated land and people'.[94] Woven together of material drawn from the forty-odd printed weekly newspapers published in the cities of the Holy Roman Empire, histories of this kind made it possible to imagine the proximate future not as the fulfilment of a preordained plan, but as empty, like the still-unprinted pages of a newspaper, waiting to be filled with the acts and events of the powerful.[95] This was precisely that world of 'conjunctures' (*Conjuncturen*) and 'trends' (*Läufe*) the Elector so often invoked in his communications with the Estates.

In his 'royal memoirs', a confidential text intended for the eyes of his successor, Louis XIV observed that kings owe an

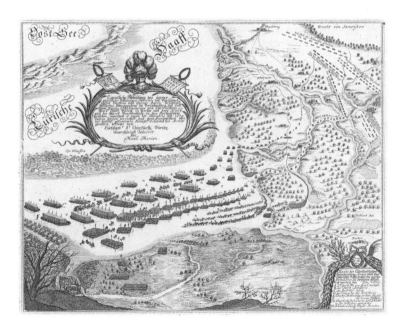

FIGURE 1.2. Engraving from the *Theatrum Europaeum* showing how the Great Elector led his forces into the Duchy of Prussia in 1679, surprising the Swedish army encamped there. *Source*: Anon., *Theatri Europaei Eilffter Theil Oder: Außführlich fortgeführte Friedens und KriegsBeschreibung* [...] (Frankfurt/Main, 1682), 1466. Collection of the author.

account of their actions 'to all ages'.[96] The Elector never unfolded a cult of historicised self-memorialisation to rival that of his French contemporary, but he did begin consciously to perceive himself and his achievements through the eyes of an imagined posterity. From 1650 onwards, there were efforts to secure the services of a court historian. The first appointee was the librarian Joachim Hübner, but Hübner's oeuvre never materialised, because he was dismissed in 1661 after complaints about his refusal to attend church.[97] In 1664, the Elector appointed Marten Schoock of the University of Groningen in the United Provinces and paid him a handsome salary to write a history of Brandenburg. A first section of the projected *Historia marchica* was completed in manuscript in 1667, but its quality was so poor, one nineteenth-century commentator acidly remarked, 'there is no reason to regret the fact that the work was cut short by Schoock's premature death' one year later.[98] Two other appointees, the French adventurer and Calvinist convert Jean Baptiste de Rocolles and Martin Kempen, a Königsberger of Netherlandish descent, took up and abandoned the task without producing anything of note.

Gregorio Leti's meandering two-volume chronicle of the House of Brandenburg, published in Italian and French in 1687, was not officially commissioned, but the Elector did reward its author with a medal worth a hundred ducats and a cash gift of five hundred thalers.[99] Leti's book was a fantastically chaotic string of vignettes and descriptions, interspersed with formulaic passages of panegyric on the Elector and his most prominent officials. But it is interesting to note that the first volume was criticised in Berlin for failing to do justice to the Elector's achievements at the Battle of Warsaw in 1656— an indication that Warsaw had by now entered public awareness as a historical landmark in the reign.[100] Neither Schoock's antiquarian survey nor Leti's rambling encomium left any discernible impact on the later historiography of Prussia.

Far more successful was Samuel Pufendorf, appointed court historian in 1686, whose comprehensive and sophisticated account of Frederick William's reign marked a new departure in Brandenburg historiography. The choice of Pufendorf was telling. In a long career as a jurist, political theorist, and historian, Pufendorf had established himself as one of the stars of academic Europe. By the late seventeenth century, he was the most widely read philosopher of natural law on the continent. Unlike many of his university colleagues, he was read outside the academic world by senior officials, military commanders, and even monarchs.[101] It is not difficult to see what attracted the Elector about Pufendorf and his writings. An astute (though also critical) German reader of the British political theorist Thomas Hobbes, Pufendorf grounded his arguments for the necessity of the state in a dystopian vision of ambient violence and disorder.[102] The law of nature alone did not suffice to preserve the social life of man, he argued in his *Elements of Universal Jurisprudence* (1660). Unless 'sovereignties' were established, men would seek their welfare by force alone; 'all places would reverberate with wars between those who are inflicting and those who are repelling injuries'.[103]

Hence the supreme importance of states, whose chief purpose was 'that men, by means of mutual cooperation and assistance, be safe against the harms and injuries they can and commonly do inflict on one another'.[104] The trauma of the Thirty Years' War resonates in these sentences. Here was an eloquent philosophical answer to the resistance that the Elector had encountered from the provincial Estates. Since it was impossible in peace or war to conduct the affairs of a state without incurring expenses, Pufendorf wrote in 1672, the sovereign had the right to 'force individual citizens to contribute so much of their own goods as the assumption of those expenses is deemed to require'.[105] He wrote extensively on the place of consent in relationships of political subjection, arguing that obligations to the sovereign could never be the consequence of compulsion alone; they could have real force only if the subject had or were provided with good reasons for acquiescing in the obligations imposed—the benevolent intentions of the sovereign, for example, or gratitude for past benefits, or the acknowledgement that the sovereign may be better able to see to the subjects' interests than the subjects themselves can.[106] The harmonic resonances between these lines of thought and the arguments advanced in the Elector's communications with his Estates are difficult to miss.

But Pufendorf was also a celebrated historian. His most famous political tract, known as the 'Monzambano', was a trenchant and controversial critique of the political organisation of the contemporary Holy Roman Empire, but it opened with a widely praised sequence of chapters setting out the history of the empire's political institutions.[107] And his *Introduction to the History of the Principal Kingdoms and States of Europe*, published in 1682 during Pufendorf's tenure as official historian to the royal court at Stockholm, opened with a plea for the importance of studying the history of the recent past. It was all very well, Pufendorf wrote, for young people to spend years reading Cornelius Nepos and Livy, 'but to neglect the history of later times is a notorious piece of indiscretion and want of understanding'. Those entrusted with the management of public affairs in particular would benefit more from studying the contemporary history of their own country and its neighbouring territories than from poring over the accounts of ancient conquests in the Roman classics. And the chapter dedicated to Germany offered, among other things, an analysis of the threats posed to Germany (or not) by every nearby power, from the Swiss and the Italians to the Poles, the Danes, the Swedes, and the French.[108]

It took some time to persuade Pufendorf to leave Sweden and take up a post as the court historian in Berlin. Pufendorf conveyed his formal agreement to the Brandenburg envoy at Stockholm in the summer of 1686, four years after the first approach, but it was not until mid-January 1688, after some wrangling with his current employers, that he arrived in Berlin. By this time, the Elector had only a few months to live. Pufendorf was given free access to the Electoral archives and provided with the services of a full-time research assistant.

Packed with material closely paraphrased from the archives and running to over fourteen hundred densely printed pages in the 1695 Latin edition, Pufendorf's *De rebus gestis Friderici Wilhelmi Magni* (over twelve hundred pages in Erdmann Uhse's slightly abridged German translation of 1710) does not make easy or enjoyable reading.[109] There is no broad sweep to the narrative and no attempt to situate the protagonists within a current of change. The counsellors, courtiers, and family members around the prince are scarcely visible in their individuality. The Elector himself appears only as the personification of his monarchy—we learn next to nothing of his pastimes, intellectual interests, tastes, or relationships. And yet in two respects Pufendorf did succeed in endowing his narrative with historical momentum.

First, he acknowledged the importance of the *domestic* consolidation of Electoral sovereignty. At the centre of Pufendorf's story is the monarchical executive: 'The measure and focal point of all his reflections was the state, upon which all initiatives converge like lines towards a central point'.[110] Personified by the Great Elector, the Brandenburg state in Pufendorf's account projects and consolidates its power both outwards and inwards. Pufendorf offers detailed accounts—even more so in the Latin edition of 1695 than in the German translation of 1710—of the conflicts between the Electoral administration and the Prussian, Kleve, and Magdeburg Estates. In Ducal Prussia after the Peace of Oliva (1660), for example, he juxtaposes the efforts of the Elector to consolidate his sovereignty within Ducal Prussia with the Estates' insistence that their age-old privileges (irreconcilable with the assertion of Electoral sovereignty) be reaffirmed. He relates how the Electoral administration circumvented this corporate resistance by instructing the Calvinist Prince Radziwill, governor of Ducal Prussia, to approach the most influential grandees individually: 'he was to get those who held the highest offices in the land to swear an oath [of fealty] according to the new formula after the acquisition of sovereignty, not all at the same time, however, but rather one by one and as the opportunity arose'. He should begin with those who he knew were willing to swear such an oath, 'so that the others would follow their example, and those who refused should be threatened with removal from their posts and he should not appoint anyone new to any office, except for those who promised that when the meeting [of the Estates] was convened they would support the Elector in his wish'.[111]

In Magdeburg, as in Prussia, Pufendorf depicts the central administration rolling back the traditional power of the Estates by playing the city of Magdeburg off against the countryside.[112] When the city of Königsberg continued to agitate against the new regime in the name of its traditional rights and status, the Elector, Pufendorf reports, 'did not conceal his anger and displeasure at such obstinate behaviour'. 'His Electoral Highness Himself decided to push the matter through by his own authority, but he also took a good number of troops with him, to tame the disobedient ones'. The passage in the text where Pufendorf describes the resolution of the quarrel in the Elector's favour is printed opposite an engraving showing the Ducal Prussian Estates swearing an oath of fealty to their new sovereign in the court of the Königsberg Palace on 18 October 1663.[113]

In drawing this dynamic picture of the state in its struggle to overcome the structures of provincial privilege, Pufendorf was able to draw not only on archival documents but also the earlier history composed by Elias Loccelius (also known as Lockelius or Löckel), Lutheran pastor at Bärwalde in the Neumark and later (from 1674) in Crossen. Completed after decades of research and writing and presented to the court in manuscript in 1680, Loccelius's compendious *Marchia Illustrata* represented a transitional phase between the naïve chronicles of sixteenth-century Brandenburg and the analytically driven historical treatise of Pufendorf. Loccelius's rigorously chronological approach, his decision to begin with the creation of the world by God, and his inclusion of disparate fragments of information—the price of rye, the appearance of comets, multiple suns or spots of blood in bowls of peas—recall the baggy and credulous chronicles of the Middle Ages. But there are also passages of impressive complexity and depth, especially on the subject of the devastations of the Thirty Years' War, the protests of the Prussian Estates in the early 1660s, and the Elector's pacification of rebellious Magdeburg.[114] Indeed, there is little reason to doubt that Pufendorf's account of these latter episodes was drawn substantially from Loccelius.

Pufendorf did not go so far as to articulate the linkage between these domestic measures and the outward projection of power and prestige, but his translator, Erdmann Uhse, made the connection explicit in his preamble to the edition of 1710, when he observed that the acquisition of undiluted territorial sovereignty 'paved the road to [Prussia's later acquisition of] the royal crown' in 1701.[115] And of course Pufendorf himself had often made the argument that the sovereign's ability to provide protection against external threat and inner mayhem justified his claim on a portion of his subjects' resources.

The other moment of dynamism in Pufendorf's narrative relates to his depiction of sovereign decision making. What we would describe as the 'historical events' of that era play a subordinate role in his account of the Elector's reign; they are viewed primarily through the prism of the choices faced by the Elector and his advisers. And this is precisely where Pufendorf's otherwise rather one-dimensional account acquires analytical texture. In 1645, for example, the Elector was invited by King Wladislaw IV of Poland (1632–48) to send a delegation of Reformed clergy to an event that would become known as the Colloquy of Thorn, a conference of Reformed, Lutheran, and Catholic clergy whose ostensible purpose was to allow peaceful and informed debate of the issues that divided the confessions. In reconstructing the response of the Elector and his aides, Pufendorf laid bare a logic tree of options, in which the consequences of each possible course of action were weighed up.

'When it was discussed [among the Elector's counsellors] whether the Elector should acquiesce in this request', Pufendorf wrote, 'the votes diverged'. The counsellors liked the idea of an irenic summit of this kind and the Polish city of Thorn was believed to be a safe location. Yet there were also reasons why one might not accept the invitation. The fact that the Polish bishops appeared to be controlling the event, arrogating to themselves the right to determine the format of the discussion and even the size of the delegations, was a cause for concern. Then there was the danger that a conference of this kind might intensify the tensions between the Reformed and the Lutherans in Prussia. The Colloquy might also have deleterious effects on the status of Polish Protestants. And what if the Catholics claimed that they had won the argument and used it as missionary propaganda? But then, on the other hand, if the Brandenburg Calvinists decided to stay away from the event, the Catholics might exploit their absence as evidence that the Reformed were not confident of their cause. And it was surely one's duty to bear witness to the truth at every opportunity. This would be a chance to present the Reformed doctrine in a clearer light and thus to defend it from the misrepresentations of enemies.[116] These contending viewpoints were not assigned to individual named persons from among the Elector's entourage; rather they were woven together using a kind of free indirect speech. Their purpose was not to commemorate the role played by specific advisers, but to expose the nature of the decision-making task itself.

Again and again, Pufendorf unfolded decision positions in this manner, granting the reader a view of each predicament before its resolution had been found and exposing the ratiocinations of the decision maker and his advisers. In 1678, for example, the Elector faced a plurality of potential threats. In the course of an exhausting four-year campaign, he had succeeded in driving every last Swede out of Pomerania. But this was not enough to place him in possession of his claim, because Louis XIV had no intention of leaving his Swedish ally at Brandenburg's mercy. France, whose powers were waxing as the Dutch Wars came to an end, insisted that the conquered Pomeranian territories should be restored in their entirety to Sweden.

Pufendorf offered a detailed account of the issues involved, together with the potential consequences of choosing each of the options on offer. 'Regarding the question of what the Elector should undertake on the military front this year', he wrote, 'they [the Elector and his advisers] were at first undecided'. The Dutch had urged the Elector to concentrate his forces against France in the west and merely hold off the Swedes in Pomerania. There was something to be said for this course, because concentrating his forces there would motivate the Dutch to stay in the fight and discourage the French from breaking into Kleve and using it as a bargaining chip at later peace negotiations. On the other hand, if the Elector went to the Rhine, he would expose Prussia, Pomerania, and the Mark to danger and alienate his ally the King of Denmark, who was also at war with Sweden and was urging him to deploy his forces in Pomerania. And yet if he concentrated on securing Pomerania and driving out the Swedes, this might well leave France in a strong enough position after the cessation of hostilities to demand the return of the conquered Pomeranian territories to its Swedish ally.[117] What is interesting about these decisional moments in Pufendorf's narrative (and they are very frequent) is how they situate the decision maker within a threat map in which his task is to balance options, each of which implies a possible future. 'Impending danger' [bevorstehende Gefahr] is as central to Pufendorf's narrative as it was to the arguments levelled against the Estates by the Great Elector.

Making decisions was hard in part because the process had to take into account the existence of other decision makers. In a discussion of the Elector's foreign policy at the beginning of the Northern War, for example, Pufendorf reconstructed the efforts of the councillors to second-guess the king of Sweden. Would the Swedes attack the Commonwealth of Poland? 'It was difficult to believe that the Swedes would breach a peace treaty that still had six years to run. . . . On the other hand, Sweden had seldom been free of inner turmoil during long periods of peace; war might thus seem a good means of countering these. The king was still young, undaunted, bold and desirous of acquiring fame by feats of arms'. Yet he also lacked an heir, faced domestic rivals, and risked domestic rebellion if he raised taxes to fund a campaign.[118] In this passage, the

Elector was depicted as trying to anticipate the behaviour of another decision maker whose predicaments and calculations were no less complex than the Elector's own. Running through all of these episodes was an interest in choice-making situations that was not merely historical, but philosophical.[119]

Pufendorf thus fashioned an unprecedentedly sophisticated account of the place of a sovereign decision maker within the European states system. What strikes the reader about his handling of international relations is the open-endedness of the predicaments in which the state finds itself. The predicaments are open-ended because the future behaviour of the other states in the system can never be predicted with certainty. Among Pufendorf's most influential interventions in the earlier essay known as 'Monzambano' was his demolition of the *translatio imperii*—an influential thesis according to which the Holy Roman Empire of the German Nation, as the inheritor and continuation of ancient Rome, was the 'fourth monarchy' prophesied in the Book of Daniel. By rejecting this claim to continuity with the ancient past, Pufendorf 'deprived the empire of a genetic, historical self-justification'.[120] At the same time he dislodged the contemporary history of the empire and, by extension, of Europe from the diachronic grip of prophecy, allowing it to unfold under secular auspices as the unforeordained outcome of interactions among states jostling for power and influence.

The interaction among powers in the same synchronous time envelope was the very antithesis of tradition and continuity, because the interests of states and the possible actions implied by them were constantly changing. While it was true, Pufendorf conceded, that the interests of a state were determined in part by immutable factors, such as 'the situation and character of the country', they were also a function of 'the condition, strength and weakness of the neighbours, with whose alteration the interest also changes'.[121] This was the flux that Pufendorf's history was made of. This was not a world of pure contingency, because the interaction among powers continued to be governed by the relation of force and the imperative of self-preservation. But the laws governing this 'system' merely described processes; they did not predict outcomes. Under such a dispensation, acting historically in the present meant discarding tradition, apprehending the multiplicity of possible futures, identifying the threats posed by each, and selecting among them. And therein lay the chief strength of Pufendorf's Great Elector as a sovereign decision maker. 'When opinions differed greatly on a complicated matter', Pufendorf wrote in a concluding appraisal of his protagonist, 'he chose one of them in accordance with his thoughts and the outcome subsequently showed that [he had chosen] the best'.[122]

Conclusion

It is worth reflecting on the dynamism of the idea of sovereign authority projected through the public utterances, actions, and historiographical articulations of the Elector's regime. Gathering authority and resources to itself, the state tears through the bonds of tradition, emancipating itself from the legacy of a provincial past, anticipating possible futures, and inventing new instruments to confront them. It is a time machine, an engine that makes history happen. Two centuries later, Max Weber would capture this confrontation in the tension between 'traditional' and 'rational' forms of rule: while the estates founded their claims on 'the sanctity of immemorial traditions', Frederick William did away with the need, still present in traditional structures, to legitimise 'rules which in fact are innovations . . . by the claim that they have been "valid of yore", but have now been recognized by means of "Wisdom"'.[123] Of course we have to be careful here about imputing to the Elector thoughts that are ours, not his. The danger of reading into his utterances the 'hypotheses and patterns of interpretation' of a later age is especially great in his case, because he was later elevated by historians to pivotal status as the founder and anticipator of the modern Prussian state.[124] The Great Elector was not driven by a vision of 'modernisation', nor did he seek consistently to unitarise or centralise his state—on the contrary, he recorded in his will an order to the effect that his patrimony should be divided upon his death among several of his male offspring, a decision that, had it been carried out by his successor, would have put an early end to Brandenburg-Prussia's long journey to great-power status. He possessed neither an elaborate vision nor privileged knowledge of the future.

On the other hand, as we have seen, his words and actions did betray a markedly preemptive and dynamic understanding of his place in historical time. The past appeared under a pall of destruction, walled off from the present by the great peace of 1648. The lesson of that past was that to stand still would mean sliding backwards into mayhem. The future appeared under a sign of threat, partly for the reason that, as Jeremy Bentham observed, 'of the invisible future, fear is more powerful than hope'.[125] The anticipation of impending peril lay at the heart of Pufendorf's account of sovereignty and its claims on the citizen. And the same trope ran like a red thread through the Elector's arguments against the defences of tradition offered by his estates. Underpinning this existential condition was the Elector's youthful memory of the Thirty Years' War, whose trauma resounds in the doleful phrases of the Political Testament to his heir: 'For one thing is quite certain, if You simply sit still, in the belief that the fire is still far from Your borders: then Your lands will become the theatre on which the tragedy is played out'.[126] Only by pressing forward, disarming

threats in advance, and choosing among futures could one secure oneself against the 'troubles' and 'difficulties' that were
the signature of the international system. And this required in
turn that the claims of 'tradition'—both as a way of justifying
domestic power structures and as a framework for conceptual-
izing the relations among states—be drastically curtailed.

The Elector and his historiographer did not carve out this
path in solitude. His appeal to the futurity of the state should
be set in the context of a broader European shift in political
and historical awareness that was not confined to the Protestant territories. In the late fifteenth and early sixteenth
centuries, forms of political rationalisation grounded in the
application of universal principles made way for a new framework in which the future appeared as 'available for manipulation' (verfügbar). The early seventeenth-century 'wish-lists' of
scholars such as Francis Bacon and Jakob Bornitz exemplified,
as Vera Keller has shown, a reorientation of knowledge away
from the past towards an open future, now imagined as an
'ever advancing frontier' of understanding. The seventeenth-
century 'scientific revolution' brought not the triumph of
certainty, as has sometimes been claimed, but rather a 'will-
ingness to engage with doubt, probability, and the murkiness
of knowledge in motion'.[127] Providential and prophetic sche-
mata may still have been invoked as guarantees for the remote
future concerned with the end of days, Peter Burke has suggested, but the immediate and medium-term future opened
up in the seventeenth century as a space for discretionary
human action.[128] And in the process, as J.G.A. Pocock argued,
Europe relinquished the idea of history as providentially ordained.[129] Precariously situated on the advancing frontier of
events, the state was obliged, as Andrea Brady and Emily Butterworth have put it, to be 'cognizant of multiple futures in
order to secure its desired one'.[130]

The Elector's mobilisation of the future against the inherited structures of privilege was thus symptomatic of a broader cultural change, as was Pufendorf's centring of his history of the reign on moments of decision. And yet the 'historical culture' of late seventeenth-century Brandenburg was also distinctive in one important respect, in that it aligned the holder of sovereign authority and the advancement of the fortunes of the state with the overriding of tradition and the disruption of continuity.[131] In the context of the royal histories of early modern Europe, this was unusual. The greatest historian of early modern Spain, Juan de Mariana, whose *General History of Spain* remained the model for seventeenth-century Spanish historians, offers a narrative of impressive subtlety and depth in which the interplay of diverse trains of events are depicted in a dynamic and engaging way. But in Mariana's account, the pretensions of kings are the disasters of their states; they bring wars, diseases, and financial ruin. Their sequestrations of the wealth of their subjects are not exactions licensed by need, but acts of wanton theft.[132] The argument from necessity could not be advanced here, because Mariana saw in the external threats to Spanish security the consequences of provocations issuing from the Spanish monarch himself.[133] And this was in keeping with Mariana's political understanding of monarchy: a king could govern well only if he ceded control of his government to senior churchmen and refrained from altering in any way the fundamental laws and traditions of his lands, especially those that governed taxation and religion.[134] It was a far cry from Pufendorf's sympathetic account, which tended to baptise the operations of monarchical power in approving rhetoric and saw the monarch as beleaguered by external threats that justified his interventions in domestic power structures.

In France, historians of the royal house constructed a myth of unruffled continuity that effaced the changes of dynasty and embedded the history of kings in an 'immobile dynastic time punctuated by the accession and the disappearance of princes who, with their qualities and faults, took part in the sacredness of power and the permanence of an ethical and political ideal'. The result was a highly conventional narrative tradition, in which new authors preferred to market themselves as the 'continuators' of established chronicles.[135] The cult around Louis XIV, to be sure, disrupted this pattern to some extent. It produced an outpouring of panegyric from historians, some of whom were so enthusiastic in their praises that they doubted whether the whole of history could contain anything of interest to compare with a monarch who had superseded all the ages. But the apotheosis of the 'sun-king' also implied, as Chantal Grell has shown, a devaluation of the future, which could never be expected to rise to the challenge of the present, and thus disqualified 'progress' as a framework for thinking about the future.[136]

In Britain, the Whig historiography that sprang up in support of the Dutch 'usurper' William III after 1688 insisted that the new regime was not an innovation, but a 'restoration' and a vindication of 'ancient rights'. Whig historians invoked a recursive continuum time, in which recent events were charged with meaning by ancient precedents: William III was the new King David; the 'Revolution' of 1688 was the return from Babylonian exile. The present and near future were imagined as foreordained, as a realignment with long-standing rights and verities, belying the reality that one legal system had been overturned and another inaugurated.[137]

This is the kind of history the Estates of Krefeld might have written, if they had prevailed over the Elector and his councillors, installed a monarch of their own choosing, and hired a historian of their own. Set against this background, the historical culture that began to emerge around the Electoral

authority stands out for its vision of the princely authority
as an institute that ruptures—must rupture—the threads of
continuity in order to meet new exigencies and make history
happen. And this in turn is a reminder that we must rescue
this era from the vast condescension of modernisation theory. To blend the Great Elector and his court historian into
an ocean of time extending from Homer to Chateaubriand, in
which history was a storehouse of examples and the present
lived under the authority of the past, does poor justice to the
open-endedness and dynamism of their historicity, their will-
ingness to challenge tradition and to privilege the future over
the past.[138]

In 1701, thirteen years after the Great Elector's death, his
son was elevated into the ranks of the German kings. At a coronation staged in Königsberg on 18 January 1701, Frederick III
of Brandenburg became Frederick I, 'king in Prussia'. The ceremony reveals how deeply the public life of the state was imprinted by the historicity of the Great Elector's time. Although
many details of the ritual and the festivities associated with it
were derived from the traditional representational culture of
European royalty, the design of the coronation ritual and its
accoutrements was in fact an extravagant exercise in bricolage.
The know-how that informed the ceremony derived from the
printed canon of 'Ceremonialwissenschaft', the highly medi-
ated and rationalised corpus of knowledge that was enjoying
a boom in the last decades of the seventeenth century.[139] From
this resource, fragments of diverse 'traditions' were assembled,
modified, and recombined in such a manner as to achieve a
highly focused array of effects.

This artificiality is in itself unsurprising—all coronations
incorporate an element of invention and there existed no direct precedent for a royal ritual in Brandenburg-Prussia. What
is interesting and distinctive about the Prussian case is the fact

that the makers of the coronation were proud to acknowledge the artificiality of the spectacle. It has often been observed that coronation rituals falsely assert their continuity with an ancient tradition in order to adorn themselves with an authority that transcends time. But the designers of the Prussian coronation adopted an overtly instrumental approach to their task. It was essential, the Prussian envoy in Warsaw wrote in June 1700, that a bishop be engaged to oversee the ecclesiastical part of the proceedings and that these include a ritual anointment of some kind, since omitting these features might jeopardise the Elector's future claim to the potentially useful title *Sacra Regia Majestas*.[140] The use of a bishop along the lines seen in the recent Swedish coronation, another advisor suggested, 'will give a great effect' (donnera un grand lustre).[141] Publicists and councillors alike were quick to point out that the function of the anointment (Salbung) was purely symbolic. This was not a traditional sacrament, but merely an edifying spectacle designed to elevate the spirits of those present.[142]

The publicity surrounding the Prussian coronation of 1701 stressed precisely the newness of the royal foundation. To be sure, there was some talk in the summer of 1700 of the 'discovery' in the works of the sixteenth-century geographer Abraham Ortelius that Prussia (meaning the Baltic principality of Prussia) had been a 'kingdom' in ancient times, but no one seems to have taken this seriously.[143] Even Johann von Besser's effusive coronation chronicle stated only that this was 'a belief held by some'. Instead of submerging the new king in an imagined continuity, the publicists celebrated him as a self-made monarch. There was no talk of blood or ancient title. The remarkable thing about the new king, Besser observed in a foreword addressed to Frederick I, was that 'Your Majesty came to His throne entirely through His own agency and in His own Land'. It was a matter of pride that the Prussian monarch had acquired his throne 'neither by inheritance, nor by succession, nor through elevation, but rather in an entirely new way, through his own virtue and establishment'.[144]

We can discern in these arrangements a further elaboration of that rejection of tradition that had informed the arguments of the Electoral administration in its disputes with the provincial estates during the reign of the Great Elector. The coronation ritual, after all, carried a powerful anti-Estates message. The Estates of Ducal Prussia were never consulted over the coronation and were alerted to the event only a few weeks before it was due to take place. Moreover, the king, in contrast to the prevailing European practice, crowned himself and his wife in a separate ceremony before being acclaimed by his Estates. A description of the coronation by Johann Christian Lünig, a renowned contemporary expert on the courtly science of ceremony, explained the significance of this step. 'Kings who accept their kingdom and sovereignty from the Estates usually only . . . mount the throne *after* they have been anointed: . . . but His Majesty [Frederick I], who has not received his kingdom through the assistance of the Estates, or of any other [party], had no need whatever of such a handing-over'.[145] The message was clear: power was what defined the legitimacy of the Brandenburg-Prussian state, not tradition, inheritance, or continuity with the past. This was the idea at the heart of the coronation ritual, and it had been the animating thought behind Pufendorf's *De rebus gestis*. Pufendorf had been dead for seven years by the time the coronation took place, but he would have welcomed its bald artificiality.

CHAPTER TWO

The Historian King

WHEN THE ENGLISH MUSIC HISTORIAN and composer Charles Burney visited Prussia in 1771, he managed to get an audience with Johann Joachim Quantz, Frederick II's instructor in flute and composition, who had been at the court since December 1741. Quantz's position at court was unique. Frederick paid his teacher the princely sum of two thousand thalers a year—by contrast, C.P.E. Bach, the king's harpsichordist (later clavichordist and fortepianist), received only three hundred. In retrospect, this seems odd: of the two men, Bach was the more innovative and exploratory composer and musician. He was less floral than Quantz; he used starker and leaner thematic material, expanding the sound-world of the baroque. His influence on the subsequent development of European music was immeasurably greater than Quantz's. Yet Frederick stuck to his flute master for forty years, according him an extraordinary authority over the musical life of his court.[1] Burney was astonished by the steadfastness of the king's musical taste:

[Mr Quantz] told me that His Majesty . . . played no other concertos than those which he [Quantz] had expressly composed for his use, which amounted to three hundred, and these he performed in rotation. This exclusive attachment to the productions of his old master may appear somewhat contracted, however, it implies a constancy of disposition but rarely to be found among princes. . . . It is an indication of a sound judgement and of great discernment, in His Majesty, to adhere thus firmly to the productions of a period which may be called the Augustan Age of music; to stem the torrent of caprice and fashion with such unshaken constancy is possessing a kind of *stet sol* by which Apollo and his sons are prevented from running riot or changing from good to bad and from bad to worse.[2]

It is hard to think of a document that better conveys the steady-state quality of the culture at Frederick II's court. The king could, like so many of his contemporaries, have chased every new fashion; instead he chose to replay and replay the same corpus of works by the same master, maintaining the rotation system for forty years. He favoured the conventionalism of Quantz over the developmental, exploratory path of C.P.E. Bach.[3] The metaphor of the *stet sol*, a device by which the rays of the sun could be fixed and projected onto a wall through an aperture or prism, captures precisely the stasis of the frederician microcosm, a world in which time seemed to stand still and the operations of taste and fashion—of history—were suspended. And this was a direct expression and articulation of the king's power: although, as Burney conceded, there were small avant-garde 'schisms' in Berlin's musical life, anything that did not conform to the dominant taste (Quantz in instrumental music, the Grauns and Hasse in opera) was unlikely to prosper.[4]

The resulting stagnation should not be written off as evidence merely of the king's cultural conservatism. There was more to it than that. It reflected a preference for recursive, nondevelopmental paradigms that can be discerned across a wide range of his activities. This chapter explores the relationship between the king's historicity and his distinctive temporal awareness. Frederick II's philosophical understanding of history was indebted to the fashionable linear stadialism of the late Enlightenment. But his temporality—his intuitive grasp of the felt texture of time—was strikingly recursive and nonlinear. He experienced—and helped to bring about—momentous geopolitical change during his reign, yet his sense of time gravitated towards an aestheticised stasis. The chapter explores this tension and enquires after possible reasons for it, focusing first on his historical writings and then on a range of other political and cultural practices—his reaction to processes of socioeconomic change, his preferences as a collector of paintings, and the arrangements he made for his own burial and memorialisation.

But before I turn to the king's writings, it is worth recalling four important differences between his reign and that of his great-grandfather, the Great Elector. First, whereas the Great Elector was an institution-builder who ruled from the midst of his councillors, inhabiting a place at the centre of an executive structure he was himself gradually assembling, Frederick took up a position at one remove from the formal structures of the state. There was a royal court in Berlin, but for much of the latter part of his reign, Frederick never attended it.[5] Unlike his ancestor, he had little contact with the day-to-day work of the ministries and little contact with his ministers, whose role was usurped by the king's own secretaries. Frederick listened to officials and friends he trusted and took advice on many questions, but the kind of collective brainstorming of political options that took place around the Great Elector in the Privy Council was unknown in Frederick's time. The building he was most enduringly associated with was not the city palace in Berlin, or the vast Neues Palais constructed outside Potsdam after his return from the Seven Years' War, but the small summer palace of Sans Souci, which could scarcely accommodate guests, let alone support the day-to-day business of a king ruling from the heart of government. By contrast with the Great Elector, who had spoken above all of his 'sovereignty', Frederick often referred to 'the state', invoking it as a transcendent abstraction, but in reality his reign saw a marked personalisation of power. And this rhetorical self-distancing from the structures of the state left its imprint, as we shall see, on the temporal texture of his reign.

Second, whereas the Elector was a passionate adherent of the Reformed faith, Frederick, probably a Voltairean deist, adopted a sceptical, non-confessional standpoint. Although he took his scepticism to mark a civilisational advance on the blind faith and superstition of many of his more devout contemporaries, he lacked that sense of belonging to an imperilled vanguard religion that had been so important to his grandfather. Third, the struggle with the estates that had so preoccupied the Great Elector was obsolete by Frederick's time. It was not the power and independence of the provincial nobilities that troubled this king, whose own private habitus was strikingly aristocratic, but their vulnerability to socioeconomic change. The linkage between the consolidation of state authority and the political neutralisation of domestic elites thus forfeited its utility and legitimating power.

Finally, the geopolitical settings were fundamentally different. When the Great Elector came to the throne in 1640, he inherited a monarchy broken and paralysed by the Thirty Years' War. Berlin was so ruined and so exposed to the depredations of foreign troops that it was at first impossible to take up residence there. The army was nonexistent. The

Brandenburg-Prussia Frederick II inherited one hundred years later was quite different. It faced no imminent geopolitical threats and possessed a large army that, though it had been only sparingly used, was acknowledged to be one of the best in Europe. The two reigns were thus animated by quite different logics. The Elector's Brandenburg was still, for all its efforts and accomplishments, a small player in a world where the big players decided the important outcomes. By contrast, Frederick's reign opened with one of the most unexpected and shocking initiatives of modern European diplomatic history— the unprovoked Prussian invasion of the Habsburg province of Silesia in December 1740. The king fought three 'Silesian Wars', in 1740–42, in 1744–45, and again in 1756–63, to retain this valuable acquisition. Although he was often tactically on the defensive, the reign was inaugurated and defined by Prussia's preemptive application of overwhelming force in 1740, and again in 1756, when he launched a preemptive invasion of Saxony in order to prevent his opponents from using it as a base for their operations against him. Prussia had become a shaper of the European order.

Why Should a King Write History?

As a young man, the future Frederick II styled himself the *roi philosophe*, and the term has since become a kind of logo for his reign, defining a moment in Prussian and European history when power and philosophy entered into a uniquely intimate partnership. In reality, Frederick was far more influential as a historian than he ever became as a philosopher. His theoretical treatises, though elegantly composed, are light on intellectual substance and lack originality. They seem more concerned with striking poses than with solving real problems. His historical writings, by contrast, mark out a new point of departure. The *Mémoires pour servir à l'histoire de la maison de Brandebourg*, the most elegant and original of the historical texts, was and remains to this day a tour de force. This concise, artfully constructed narrative achieved such an attractive and plausible synthesis that it shaped—and continues to shape— the historical memory of Brandenburg-Prussia. It is the *roi historien*, not the *roi philosophe*, whose influence has endured.

About the seriousness of the king's historiographical enterprise there can be no doubt. He returned to it at intervals throughout his reign, producing new texts, but also reworking old ones. The first study was the 'History of the First Silesian War', begun in 1742. Four years later, after the Peace of Dresden, a 'History of the Second Silesian War' followed; Frederick now revised the earlier piece and worked the two essays into an ensemble. They were revised once again under the new title *Histoire de mon temps* in 1775. The *Mémoires pour servir à l'histoire de la maison de Brandebourg*, which surveyed the history of the Hohenzollern lands and dynasty before his own accession to the throne, was the product of nearly two years of intermittent writing and research in 1746–48; parts of it were presented as papers to the Akademie der Wissenschaften in Berlin. Only in 1751 was this text—in a heavily revised and abridged version—published under the title by which it is known today. Further texts followed after the end of the Seven Years' War, covering intervals of time spanning the period between the outbreak of the Seven Years' War in 1756 and the aftermath of the War of the Bavarian Succession in 1778.[6]

Most of the writing was based on genuine documentary research, though not necessarily always the king's own. In the early years, Frederick had key documents brought to him in Potsdam; later he used ministers and officials as 'research assistants'—Maupertuis provided data on cultural history, Podewils, Finckenstein, Hertzberg, and others wrote compact essays on political events, Prince Leopold of Dessau reported on the old Brandenburg military establishment, the General-direktorium on coinage, and the Chamber of the Kurmark on demography and settlement history. The rector of the Friedrich Wilhelm Gymnasium in Berlin, Georg Friedrich Küster, provided a long chronology compiled from the most important chronicles. In short, this was a project of abiding importance that accompanied the king throughout his long life on the throne.[7] The frequent redactions and reworkings show that these texts were intended not as one-off snapshots of specific moments, nor merely as works designed to manipulate specific constituencies, but as components of an ambitious, overarching history of the Brandenburg-Prussian lands whose value would endure.

This deep commitment to historical reflection was unusual—it is difficult to think of another European monarch, in Frederick's era or any other, who invested so much imagination, talent, and energy in the business of writing history. Why did he do it? In answering this question, we have first to distinguish between motives and justifications. The king was quite clear about the latter. First, there was the need to put his country on the historiographical map, to 'establish Prussia's place in history'.[8] Among the European states, he declared in the 1748 foreword to the first draft of the *Mémoires pour servir à l'histoire de la maison de Brandebourg*, Brandenburg-Prussia alone lacked a history of its own. 'Even the insects' had been honoured with a multivolume study—this was a reference to René-Antoine Ferchault de Réaumur's encyclopaedic *Mémoires pour servir à l'Histoire des Insectes*. Frederick adapted Réaumur's title to his own purposes, a characteristically wry and distanciating move, but also a reminder that the relationship between the natural sciences and historical writing was closer in this era than one might suppose.[9] Then there were the various conventional justifications of a more general nature for the study of history. In the *Discours Préliminaire* of 1751, a revised introduction to the *Mémoires*, the ironic playfulness of the earlier Avant-Propos made way for a more earnest appeal to familiar topoi. History was 'regarded as the school of princes', the king declared; in 'pronouncing on the reputation of the dead, it implicitly judged the living'. The opprobrium it attached to base men in the past was 'a lesson in virtue to the present generation'. For every individual, history had a cosmopolitan potential to expand the compass of experience. To know it was 'to have lived in all ages, to become in effect a citizen of all places and of all countries'.[10] Historical knowledge, he suggested, was also constitutive of identity, of meaningful participation in the culture and institutions of one's own country. We might readily forgive an Englishman his ignorance of the regnal dates of the kings of ancient Persia, or the 'infinite number of popes who have governed the church', but we would be shocked to find him ignorant of the origin of his parliament, the customs of his island, or the 'various races of the kings who have reigned over England'.[11]

These observations are justifications for the study of history in the most general terms. They may explain why it is a good thing for history to be written and read, but they do not account for Frederick's own commitment to writing it. On this question the king's testimony is more oblique, as one would expect of an individual whose texts and utterances were generally rhetorical and performative, rather than expressive.[12] A central and abiding motive appears to have been the desire to establish and control the narrative of his own time, not just for the present (the Mémoires was the only text to be published in the king's lifetime), but for posterity: 'C'est à vous, race future, que je dédie cet ouvrage', he wrote in the 1746 preamble to the *Histoire de mon temps*.[13] 'It is for posterity to judge us', he wrote in the revised preamble of 1775, 'but if we are wise we can pre-empt it by judging ourselves'.[14] Several preoccupations were intertwined here: first there was the need to ensure that narrative authority did not fall into alien hands, such as those of some 'future Benedictine monk of the nineteenth century' who might otherwise be empowered to tell the king's story.[15] Linked with this concern was Frederick's need to defend and legitimate controversial aspects of his own policy, such as his challenges to the traditional authority structures of the Holy Roman Empire, or his frequent breaches of treaty obligations.[16] In general, as Jürgen Luh has shown, Frederick showed a concern for fame and posthumous reputation that was unusual in its intensity, even among his monarchical contemporaries, though in his determination to shape and control his own place in history he resembles the twentieth-century British statesman Sir Winston Churchill.[17] Then there was the desire (possibly tactically motivated) to memorialise the feats of his boldest and most skilful officers: 'I shall not fail to speak of the immortal glory that so many officers earned [in battle]', he wrote in the 1746 preamble to the *Histoire de mon temps*. 'I dedicate this feeble essay as a monument to my gratitude'.[18]

The orientation towards a remote posterity also underscored the king's claim that the historical accounts of his own time represented a disinterested and truthful depiction of events. After all, a narrative addressed to future generations could not be accused of pursuing propagandist or self-interested motives, or of making concessions to contemporary sensitivities; the writer was delivered from the need to take account either of the reading public or of his princely colleagues; he could 'say aloud what many persons think in silence, painting princes just as they are'.[19] The sovereign status of the author was a further guarantee of authenticity. The king had privileged access, for one thing, to the secret archives of the state—Frederick had sought and gained permission to consult his own royal archives, he joked in the 1748 preamble to the Mémoires.[20] And there was the question of the author's personal experience. Most histories—this was a point to which Frederick repeatedly returned—consisted mainly of 'lies and absurdities' cooked up from rumour and dubious second-hand testimony.[21] By contrast, Frederick's history would speak of high matters of state with the authority of one who had wielded real power. The aim was to achieve in his own writing the immediacy of those passages in *Anabasis* where Xenophon describes the retreat of the ten thousand men under his own command, or the letters in which Cicero speaks to his friend Atticus of the political events of the day; these texts remain fresh because 'it is one of the actors in the great scenes who speaks'.[22] And this in turn ensured that works like the *Histoire de la guerre de Sept Ans* would be instructive to those future rulers and military commanders of his state who might once again find themselves locked in conflict with Austria.[23] So crucial was the authority bestowed by the experience of power that Frederick even challenged Voltaire's qualification to write political history—despite his otherwise warm admiration for the French philosopher's work.[24]

Were Frederick's historical writings acts of interior reflection, or were they rhetorical manoeuvres, whose purpose was to project a particular image of the monarch, or to justify specific courses of action? Frederick went to great lengths to evacuate any sense of a private subjectivity from these writings, announcing in the foreword of 1775 to the *Histoire de mon temps* that he would speak of himself only when necessity demanded and that when this occurred he would speak of himself, in the manner of Caesar, in the third person, 'in order to avoid the odium of egoism'.[25] In the preamble to the *Histoire de la guerre de Sept Ans*, he put it even more forcefully: 'I would have found it unbearable, in a work of such length, always to speak of myself and in my own name'.[26] But this erasure of his own person sits in a strained relationship with the author's claim that his identity and experience as sovereign bestowed a privileged vantage point. The labour invested in these works may, as Johannes Kunisch has suggested, have performed a psychological function. Frederick was intermittently troubled by spasms of self-doubt, especially in relation to battles where he felt his judgements had been flawed, and the vivid dreams that he described to his confidante Catt suggest that he continued to crave the approval of his dead father.[27] Perhaps the narration and re-narration of the events of his reign helped to effect an inner settling of accounts—the hypothesis is plausible, if not verifiable.

An alternative view of the historical writings emphasises their communicative and propagandistic function—an approach exemplified by Andreas Pečar's plea for a contextual and rhetorical reading of the king's literary works. The historical and political essays were not, Pečar argues, statements of personal conviction, or acts of psychological clarification, but political instruments designed to achieve a specific end. It is worth noting in this connection that although the *Mémoires pour servir à l'histoire de la maison de Brandebourg* was the only historical text to be published during the king's lifetime, a number of the other essays and fragments were circulated to a more or less narrow circle of readers. Pečar reads the *Réflexions sur les talents militaries et sur le caractère de Charles XII, Roi de Suède*, for example, as an encoded communication between the king and his senior officers. Its purpose was to address criticisms circulating among the political and military elites of Brandenburg-Prussia during the dark years of the Seven Years' War. Critics of the king's drive to seize the military initiative—strategically and tactically—had often made a link between Frederick II and Charles XII, suggesting that the Prussian king's errors—his insistence on seeking a fight at Kunersdorf, for example—derived from a desire to emulate the Swedish adventurer. The aim of the *Réflexions*, with their comprehensive critique of Charles XII, was to disarm these concerns without encouraging a more direct discussion of the king and his handling of the war.[28]

However we weigh the respective validity of these two approaches—and they seem to me complementary rather than mutually exclusive—the question remains, why did Frederick become so invested in the writing of *history*? Other literary formats could have served the king's psychological needs and his political purposes. Why was it history—in the sense of an impersonal, synthetic narrative of the Brandenburg state's development over time—that absorbed so much of his talent and attention? Frederick's admiration for the historical works of the French Enlightenment was clearly an important factor. He was deeply impressed by Montesquieu's *Considerations sur les causes de la grandeur des romains et de leur décadence* (1721). It was the 'philosophical' quality of this work that Frederick found engaging: the power and consistency of its central animating idea (that the expansion of Rome was rooted in the temperament of the Roman 'national spirit'), the quest for 'useful truths', and the ambition to rise above the specificity of the subject matter to an awareness of what was generic or universal.[29]

An even more important influence was Voltaire. No other individual held a comparable fascination for the Prussian king, and more than any other work, it was Voltaire's *Siècle de Louis XIV*, a sweeping, panoramic cultural and political history of seventeenth- and early eighteenth-century France, that Frederick admired. Everything in this work was outstanding, Frederick wrote to Voltaire in 1738, after he had seen parts of it in manuscript. It was brim-full of brilliant insights, impartial in its judgements, and free of anything false or tasteless; Europe had never seen such an accomplished work—it was superior to anything produced in antiquity. The *Mémoires pour servir à l'histoire de la maison de Brandebourg* was written during the late 1740s, at a time when the literary exchange between the two men was at its most intense; it was revised, with the Frenchman's help, during Voltaire's visit to Berlin 1750–51; no one who reads it alongside the *Siècle* could fail to see the many affinities of structure, tone, and style.[30] These are so obvious, in fact, that many contemporaries believed the published version of the *Mémoires* had been ghostwritten by the French philosophe.

Frederick's Historicity

To read Frederick alongside Voltaire is to situate him horizontally, within the framework of the Enlightenment's distinctive historicising sensibility.[31] And Frederick's historical works do bear the imprint of Enlightenment. His reflections on his own vantage point as a writer of history were characteristic of the methodological self-awareness of enlightened historiography and reminiscent of the 'perspectivism' of the Göttingen historian Johann Martin Chladenius, whose primer on historical interpretation appeared in 1742.[32] They are also trenchantly secular. The history of religion, the king implies in a passage from the *Mémoires*, is a subcategory of the history of culture, for religion, like manners and customs, has changed over time. 'Everything that was added to it was the work of men; like them, it was doomed to perish'. Frederick made no effort to conceal his instrumental and coolly impartial view of the Christian confessions: 'All the [Christian] sects', he observed, 'contribute equally to the wellbeing of the state'. The Christian confessions were all the same in the eyes of the civil authority, which left to each individual subject the choice of which path he would like to take to heaven. The state needed to take no interest in the religious convictions of the subject, 'provided he is a good citizen—that is all that we demand of him'.[33] In his anonymous foreword to an abridged edition of Fleury's *Histoire Écclésiastique* (1766), Frederick indulged in an anticlerical mock-historical tirade of Voltairean intensity: here the evolution of Christianity was depicted as the work of fanatics, manipulators, and credulous morons. There were even flashes of that deconstructive contextualizing logic that would power the 'Biblical criticism' of the early nineteenth century: Frederick suggests, for example, that the dogma of Christ's divinity was rooted in an overly literal interpretation of the phrase 'son of God', used by the second-temple Jews to denote a man of virtue.[34]

Frederick's writings also reveal a characteristically enlightened (and Voltairean) sense of the processual character of history, its progression through stages of maturation and refinement. Reflecting on the athletic prowess of his ancestor Elector Albrecht Achilles (1414–86), a fabled participant in tournaments, Frederick reflected on how values had changed in Brandenburg and Europe since the fifteenth century: 'in those coarse times, bodily agility enjoyed the same respect as in the times of Homer. Our century, more enlightened, accords its esteem less to military virtue than to talents of the mind and to those virtues which, in elevating a man above his condition, allow him to trample the passions beneath his feet and make him benevolent, generous and solicitous'.[35] This sense of history as an inexorable advance could articulate itself in a vertiginous sense of the distance between past and present. 'What a difference between the centuries!' Frederick exclaims in the chapter of the *Mémoires* dedicated to the 'history of morals, customs, industry and the progress of the human spirit in the arts and sciences'. Nations divided by vast oceans could scarcely differ from each other more in their customs than the Brandenburgers 'differ from themselves, if we compare those of the age of Tacitus with those of the age of Henry the Fowler, and those of the age of Henry the Fowler with those of the time of [Elector] John Cicero, or finally these latter with the inhabitants of the Electorate under Frederick I, king of Prussia'.[36]

It is perfectly legitimate to view Frederick's historical writings—and specifically the *Mémoires*—both as a reply to Voltaire and as an act of self-alignment with the style and values of the Enlightenment. But they should also be understood as the continuation—and modification—of a specifically Brandenburg-Prussian train of thought on the state and its history, articulated not merely in books of history as such but also, as we have seen, in the political utterances, testaments, and public performances of Frederick's most recent forebears. Frederick was not the first person to have tackled the history of his kingdom, and not the first member of his house to ponder on the meaning of 'history' to a European state that had only recently emerged from impotence and obscurity.

The previous chapter argued that by the 1690s the nascent historiography of the Great Elector's reign had begun to incorporate the notion that the state represented the forwards-moving, innovating, tradition-breaking power in Brandenburg-Prussian history. When Samuel Pufendorf devised his narrative of the Elector's reign, he embedded his account of Brandenburg's external relations within an unprecedentedly dynamic and subtle account of its place within the European states system, identifying the Elector as the choice maker who resolved the open-ended predicaments generated by a system in which the future behaviour of other states can never be predicted with certainty.

But Frederick II was dismissive of these antecedents: 'I do not count a Hartknoch or a Pufendorf as historians; they were authors of great industry, it is true, who compiled facts, whose works are historical dictionaries rather than histories as such. I do not count Lockelius, whose book is no more than a diffuse chronicle in which one is forced to pay for one interesting event with one hundred pages of boredom: these sorts of authors are mere workmen, who amass, scrupulously and without discrimination, quantities of material that remain useless until an architect can shape them into the form they should have'.[37] The seventeenth century, Frederick observed in one of the supplementary chapters of the *Mémoires*, did not produce 'a single good historian'. 'Pufendorf wrote a history of Frederick William in which, to be sure of omitting nothing, he left out neither his chancellery clerks, nor any of the chamber valets whose names he could find out'. Pufendorf, Frederick claimed, shared the general fault of German writers, who wrote as pedants rather than as men of genius, in a clumsy and dragging prose overloaded with inversions and epithets.[38] This is, needless to say, a grotesquely unfair appraisal of Pufendorf's *De rebus gestis*. But it was typical of an era in which Pufendorf was old-hat, and 'philosophical' historians in the manner of Montesquieu and Voltaire denounced their seventeenth-century predecessors as mere antiquarians and dry-as-dust erudites.[39]

All the same, Frederick did admit, in a statement setting out his method of research, that he had 'consulted' the chronicles of Lockelius, Pufendorf, and Hartknoch when he was preparing to write the *Mémoires*. We know that he used the German translation by Erdmann Uhse of Pufendorf's biography of the Great Elector (one might add in this connection that since Frederick never read the book in the original Latin, he was in no position to criticise the author's prose style).[40]

And of course the king was deeply familiar with the Political Testament of his great-grandfather, Frederick William the Great Elector. He may even have appreciated the historiographical power of the Testament—certainly he saw his own Political Testaments, which were partly modelled on the Great Elector's, as 'siblings' of his historical writings.

Does Frederick's history of the Mark Brandenburg before his accession to the throne represent a further development of the train of thought I have traced in the earlier period, or a break into something new? The answer to this question must be equivocal. One of the most striking features of the *Mémoires*, if we place them against the background of Loccelius, Pufendorf, Hartknoch, and the archival record from the reign of the Great Elector, is the almost complete erasure of any hint of conflict between the crown and the Estates. Loccelius's otherwise rather naïve chronicle of the history of the Hohenzollern lands referred explicitly to the protests of the Prussian estates against the policies of the Great Elector in the aftermath of the Northern War of 1655–60 and to the Elector's pacification of rebellious Magdeburg.[41] Pufendorf, as we have seen, drew on these passages when he traced the same theme in his *De rebus gestis*.

The Estates theme is even more strongly present in Christoph Hartknoch's magnificent histories of the land of Prussia, which located the central meaning of the province's history in the defence of its ancient liberties by freedom-loving patriots who had never tired of resisting despotism.[42] Hartknoch insisted on the continuity between ancient rights and modern privileges. He dated the customary liberty of the Prussians back to the country's 'oldest inhabitants', the Sarmatian Vends, who had governed themselves through a 'popular republic' founded on the acquiescence of the entire Prussian nation, of whom it was said, 'They have no particular lord, but rather in plenary council they deliberate as they see fit upon the issues arising and when they intend to undertake something, the will of all must be in support of it'.[43] And this state of freedom must have persisted, Hartknoch argued, because as late as the eleventh century, the chronicler Adam of Bremen had reported of the Prussians, 'They will not suffer a king among them'.[44] From their ethnically mixed primordial commonwealth, composed of Prussians, Poles, Lithuanians, Sarmogitians, Curonians, Livonians, Czechs, and others, the Prussians of Hartknoch's day had inherited their modern liberties. In his history of 'new' or modern Prussia, Hartknoch traced this tradition into the fifteenth and sixteenth centuries, when the Estates representing the cities and the rural hinterland of Prussia had defended their privileges by working together against the high-handed impositions of the Teutonic Knights.[45] In short, Hartknoch was an exponent of the privileges and liberties of Prussia, whose history he saw exemplified in the struggle of the political elites of town and country against monarchical power, whether it came from the kingdom of Poland, the High Masters of the Teutonic Order, or their successors, the Hohenzollerns of Brandenburg.[46]

This conflict between crown and estates was completely absent from Frederick's narrative of the history of his lands. Frederick achieved this erasure in part by a kind of sleight of hand: he back-dated the suppression of the Estates to the reign of Georg Wilhelm, and specifically to the period in office of his powerful minister Count Adam Schwarzenberg, during the Thirty Years' War. Schwarzenberg, the scion of an old Catholic family in the County of Mark (a Brandenburg dependency since 1614), served intermittently as a member of the Privy Council during the 1620s and 1630s. When the Elector fled war-torn Brandenburg for Königsberg in 1638, Schwarzenberg acquired almost dictatorial powers. In an effort to recover some measure of control over the territory, he attempted with not much success to raise a small Brandenburg army, using financial contributions extorted from the obstreperous nobilities of the Brandenburg-Prussian provinces.

In Frederick's account, Schwarzenberg became the grave-digger of provincial corporate liberties. Before the Thirty Years' War, Frederick writes, the Estates were still 'masters of the government'; they accorded subsidies, they controlled duties, they fixed the number of troops and paid them, they were consulted on all measures necessary for the defence of the country, and the laws and policing were administered under their supervision. It was Schwarzenberg who single-handedly broke their power: 'Schwarzenberg, all-powerful minister of a weak prince, drew to his person all the authority of the sovereign and of the Estates: he imposed contributions by his own authority and nothing remained to the Estates of that power that they had never abused, but . . . blind submission to the orders of the court'.[47]

What is remarkable about this portrayal of Schwarzenberg is not only its partisan character (it reproduces exactly the histrionic viewpoint of the Estates in their opposition to Schwarzenberg's policies) but also its drastic overstatement of the minister's impact.[48] Schwarzenberg's 'dictatorship', an emergency response to conditions of extreme duress during one of the worst phases of the Thirty Years' War, lasted in reality only for scarcely two years (1638–40). This brief and unsuccessful experiment in absolutist rule by proxy did not terminate or even seriously diminish the powers of the Estates. On the contrary, it was the Great Elector (acc. 1640) and his successors Frederick III/I (1686–1713) and Frederick William I (1730–40) who gradually changed the terms of the relationship between the central authority and the rural elites, imposing new and permanent taxes, establishing and maintaining the standing army (in place of the old province-based militias), reconfiguring the legal status of noble landholding, and much else besides.

Frederick knew this perfectly well: the conflict with the Estates had been one of the central themes of the Great Elector's reign, not to mention of his Political Testament. Pufendorf and even Lockelius had placed this struggle at the centre of their respective narratives, as had Hartknoch, whose histories of the Polish-Lithuanian Commonwealth and Royal and Ducal Prussia were scrupulously attentive to the domestic constraints on sovereign power.[49] Yet it left no trace whatsoever on Frederick's account of his great-grandfather's rule. Even at those moments in his narrative when the topic was especially apposite, Frederick scrupulously avoided any mention of it. There is a passage, for example, in the *Mémoires* where Frederick compares the reign of the Great Elector with that of Louis XIV of France; yet even when he comments on Louis's early struggle with the French nobilities at the time of the *Fronde*, he draws no parallel with the Great Elector, whose early years in power were also marked by frequent standoffs with the provincial nobilities over taxes, the raising of troops, and the power to appoint officials.

Frederick's omissions are all the more striking for the fact that Voltaire's historical works offered the template of a narrative linking sovereignty and conquest with the subordination of domestic elites. His *Henriade* (1723), which Frederick held to be one of the greatest epic poems ever composed, superior even to Homer's *Odyssey* and *Iliad*, describes the hard-won victory of the French monarchy over an effete and self-serving elite who have exploited bigotry and religious passions to stifle the powers of the crown. The 'Estates' assembled at Paris against Henry IV are a playground for factions and cabals; their debates resound with 'infernal cries'.[50] In the *Siècle de Louis XIV* (1751), which Frederick read in manuscript, the

Paris parliament is depicted as the mouthpiece of a pretentious, undisciplined, and lazy nobility who oppose the legitimate fiscal and political measures of the state in the name of a bogus appeal to 'ancient laws' and 'sacred rights'. A happy state, Voltaire observes at various points, is a state in which the nobility has been brought entirely into the service of the state; only by this means can the 'tyranny' and 'Gothic barbarism' of the old seigneurial system be overcome.[51] In short, Frederick's decision to exclude from his narrative the domestic consolidation of electoral and royal power in Brandenburg marked a departure from the practice of his mentor, who celebrated absolute monarchy in France precisely for the fact that it represented the victory of a more rational and powerful form of governance over the particularist authority of the old seigneurs.

Hegemony without Conflict

Why did Frederick alter the record in this way? The answer must partly be that a narrative emphasizing the conflict between the central executive and the Estates no longer seemed opportune. The epochal process of subordinating the provincial nobilities to the central authority was now largely accomplished. All that remained of the power and autonomy of the old Estates was a 'corporate latency' expressed in the local power networks of the provincial elites.[52] And the impact of this depletion of their political power was heightened by economic decline. During the second half of the eighteenth century, the landed nobility entered a period of crisis. The wars and economic disruption of the 1740s and 1750s–60s, aggravated by government manipulation of the grain market through the magazine system and demographic overload through the natural expansion of estate-owning families, placed the landowning class under increasing strain. There was a dramatic growth in the indebtedness of Junker estates, leading in many cases to bankruptcies or forced sales, often to commoners with cash in hand. The growing frequency with which estates changed hands raised questions about the cohesion of the traditional rural social fabric.[53]

Frederick was much more socially conservative than his father had been.[54] Unlike his father, Frederick himself—notwithstanding his studiously managed image as a thrifty and ascetic figure—cultivated a pointedly aristocratic lifestyle.[55] The nobilities were, in his view, the only group capable of serving as officers in the military; partly because they were the only social stratum with an inborn sense of honour. From this it followed that the stability and continuity of noble property were crucial to the viability of the military state. Whereas Frederick William I had deliberately set out to dilute the social preeminence of the nobility, Frederick adopted a policy of 'conservation' whose objective was to prevent the transfer of noble land into non-noble ownership. There were generous tax concessions, ad hoc cash gifts to families in financial straits, and efforts—largely futile—to prevent landowners from over-mortgaging their estates.[56] When these measures failed, Frederick's immediate response was to tighten state control of land sales, but this proved counterproductive. Transfer controls involved an aggressive curtailment of the freedom to dispose of property. The administration thus had to reconcile conflicting priorities. It wished to restore and preserve the dignity and economic stability of the noble caste, yet it sought to achieve this by suspending one of the fundamental liberties of the estate-owning class.

The quest for a less interventionist and controversial method of supporting the noble interest ultimately led to the foundation of state-capitalised agricultural credit unions for the exclusive use of the established Junker families. These institutions issued mortgages at subsidised interest rates to ailing or indebted landowning families. Separate credit unions were established for each province (Kurmark and Neumark in 1777, Magdeburg and Halberstadt in 1780, and Pomerania in 1781).[57] The king wanted these measures to be known, and dedicated a long and rather fulsome passage of the *Mémoires depuis la paix de Hubertusbourg* to his efforts to improve the condition of the nobilities.[58] It is true that many of Frederick's pro-nobiliary measures date from the 'second reign', after the Peace of Hubertusburg (1763), but Frederick's esteem for the nobility and his regard for its special social standing as the caste called to serve the kingdom as officers and commanders were in evidence throughout the reign.[59]

In place of the conflictual model embraced by his father and great-grandfather, Frederick saw himself as leading, as it were, from within the midst of his nobilities. This is the true meaning of his observation in the *Lettres sur l'amour de la patrie, ou correspondence d'Anapistémon et de Philopatros* that 'good monarchies, whose administration is wise and gentle', are more like 'oligarchies than despotisms', because those (almost all of them noblemen in Frederick's time) who are employed in councils, in the administration of justice and finance, in foreign missions, in the armies, in domestic authorities 'all participate in the sovereign authority'.[60] In general it can be said that Frederick preferred consensual to conflict-based rationalisations of sovereignty. He thus claimed to reject Hobbes's account of the origins of sovereignty because it posited—in his view—that subjects must have made themselves entirely rightless in order to acquire the protection of their persons through submission to a sovereign. The contrary was true, Frederick argued: the primordial signatories to the 'social contract' had elevated the sovereign not under duress, but only on account of his wisdom, the protection he could provide, and the achievements they expected from a ruler; in doing so, they had said to him, 'du reste, nous exigions que vous respectiez nos libertés'.⁶¹

Frederick thus accommodated his account of the past to the priorities of his present. The past was brought into conformity with the political and social objectives of the frederician state. This was in all likelihood a conscious manipulation. He could hardly have missed the conflict theme in Pufendorf, let alone in the political testaments of the two Frederick Williams. And since the *Mémoires* were composed for publication, we might well view them as a rhetorical performance directed at the nobility whose young men had served him so well in the First and Second Silesian Wars. Frederick alluded openly to his own role as the selector of material garnered from the supposedly shapeless and indiscriminate narratives of Pufendorf and his fellows, who had simply dumped the raw material of their research on the page and left the reader to make sense of it all. He frequently acknowledged the crucial importance of selection to the construction of historical narratives, an idea he may have picked up from Voltaire, whose *Essai sur les mœurs* observes that among the plenitude of stories one could tell about the past, 'one must limit oneself and choose'. The past, Voltaire wrote, was 'a vast storehouse from which you must take whatever you can make use of'.⁶²

Nevertheless, the occlusion of domestic political conflict from the king's story created a problem, a potential aporia. The struggle with the Estates was not just an episode or a sequence of events; it had also served as a mechanism for describing and explaining the emergence and historical trajectory of the state.

The methodology exemplified in Voltaire's *Siècle de Louis XIV* represented a way around this impasse. In Voltaire's account, the military and political events of Louis XIV's reign are recounted in some detail, but only as the preconditions for the story that is really at the centre of Voltaire's account, namely the advancement of civilisation in France to a point of unprecedented refinement. What mattered about the reign of Louis XIV was not the king's treaties and wars (Voltaire regarded all wars as lamentable relapses into barbarism) but the flowering of the arts and sciences in 'the most enlightened of all eras'. Following the master's model, Frederick appended to his brief political history of Brandenburg three cultural-historical essays that focused on the history of superstition and religion, the history of 'morals, customs, industry, the progress of the human spirit in the arts and sciences', and the 'modern and ancient governance of Brandenburg'. All are informed, as we have seen, by a strong sense of stadial progression.[63]

Voltaire's paradigm of the 'era'—a secularised version of the salvational succession of 'world monarchies' foretold in the Bible—helped Frederick to float his account of the evolution of the Brandenburg-Prussian state free of its domestic origins in the conflict with the Estates. His narrative thereby acquired an attractive forwards momentum that derived not from an account of the consolidation of sovereign authority and power at the cost of traditional social and political formations, but from the appeal to a broader civilisational idea that Voltaire helped to establish as a commonplace of Enlightenment temporality, an idea that celebrated the present as the telos of all human striving. And yet Frederick did not simply adopt Voltaire's model wholesale. For whereas Voltaire had subordinated affairs of state to a higher set of values embracing all domains of cultural life, Frederick, as Ulrich Muhlack has shown, reversed the priorities, placing the state and its doings at the centre of his story. 'The state' is not a mere enabling condition for the progress of the human spirit; it is the chief actor of the drama. Inasmuch as culture and customs receive serious consideration, they are weighed up from the vantage point of their utility to the state. Thus the religious denominations, for example, were assessed in terms of their ability to generate good 'citizens' (Staatsbürger). Morals, customs, and the arts and sciences were appraised for the benefits they yielded to the state.[64]

But this frederician 'state' was not itself depicted as historically emerging; its career was not defined as a progression. For the Great Elector and Pufendorf, the process by which the nascent Electoral state argued itself into existence by disputing the claims of the holders of traditional authority lay at the centre of the historical narrative of Brandenburg-Prussia. In Frederick's writings, by contrast, the state figured as an extra-historical fact and a logical necessity.[65] The result of Frederick's idiosyncratic adaptation of Voltaire is a curiously unresolved narrative. The vectors of change so forcefully drawn in the writings of Pufendorf, Hartknoch, and the Great Elector make way for diffuse currents of change whose ultimate sources remain obscure. Change is ever present in the king's reflections on the past, but it has become an attribute of reflective consciousness. It is not anchored in a specific historical process. The domestic setting for the exercise of power becomes shadowy and immaterial. The councils and debates that were so central to Pufendorf's narrative disappear from view, and with them the sense that each sovereign decision represents the irreversible choice of one possible future out of many.

Whereas Pufendorf had written his biography of the Great Elector as a story about change driven by unforeseeable contingencies, Frederick insisted that history embodied the operations of certain immutable and universal laws. 'Fragility and instability are inseparable from the works of men', he observed, but 'the revolutions that shake monarchies and republics have their origin in the immovable laws of nature'. By this, the king meant above all those human passions that drove successive generations of actors to alter the scenery of the great theatre of history. 'Without these upheavals . . . , the universe would no doubt have remained the same; there would have been no new events'.[66] Amidst all the destruction and transformation that attended human affairs, one could thus discern the eternal recurrence of certain motifs—the rebellious power unleashed by ambition was the one to which the king most often returned, not only in the historical essays, but also in the *Anti-Machiavel*, composed when Frederick was still Crown Prince in Rheinsberg. At times, it even seemed to the king that there might be a cyclical, self-repeating dimension in the unfolding of history, as in the movements of nature. Anyone who addressed himself assiduously to the study of history, he suggested in the *Histoire de mon temps*, would soon see that 'the same scenes repeat themselves—one must merely change the names of the actors'.[67] Perhaps, he speculated in the *Mémoires*, the movements of the history of states resembled those of the planets, which always return to the point from which they came.[68] Such passages hint at the intimate connection between mid-eighteenth-century history and the natural sciences; they remind us of how the prestige of 'philosophy' pushed the historical writing of this era in the direction of generalisable principles. But the king's reflections were also performances. Affecting the pose of the philosopher who has seen it all before, they take us a long way from that sense of hard-won historical accomplishment that animated the 'Fatherly Instruction' and Pufendorf's epic overview of the Great Elector's reign.

Times of Decision

Frederick could, to be sure, display an acute awareness of the changes wrought by the passage of historical time. If a commander from the era of Louis XII were to reappear in his own time, Frederick observed in the *Anti-Machiavel*, he would be shocked by the immensity of present-day campaign armies and by the ability of princes to maintain them in peace-time as well in war.[69] 'What would Machiavelli himself say, if he were to look upon the transformation of power relations in Europe, so many great princes who in his time were of no significance in the world and yet play a role today; the power of kings firmly anchored, the manner in which rulers conduct their negotiations, these plenipotentiary spies they maintain at each others' courts, and this equilibrium of Europe, which rests upon the coalition of several weighty princes against ambitious disturbers of the peace.'[70] So fundamental were the differences between his own epoch and that of Machiavelli, Frederick observed, that many of the Italian writer's observations were now simply obsolete. The 'fundamental transformation in large things and in small' that had taken place since the age of Machiavelli meant that 'most of [his] thoughts can no longer be applied to the life of states in our own time'.[71]

And yet there are numerous other passages in which a sense of historical development seems strikingly absent. Frederick deployed exempla from Greek and Roman antiquity in much the same way as Machiavelli himself had done. History, he argued, should be a timeless storehouse of good examples—only the lives and deeds of 'good princes' should be preserved; this would make history books thinner, but also more edifying.[72] He applied this insight to the instruction of his young nephew and heir: 'His memory should not be wearied with the sequence of princes', Frederick told the young man's tutor, 'as long as he learns the names of the outstanding men who played a great role in their country'.[73] Accounting for the great variety of state forms that could be observed in the present, Frederick appealed not to historical causation, but to the 'fruitfulness of

nature' that could bring forth such variety, even within one spe-
cies.[74] The history of states, he suggested, could be likened to
a biological life cycle, in which change was confined within an
eternally self-repeating sequence: 'Just as an individual person
is born, lives for a time and then dies of illness or old age, so republics are established, flourish for a few centuries, and eventually fall prey to the ambition of a particular citizen or to the
weapons of their enemies. Everything has its own time-frame,
including all principalities, even the greatest monarchies have
only their allotted time and there is nothing on earth that is
not subjected to the law of change and decay'.[75] For Pufendorf,
the pressure of the future had imposed choices and decision-
making tasks that defined the sovereign office.

For Frederick, sovereign decisions of this kind, in which the
prince selected among alternative futures, carried less weight.
The difference can also be discerned in Frederick's reflections
on how the prince should prepare for the future. In this connection, Frederick distinguished between what we might call
incremental and stochastic modes of preparation. The former
presumed continuity with the present, and the latter did not.
On the one hand, Frederick argued in the Political Testament
of 1752, the ruler should continue augmenting his existing as-
sets. There were still many areas with abundant arable land on
which new communities of farmers could be settled. Drainage
projects would provide yet more land for cultivation. The silk
'industry' was still in its infancy: in six years, the kingdom's
mulberry tree plantations would be ready for the harvesting
of leaves to feed masses of silkworms. The knife and scissor
factory at Neustadt should at some point be expanded. The volume of trade must continue to increase, and so on.[76] All these
enterprises should form the strands of a single 'project' that
lived inside the head of the prince, Frederick explained. For
'the well-run government of a state must possess as watertight

a rationale as any philosophical system. All measures must be well thought-through; finance, politics and the military must all strive towards one common goal, namely the strengthening of the state and the growth of its power. But a system can only spring from one head'.[77]

On the other hand, the responsibilities of the prince also included 'political daydreaming' focused on future scenarios completely detached from the conditions of the present. Such 'chimerical politics' required the sovereign to abstract himself from the reality of his own time and to wander in 'the unending pastures of imaginary designs'. The importance of these designs lay in the possibility, however remote, that they might one day become realisable in practice.[78] It might one day, for example, be possible, in the event of a war with Austria, for Prussia to conquer Bohemia and then exchange it for Saxony.[79] Chimerical politics concerned itself with long-term objectives, the realisation of which was not a continuous process, but the function of unforeseeable and possibly very remote eventualities.

These reflections might appear to bring Frederick close to the kind of meticulous option selection so painstakingly recorded in Pufendorf's history of the Great Elector's reign. But the emphasis was quite different. In Pufendorf's narrative, the decisional calculus involved the unpredictable behaviour of numerous other actors. Here, by contrast, it was a question of seizing the initiative through a show of force when the opportunity arose. And the driver of these speculative scenarios was not the interplay of contingency, but the will of the prince. After all, the policy, or 'political system', of the state was the brainchild of the prince, who must 'draw up his system and then bring it to implementation'. Since the ideas composing the system were his alone, he alone possessed the capacity to ensure their success. But this in turn also implied a de-emphasis of the moment of decision; whereas for Pufendorf the decision was a moment of choice amidst the uncertainties of a rapidly changing environment, for Frederick the decision was an expression of will in support of an already clearly defined goal. 'A prince who rules on his own will not be caught off guard when there is a swift decision to be made, for he links everything to his pre-conceived final objective'.[80]

Frederick's reign was rich in large and perilous events. The Seven Years' War brought Prussia to the brink of collapse and might well have resulted in the partition and destruction of the state inherited from the Great Elector. The First Partition of Poland, though less dangerous in the short term from Berlin's perspective, was a momentous event whose consequences would reverberate into the twentieth century. Yet the shuddering, fearful vibration of great events is strangely absent from Frederick's reasoning about past, present, and future. Contingency was crowded out by will; decisions were a function of 'systems' resistant to short-term shocks and disruptions.

We can only speculate about the reasons for this curious placidity. Wishful thinking and posturing surely played a role. The man who called himself the 'philosopher king' was inclined to picture himself as detached from the turbulence of 'events', stoical in his emotional life, consistent (or so he imagined) in his pursuit of his objectives. The drama of those scenes in Pufendorf where the Great Elector, gripped in a geopolitical dilemma, heard the divergent advice of his councillors and carefully weighed up the dangers of the various courses of action available to him possessed no charm for Frederick, who strove to embody absolute autonomy, both as a man and as a prince. Finally, Frederick's intuition that history was subject to self-repeating cyclical patterns diminished the weight of the event, of the decision, and of the moment in which the decision occurred. In a world where everything that went around came around and the states were life forms passing through a cycle of maturation and decay or planets locked in circular orbits, as Frederick so often insisted, the decisions that produced victories and defeats, treaties and alliances might be quite important. But ultimately, they were products of history's essentially repetitive structure. They could not acquire the philosophical weight they had possessed for Pufendorf or would possess in a later age for Otto von Bismarck.

The Suspension of Time

In Antoine Watteau's *Love in the Italian Theatre*, eleven people, standing in a semicircle and facing the viewer, gather around a man playing a guitar. They are wearing the costumes of stock characters from the Italian *commedia dell'arte*: the playful Arlecchino, the pompous university doctor, the swaggering captain, the prima donna, and the seconda donna. Yet they are not standing on a stage. The light of a torch catches curving boughs and wisps of foliage. And in the top right-hand corner, a bright moon nestles among clouds. They seem out of place, these elaborately dressed figures in a nocturnal forest. Darkness looms around them, muting the pantomime jollity of their clothing. Separated from the stage, their signalling costumes take on 'all the sadness of depleted signs'.[81] And they are chronologically displaced, too. In 1716, when Watteau painted this image, the *commedia dell'arte* was already in decline. In 1766, when its presence in the picture gallery at Sanssouci is first recorded, it evoked an indistinct and distant past.[82]

Frederick II was an avid collector of the paintings of Watteau. He acquired so many of the French artist's paintings that Berlin-Potsdam today remains, after Paris, the second most important location of his works. Watteau (1684–1721), the most celebrated painter in the *fêtes galantes* manner, was renowned for dreamlike pastoral scenes inhabited by archetypal

La jeleuse Italie offra yant les Amours, / Les fait marcher de nuit, les contraint au mistère; / Mais une Serenade y supplee sous d'oceurs; — L'AMOUR AU THÉÂTRE ITALIEN. / Escus de la scène peinte du Tableau original du tableau de Mr le Roué — Un geste, un seul regard conduit où rompt l'Affaire; / L'impatient François en intrigue profère / Des chemins moins couverts les croyés vous plus courts?

FIGURE 2.1. Antoine Watteau, *Love in the Italian Theatre* (1718); engraving by Charles Nicolas Cochin père, 1734. *Source*: © The Trustees of the British Museum.

costumed figures. What strikes us most about these images is their timelessness; the persons depicted in them seem to float in a shimmering world that is half theatre and half myth. They play or listen to music, engage in conversation, or simply take their ease, without any apparent purpose beyond savouring the delight of the moment. In an appreciation of the 'universe of Watteau', the French writer on the history and philosophy of art René Huyghe tried to capture the unique atmosphere of Watteau's oeuvre: 'Visible, fictional, they are there before us. In the mirror of their false presence, those symmetrical faces, of "never" and "always", recognise each and reconcile themselves to each other. Doubtless they have always been like this; doubtless they have never existed. Are they alive? In the streams,

seemingly immobile, one sees the imperceptible current flow,
which carries everything away. . . . Already they are leaving us;
they [Watteau's figures] abandon us; tender and distant, un-
aware of our presence, they gently pivot and, step by step, de-
part'.[83] In a posthumous critique, the antiquarian Anne Claude
de Caylus, a friend of the painter, noted that Watteau's com-
positions 'neither possess a subject matter of any kind . . . nor
express any passion' and that they therefore lacked 'one of the
most piquant dimensions of painting, namely action', the one
thing capable of endowing any composition with 'that sublime
fire that speaks to, seizes and leads the spirit'.[84] What troubled
Caylus about Watteau, as Thomas Kavanagh has noted, was
the failure of his paintings to provide a 'springboard to narrative'. The moments conjured in Watteau refuse to be aligned
with anything we could call *history*; they 'fail to come together
towards the evocation of a larger, more inclusive temporality
embedding the now of those individual moments within some
sustained story they serve to illustrate'.[85]

Frederick never set down in writing the reasons for the
unusual ardour with which he pursued works by Watteau,
but his writings reveal beyond doubt that he saw in them
something that captured the texture of his own lived existence. 'Paint yourself in Watteau's brush strokes', he urged
his friend and former tutor Jordan in 1742, 'not in Rem-
brandt's!'[86] In an erotic homage to his lover Count Algarotti,
Frederick declared that the spirit of the handsome young
count (addressed in this context as 'the beautiful swan of
Padua') seemed to transport him into a picture gallery, where
'the enchanting spectacle of the most beautiful paintings
never ceases to vary' and where 'the last are the most beautiful of all'. The last painter named in the list that followed was
Watteau, as if he were the painter whose scenes best captured
the momentary intensity of the orgasm, a subject to which he

also dedicated a poem.[87] Writing to his sister Amélie in April 1761, in the darkest year of the Seven Years' War, he observed that 'the true painting of our situation is not by Watteau, but in the Spanish style that uses dark colours and paints only the most gloomy subjects'.[88]

It is true that Frederick's interests as a collector broadened during his reign. In the years 1755–79, he began to bid internationally for monumental paintings of the courtly representative type—during this period he acquired paintings by Rubens, van Dyck, Raphael, Correggio, and Titian, among others. But these purchases did not imply a fundamental break in the king's personal taste; rather they marked, as Astrid Dostert has noted, his transition from a 'royal private collector' to a 'collecting king'.[89] Works in the *fêtes galantes* style continued to dominate in the rooms privately frequented by the king at Sanssouci.[90]

That the king should have taken such an interest in Watteau might not seem especially surprising—the artist was expensive in the 1730s and 1740s precisely because a craze for his works was sweeping Europe. But even against this background, the determination with which Frederick collected Watteau and other *fêtes galantes* painters was unusual, especially for a monarch—the *fêtes galantes* style was associated by contemporaries with the artistic preferences of Parisian financial circles.[91] Particularly interesting is the intensity of Frederick's identification with these images, his inclination both to project himself into their timeless landscapes and to imagine his own existence as 'painted' in Watteau's brushstrokes, as if the painter had not merely grasped a specific iconography, but evoked a kindred form of consciousness. Watteau's paintings portioned out time in suspended moments, cut adrift from the recent past and the imminent future. In this way they captured Frederick's own sense of the texture of time. In an *Ode on*

Time, first published in an edition of 1761, Frederick remarked that there was 'no power on earth so firm / as not to be swept away [by time]':

Nothing stops your violence
And the very moment in which I think
Has already fled far from me.

. . .

And like an indivisible point
Or an unconscious atom
[Time] passes, and I pass with it.[92]

Henri de Catt, the Swiss scholar who was for a time the king's tutor in French oral and written expression, recalled a conversation with Frederick in the summer of 1758. He found the king engrossed in a numerical calculation. The following dialogue ensued:

Frederick: 'Ah good day, dear fellow, guess what I am calculating'.
De Catt: 'Your treasure— . . .'
F: 'Alas, I no longer have any and the little I have will soon be spent, so take a guess'. [This exchange took place during the third year of the Seven Years' War.]
De C: 'Perhaps you are calculating what you have already spent during this war?'
F: 'I know only too well, I don't need to calculate it: go on, don't be scared, guess!'
De C: 'Your Majesty could be calculating so many things that it would be difficult to happen upon what you are calculating right now'.
F: 'So you won't hazard a guess? Monsieur, I am calculating how many minutes I have lived. And I've already been working away at this calculation for an hour. What a sum—and how

many lost minutes! This time that flies without ceasing, this time that drags with it days, hours, minutes, is received with indifference and often without paying the slightest attention, and nature cries out to us at every moment: "Mortals, use your time; don't ever forget the value of that moment on which rests the immensity of time and don't let trifles accelerate the flight of your days"'.[93]

That reference to the moment 'on which rests the immensity of time', that paradoxical conflation of the instant with the entire expanse of eternity, is surely the clue to Watteau's meaning for the king. And if Watteau captured the fleetingness of all human experience, it was the idealised heritage of Greco-Roman antiquity that anchored these momentary units of experience within a larger timescape. A good literary education, Frederick insisted in a memorandum of 1760, must pleat the study of antiquity together with readings of the moderns, establishing an understanding of poetic beauty by comparing passages from the authors of antiquity with modern authors who had treated the same subjects.[94] For Frederick, the 'classical' was not historically or chronologically bound; it was a treasury of images and attitudes that could live as vividly in the present as in the past.[95] In a letter to Voltaire of April 1737, he unfolded a fantasy about Rheinsberg, the palace where he spent the years before his assumption of the throne in 1740. Contrary to widespread belief, he proposed, Remus had not been killed by his twin brother, Romulus, mythical founder of Rome, but had fled into northern exile on the banks of the Grieneckersee, the future site of his own palace. Monks sent by the Vatican had searched in vain for Remus's mortal remains, but in the course of constructing the palace, builders had happened across stones marked with ancient inscriptions and an urn full of Roman coins. Hence the name 'Rheinsberg', which was in fact a corruption of 'Remusberg'. When Voltaire wrote back taking the Crown Prince to task for indulging in such implausible fancies, Frederick was offended—he had only been joking! And yet, from this moment onward, he signed all of his Rheinsberg letters (excepting only those addressed to his father) 'Remusberg'.[96]

From early youth, Frederick cultivated an intense relationship with the great historical personae of ancient Rome. 'From time to time Marius, Sulla, Cinna, Caesar, Pompey, Crassus, Augustus, Antonius und Lepidus come by for a chat', he told Grumbkow, one of his father's ministers, in January 1732.[97] The sociability cultivated by the king at Sanssouci was modelled on the Roman country-house parties celebrated by Horace, at which meals consisted of 'a simple repast enlivened by clever conversation and mockery of the stupid'.[98]

This intensely felt elective affinity with ancient Rome implied a historicity that was analogical and recursive rather than linear and developmental. Portals opened between the present and an antique past; time was pleated around the analogy between one era and another; the tyranny of the recent past over contemporary experience, so axiomatic to Pufendorf and the Great Elector, was relativised, if not entirely suspended. We can discern the imprint of this timescaping in Frederick's highly distinctive plans for his own burial. His interment was not to take place within the usual dynastic ritual framework. Instead of arranging to be laid in the mausoleum of the House of Hohenzollern, he chose for himself a plot in the terraced gardens of Sanssouci. He was, he wrote, to be burned in the manner of the ancient Romans and his ashes were to be buried alone, away from his father and ancestors.[99] Instead, Roman emperors, whose busts would be erected on columns around the grave, were to keep him company—the most important being Marcus Aurelius.[100] Frederick had read Suetonius's *Lives of the Caesars*, which relates that the Roman emperors were buried in beautiful gardens, but another model was the poet Horace, whose name occurs more than 180 times in Frederick's published oeuvre and whose *Carmina* 2.6 closes with these strophes:

> Here where gracious Jupiter grants long springs
> And warm winters, and Aulon's hillside
> scarcely envies the Falernian grapes
> of fertile Bacchus
>
> These blessed valleys will summon us two
> To that place and there you will scatter the warm ashes
> Wet with due tears
> Of your friend the poet[101]

What made this easy travel between remote historical eras possible was the transtemporal circuitry of fame. The fame of the Romans was like an elevated freeway that connected antiquity with the present, passing over the squalid, violent suburbs of the Middle Ages and the Thirty Years' War. Fame was also the bridge to a remote future and the only form of immortality Frederick was able to believe in. To live again in the memory and admiration of posterity may have been one of this king's most deeply held desires.[102] The quest for fame, he proposed in an 'Ode on Glory' penned in 1734, had been the chief motivation of the great heroes of antiquity. The fame to which they aspired had been the 'desire' that 'smoothed and polished' the metres of Homer, Virgil, and Voltaire, just as it was a consuming passion for the king himself.[103] Addressing himself to fame, the prince begged this secular deity 'in spite of cruel death' to

Save one feeble spark
Of the spirit that resides in me
Let your hand open the barrier,
And, ready to run your course
I will live and die for thee.[104]

A striking feature of these fantasies of fame—which accompanied the king throughout his life—is that they focused
solely on the person of the king himself. In ordering that his
body be burned in the ancient manner and then deposited in
the garden of his 'villa', Frederick distanced himself from the
conventional practice of European dynastic representation in
his era, which tended not to foreground the individuality of
the monarch, but to embed him or her in the succession of
the family's generations, focusing attention not on the person
of the monarch, but on the dignity of his office and his family.
By contrast, Frederick chose to be buried not as a king but as
a 'philosopher', a pose that separated him from all of his ancestral predecessors, but also from his royal contemporaries.
The same observation can be made of the palace at Sanssouci,
on whose terraces he wished to be buried. As Andreas Pečar
has pointed out, Sanssouci was not a 'residence'—it did not
project 'kingly magnificence and dynastic greatness', but was
focused rather on 'personal cultivation and private taste'.[105] In
these ways, too, Frederick resisted incorporation into a narrative larger than himself, seeking refuge instead in the timeless
renown owed by posterity to a unique personality.

To a remarkable degree, this detachment from grand narrative remained a feature of the cult that sprang up around
the memory of the king after his death in 1786. The 1780s and
1790s saw a wave of publications commemorating the dead
monarch. But the most famous and successful by far was a
two-volume compendium of anecdotes about the dead king

edited by Friedrich Nicolai, the most influential publisher of the Berlin Enlightenment.[106] In these apparently random tatters of memory (and Nicolai's was only one of many such volumes of anecdotes) the king appeared falling from his horse, responding to impertinence with an indulgent witticism, forgetting someone's name, prevailing over adversity through sheer nerve.[107] Being compact and memorable, anecdotes circulated as swiftly in oral as in literary culture, much as jokes do today. Charged with the humanity of the king, they appeared innocent of politics and history. Like the paintings of Watteau, the anecdotes of the frederician memory wave offered unique moments suspended in time that resisted integration into the grand narrative of history.

Conclusion

The contrast with the dynamic historicity of the Great Elector and his court historian Samuel Pufendorf could hardly be starker. Pufendorf had urged his contemporaries to leave aside the ancient Greeks and Romans and focus on the history of their own times. He had imagined the state as something that had to argue and fight its way into existence. For Frederick, the ancient Romans remained the salient authority and source of inspiration in past and present, infinitely superior to the centuries of zealotry and error that had followed their demise. When he contrasts his present with the 'barbarism' of the Middle Ages, he looks like a linear stadialist, but this is an optical illusion, like the apparent flatness of the earth's surface, made possible only by the vast scale of time's curvature. He thought of the state as a timeless, logical necessity—he was not interested in the historical circumstances under which it had come to acquire its modern form. Pufendorf was the theorist of discontinuity, Frederick sought to embed even the most traumatic change into the timeless continuum of unchanging laws and principles. The conflict with powerful provincial elites dominated the domestic horizons of the Great Elector and supplied one of the driving themes of the histories composed by Pufendorf, Loccelius, and Hartknoch. Yet Frederick erased this strand of his country's history in his own retelling, eviscerating the discursive framework adumbrated by Pufendorf and supplanting it with a narrative whose core was impervious to the perturbations of history.

We have already reflected on the reasons for these choices. The solipsistic, almost pathological vanity that Jürgen Luh and Andreas Pečar have identified as a central and dominant attribute of this king was clearly one important factor. No one who insisted so vehemently on his own uniqueness could wish to be embedded in the interdependencies of 'history'. Frederick prized the past above all as the storehouse of shining exemplars that spoke to and resonated with his own achievements—the rest was dust and junk, a catalogue of human follies unworthy of memorialisation or emulation. And these preferences resonated with a social politics of stasis and conservation—especially in respect to the territorial nobilities, who no longer figured as the provincial antagonists of royal power, but as the indispensable social spine of the frederician military state.

The deepest reasons for making such choices doubtless lie within the realm of what Judith Butler has called the 'psychic life of power'. We are accustomed to thinking of power as something that presses in on us from outside. But what if we ourselves are actually 'initiated through a primary submission to power'—the power, for example, of our parents? If, Butler suggests, we understand power as a force in our own formation as *subjects*, 'then power is not simply what we oppose, but what we depend on for our existence and what we harbour

and preserve in the beings we are'.[108] The potential relevance
of this line of thought to Frederick hardly needs pressing. For
a man who had endured a traumatic childhood and youth at
the hands of a brutish and sadistic parent, the encounter with
power began with the terror of a boy cowering before his father, a king who was himself the son of a king. In the setting
of a dynastic clan, where power was a function of birth and
inheritance, 'history' manifested itself in the 'line of flight' that
stretched back into the past from father to father to father.[109]
In refusing to be buried with his male ancestors, in refusing to
sire a son upon the woman imposed on him by his father and
shutting her out from his presence, in setting himself at one
remove from the state structure his father had built, in asso-
ciating himself with the remote rather than the recent past, in
imagining himself as a unique figure unbound by time, Frederick was plotting his escape from these personal entanglements, whose psychological grip on him never loosened.

Frederick's homosexuality is pertinent to these reflections.
Frederick delighted openly in the physical beauty of the men
he loved, composed poems celebrating heroes 'responding
both actively and passively to their lithe and obliging friends',
described Jesus as the 'Ganymede' of the Apostle John, and
adorned his parks with statues of Antinous and pairs of male
lovers from classical antiquity.[110] And these signals were cou-
pled with a clear rejection of heteronormative expectations,
as exemplified in his theatrical humiliations of the unwanted
wife he described as that 'incorrigibly sour subspecies of the
female sex'. The pastoral literary tradition that Frederick
prized had long been inflected with a homosexual longing
for the enactment of desire free from patriarchal and heteronormative constraints, in a space withdrawn from time and
history.[111] Frederick pointedly rejected the reproductive futurity of dynastic succession, preferring instead to invest in

perfecting an idyll in which the personal freedom and candid sociability of early adulthood might be sustained and deepened indefinitely.[112]

These not-so-private inclinations merged seamlessly with a broader vision of the state and of his own power that was ahistorical, suspended in the zero gravity of eternal laws and cyclical motions. And this vision resonated in turn with the political economy of a reign in which the need to curtail the authority of the traditional agrarian elites had made way for a regime of 'conservation' designed to protect them against the effects of rampant social change. The king's detachment from the conflictual domestic narratives of an earlier era enabled him to suspend his state like a heavenly body in the gravitational field of an international system whose movements, notwithstanding repeated recalibrations of an always precarious balance of power, were fundamentally unchanging.[113] The result was an unresolved tension between the ambient stadial historicity of the late Enlightenment and the king's own strikingly undynamic view of his place in time.

It is doubtless true that Frederick, as a *historian*, anticipated in some respects the political historiography of the 'Borussian School' whose works would refashion the history of Prussia for nineteenth- and early twentieth-century Germans.[114] To a much greater extent than his mentor and teacher Voltaire, he assigned clear priority to political and military history. And his most famous essay, the *Memoirs of the House of Brandenburg*, left a deep imprint on the memory of subsequent generations. The mordant elegance of the king's aphorisms ('men of genius are rarer in Denmark than everywhere else')[115] and the memorability of his pen portraits ensured the king's writings a vivid afterlife. Of August III, king of Poland and Elector of Saxony, for example, he wrote, 'laziness made him gentle, vanity wasteful, [he was] incapable of any thought that required combinations; though he lacked all religion, he was obedient to his confessor and though he was incapable of love, he was a submissive husband'.[116] His pen portraits of the Great Elector, the first Prussian king and his own father, among many others, resonate across the nineteenth- and twentieth-century historiography of Prussia.

Yet it would be going too far to suggest that the king's historical works anticipate or exemplify the historicist revolution that transformed German and European historical awareness in the late eighteenth and early nineteenth centuries. Rather they represent a sideways step. The philosophically consequential train of thought inaugurated by the Great Elector and his court historian and sustained in different ways by Frederick III/I and Frederick William I was left to one side because it appeared politically and culturally obsolete. In its place, Frederick embraced a diffuse and derivative historical paradigm, adapting it to his own preferences in ways that undermined its coherence. It was the *details* of the frederician edifice—the portraits and aphorisms—that exercised an enduring influence, not the underlying logic of his narrative. Frederick cannot easily be incorporated into a sequence in which modern, linear forms of historicity inexorably displace older recursive ones.

At the core of the new historiography that emerged in mid-nineteenth-century Prussia was a constellation of arguments that owed less to Frederick than to his predecessors, and specifically to Pufendorf's Hobbesian construction of the Brandenburg-Prussian state's trajectory through history. Ranke and Droysen, two of the greatest nineteenth-century founders of Prussian historiography, both placed the protracted struggle between the Electoral executive and the Estates at the centre of their respective Prussian histories, highlighting the interdependencies between the inner and outwards projection of state power. And for Georg Wilhelm Friedrich Hegel, whose influence on the development of historical thought in the nineteenth and twentieth centuries was not unimportant, the antagonism between the princely executive and the corporate holders of traditional power, between the universal and increasingly abstract authority of the state and the traditional, particularist appurtenances of provincial privilege, appeared to capture in paradigmatic fashion the very movement of history itself.

CHAPTER THREE

Boatman on the River of Time

'THE STREAM OF TIME runs its course as it should', Bismarck wrote to his mother-in-law Luitgard von Puttkamer in 1852, 'and if I stick my hand into it, I do so because I believe it to be my duty, not because I hope thereby to change its direction'.[1] Bismarck appealed to this metaphor repeatedly throughout his career. 'Man can neither create nor direct the stream of time', the retired statesman would tell visitors to his estate at Friedrichsruh. 'He can only travel upon it and steer with more or less skill and experience'.[2] The figure of the boatman steering his craft on the swirling currents of time expresses a feeling for the fluent motion of history so commonplace in Bismarck's mid-nineteenth-century environment that it scarcely marks him out as a distinctive spirit.

Between the death of Frederick II in 1786 and Bismarck's appointment to high public office in 1862, the idea of 'history' underwent a process of semantic expansion, especially in the Protestant lands of German-speaking Europe. 'History', the Prussian legal theorist Carl von Savigny had written in 1815, was not a 'mere collection of examples', but rather 'the sole path to the true knowledge of our own condition'.[3] It was a claim

Frederick II would have been puzzled by. In his view, after all, history was exactly that: a storehouse of good and bad examples. If it were not, how could it provide knowledge of one's own condition? The answer is, or was, that the word 'history' had come to denote, over and above the sum of things, events and people that composed it, an all-embracing and irreversible process of change. This is not to suggest that an awareness of epochal change was absent from eighteenth-century historical thinking—on the contrary: the historiography of the Enlightenment was marked by a strong sense of development, often conceptualised as a journey through a sequence of 'stages', resembling the milestones in the growth, maturation, and senescence of a living being. But it would never have occurred to Voltaire that it might be interesting or useful to distinguish, as Hegel did in the introduction to his *Philosophy of World History*, between the countless specific sequences of actions and events that made up the *content* of history and History itself, as an all-encompassing process of transformation.

For Hegel, whom Bismarck claimed to have read as a young man but not to have understood, history, in this inscrutably large sense, possessed an almost theological dignity, since it exposed the imprint of the progressive unfolding of reason, or 'Spirit' (Geist) through time. Not everyone endorsed this equation of history with the progress of reason. But Leopold von Ranke, a vehement opponent of Hegel's rationalist progressivism, affirmed nonetheless that History was animated from within by a movement that infused and encompassed all aspects of life: The 'Spirit that appears in the world is not conceptual [begriffsmäßig] in nature; it fills out all the boundaries of its existence with its presence; nothing in it is accidental, its appearance is explained in everything'.[4] For all the differences between them, both men shared the view, first, that it made sense to think about history in the abstraction of its absolute totality and, second, that this totality was a form of motion animated by an immanent force or principle.[5]

This was at the root of what would become distinctive about nineteenth-century historical awareness. The upheavals of the revolutionary and Napoleonic eras sensitised nineteenth-century intellectuals to the problem of discontinuity and fundamental change. The 'examples' stored in the past gradually drifted out of focus, forfeiting their claim to edify the present; what mattered now were the larger patterns of history's movement, of which all of the phenomena in the human world were 'products'.[6] As Ernst Troeltsch put it, the verb 'to become' became the active ingredient of nineteenth-century German historical consciousness: 'The continuous becoming of historical things . . . cannot be imagined purely causally as an array of discrete individual actions; rather the individual actions are melted together by a unity-of-becoming that flows through them, dissolves them into each other and thereby makes them continuous, [a unity-of-becoming] that is very difficult to describe in logical terms, but the seeing and the sensing of which is the essence of historical awareness'. The capacity to see specific actions and events not as singularities, but as dissolved in the violent flow of becoming, Troeltsch argued, was the signal faculty, the 'recognizing organ' of history.[7]

Otto von Bismarck was neither a historian nor a philosopher of history, but his thinking was historical in Troeltsch's sense. This chapter explores that quality of historicalness. At its core was Bismarck's fundamental acknowledgement that the revolutions of 1848 had inaugurated a new and turbulent form of politics. He responded to this state of affairs in ambivalent ways. He developed, on the one hand, refined political techniques in order to manage the flux and unpredictability of post-revolutionary political life. He focused his own attention and that of his contemporaries on those passing moments of opportunity in which, amidst the churn of events, decisions became possible. This 'apotheosis of the moment' transformed the statesman into a *decision maker* whose task was constantly to read the entrails of the present.

But this imagined decision maker did not operate from within the tumult of history; he stood above the fray, wielding an authority that derived from something immoveable and permanent: the power of the crown. For Bismarck, it was the monarchical state, with its enduring structures, that prevented the changefulness of history from degenerating into mere tumult and thereby guaranteed the identity and continuity of the polity. When the array of forces at play in political life threatened to undermine the state's freedom of action, Bismarck reached for authoritarian measures—laws of exception or the threat of a coup d'état—in order to stabilise the system. The simultaneous commitment to the more or less free interplay of political forces and the permanence of the monarchical state structure created a tension at the heart of his statesmanship that Bismarck never resolved.

The chapter reflects on each of these points in turn: the legacy of 1848; the flux and challenge of history; the salience of the moment in mid-nineteenth-century cultural political and cultural discourses; and the exceptional status of the monarchical state as an instrument for stabilising the system and imagining its history. The last part of the chapter reflects on what happened when the Prussian-German state established by Bismarck in 1866–71 collapsed at the end of the First World War, unsettling the state-focused form of historicity that had struck such deep roots in German cultural life.

When Bismarck reflected on the immensity of history and his smallness within it, he thought of rivers and rushing currents. But when he pondered on his own capacity to anticipate and control the flow of events, he found other, less aqueous, rhetorical figures. This chapter thus opens with reflections on one of the master metaphors of Bismarckian politics, the game of chess. More than any other metaphor, chess captured Bismarck's sense of what it meant proactively to intervene in the flow of history.

The Chess Player

For anyone who has worked on the history of nineteenth-century Germany, this caricature, published in 1875 by the satirical journal *Kladderadatsch*, belongs to the stock of canonical illustrations from the era of the *Kulturkampf*, the Culture War of the 1870s between the Prussian-German administration of Chancellor Otto von Bismarck and the Catholic Church in the German states and in Prussia in particular. We see the Chancellor and his great antagonist Pope Pius IX bent over a chessboard. The pope is playing black, in reference to the black garb of the clergy, but also to the proverbial denigration of the clericals as *Finsterlinge*, 'darklings'. The pieces are identified with floating legends in the manner characteristic of the satirical journals of this era. Some bear the paragraphic symbol for laws, another carries a flag emblazoned with the word 'Klostergesetz' in reference to the 1875 'Gesetz zur Auflösung der geistlichen Orden', a law that excluded spiritual orders of the Catholic Church from Prussian soil. The figure of 'Germania' towers over the other pieces. There is one piece bearing a resemblance to an ink pot that appears to represent the press. Next to Bismarck's right hand we see a box of captured pieces marked 'interned', in reference to the incarceration of noncompliant clerical personnel—a commonplace of the culture war years. On the pope's side are pieces marked 'Encyclica', 'Syllabus' (in reference to the 'Syllabus of Errors' condemning the doctrines of modern liberalism), and

Zwischen Berlin und Rom.

Der letzte Zug war mir allerdings unangenehm; aber die Partie ist deshalb noch nicht verloren. Ich habe noch einen sehr schönen Zug in petto!

Das wird auch der letzte sein, und dann sind Sie in wenigen Zügen matt — — wenigstens für Deutschland.

FIGURE 3.1. Wilhelm Scholz, *Between Berlin and Rome*: Bismarck
and Pope Pius IX wage culture war on the chessboard. Satirical image
from *Kladderadatsch* (1875). *Source*: Wilhelm Scholz, *Bismarck-
Album des Kladderadatsch. Mit dreihundert Zeichungen von W. Scholz*
(Berlin, 1890), 86. Courtesy of Cambridge University Library.

'Interdict'. The caption suggests that white is confident of victory. The pope says, 'That last move was rather unpleasant for me, but the game is not yet lost, I have another very nice move in reserve!' To which Bismarck replies, 'That will be your last move then, because in a few moves you will be checkmate—at least in Germany'.[8]

This is one of those caricatures that virtually reads itself for us, its field of reference so obvious that there seems little reason to enquire into it more deeply. What interests me about it is not the laboured allegorical messaging, but the choice of chess as a way of metaphorising the political struggle between Bismarck and his Catholic opponents. Chess has meant many things during its long history. In the medieval romance tradition, chess games were the opportunity for amorous encounters, though the game itself was often seen as an allegory for the tension between human effort and the vicissitudes of fortune.[9] According to the Shakespeare scholar William Poole, chess was the 'medieval and renaissance symbol of courtly, aristocratic entertainment and even of sexual equality', though it was also associated with gambling, war, and erotic license.[10] In the late sixteenth and seventeenth centuries, it often served as an allegory for political or moral conflict, in the nineteenth as a 'game of life' or a meditation on human existence.[11] But by the last third of the nineteenth century, it had also acquired other connotations. In an era when the game was passing through a phase of professionalisation with increasingly formalised international tournaments and an increasingly extended and standardised associational structure, it was esteemed above all for its logical complexity, its strategic intensity, its capacity to generate ever new situations.

In an article published by the *Chess Players' Chronicle* in 1878, the Hereford-based player Edwyn Anthony praised the

'inexhaustibility of chess' and offered a mathematical justification for his claim:

> To estimate the actual number of ways of playing even a very
> few moves is beyond the power of calculation, but to get some-
> thing of an approximation to that number is very simple. Tak-
> ing a variation of each of the openings as in Cook's *Synopsis*,
> we found that the first player has an average of 28, 31 and 33
> ways of playing the second, third, and fourth moves respec-
> tively; 29, 31 and 33 being the corresponding numbers for
> the second player. Of course both players have a choice of 20
> moves on their first move. On the hypothesis that the number
> of replies open at each move is always the same whatever the
> preceding move may have been, and that the foregoing figures
> give those numbers, the number of possible ways of playing the
> first four moves only on each side would be 318,979,564,000.

Even if one took into account the fact that the ratio of the
plausible to the possible number of moves was usually small,
Anthony noted, the variety of plays still remained enormous.
Extrapolated to the first ten moves in any game, the numbers
of ways of playing them rose to the giddy total of 169,518,829,
100,544,000,000,000,000,000, a number that the author conceded was probably an underestimate. If one imagined this
number as a sequence of actions extended across time, the implications were mind-numbing: 'Considering the population
of the whole world to be 1,483 millions (Levaseur's estimate),
more than 217 billions of years would be needed to go through
them all, even if every man, woman and child on the face of the
globe played without cessation for that enormous period at the
rate of one set per minute and no set was repeated'.[12] Calculations of this kind are typical of a contemporary discourse that
emphasised the fluxing, infinite quality of the game. In Lewis
Carroll's *Through the Looking Glass and What Alice Found*

There, published in 1872, Alice discovers, on climbing a hill, an entire landscape divided by hedgerows into square fields, like a chessboard that extends beyond the horizon and exclaims: 'It's a great huge game of chess that's being played—all over the world'.[13] In 1889, the holder of what was then called 'the chess supremacy', in effect the first undisputed world chess champion, the Austrian (later American) player Wilhelm Steinitz observed that 'the infinite variety of possible combinations in playing the game affords opportunities for the exercise, and, therefore, the training, of the logical as well as of the imaginative faculties of mind'.[14] The complexity of the game made the exercise of foresight both essential and impossible, a tension captured in the White Queen's paradoxical boast to Alice that her memory worked 'both ways' so that she, unlike Alice, could remember things that hadn't yet happened.[15] Chess was both constantly in flow and composed of a long string of discrete moments of choice on each of which the course of an entire match could turn—a feature of the game captured in the study of 'problems' that are the subject of a specialised branch of the chess literature. And chess was esteemed for the way in which it—as Steinitz put it—'afforded a test of mental skill free from the elements of chance'; in this respect it was quite unlike card games, for example, and 'utterly unsuited for gambling'.[16]

Steinitz, praised by his German contemporaries as 'the Moltke of the chessboard', was known for the forcefulness and flexibility of his play—qualities that allowed him to see off the celebrated rival masters of the era: Zukertort, Blackburne, Tschigorin, and Gunzberg. Steinitz favoured openings by which he obtained in the centre of the board 'a strong and unassailable position'. Yet, as his great-grandnephew Kurt Landsberger, the editor of his papers, notes, he was also famous for his 'wonderful resource in trying to avert defeat in apparently hopeless positions'. He recalled a famous game against his nemesis Emanuel Lasker, in which 'he was at bay, but dropping defensive operations, boldly essayed an attack at the expense of material and handled his forces with such vigour that few players could have resisted'.[17]

The use of the word 'forces' is interesting here because it takes us to the heart of what contemporaries thought was happening on the chessboard. In nineteenth-century handbooks, the pieces were denominated not just as individual tokens—'Klötze'—but also as 'forces', or 'Kräfte', embodying a principle of movement and pressure. Combinations, much pondered over in chess literature, were combinations of *forces* whose purpose was to push the opponent into a position of vulnerability.

Wilhelm Steinitz was famous not simply because he held the supremacy for so long, but also because he was credited with having placed the theory of chess on a new footing.[18] Steinitz organised his game around the insight that successful play could be driven not by a plan extrinsic to the game itself, but by a clear-eyed 'evaluation' of the balance of forces on the board at any one time. His achievement was to abstract the discourse of chess from a romantic notion of genius centred on the mental prowess of distinguished players and focus it instead, in the words of Emanuel Lasker, the master who challenged Steinitz and eventually won the world title, on 'the force of the pieces, the force of their cooperation', whose interaction resembled those 'vectors, called forces' found on the pages of 'mathematical books'.[19] Steinitz remained 'the greatest representative of the scientific tendency in chess', but his rigorous understanding of the game as a kind of embodied physics never entirely displaced the older 'romantic' admiration of daring moves and unexpected combinations. The discourse of chess continued to be marked by an unresolved tension between the quest to discern an objective 'reason' intrinsic to the game and an esteem for serendipitous moves and bold expressions of instinct and will.[20] The rhetorical escalation taking place around a game that was felt to require 'all the qualities of the fighter: force, discernment, conscientiousness, [and] undaunted courage' helps to explain why it was so widely adopted as a metaphor for politics, serving both as an 'argument for the necessity of social order' and as the ludic embodiment of the agonal principle.[21]

The chess analogy came naturally to those mid-nineteenth-century observers who tried to characterise Bismarck's qualities as a politician. 'Do not forget', the British envoy Sir Robert Morier wrote to Odo Russell, future British ambassador to the German Empire, in September 1870, 'that Bismarck is made up of two individuals, a colossal chess player full of the most daring combinations and with the quickest eye for the right combination at the right moment and who will sacrifice everything, even his *personal hatred*, to the success of his game *and* an individual with the strangest and still stronger antipathies, who will sacrifice everything except his combinations'.[22] Horst Kohl's poem 'A Victory at Chess—An Oriental Fable', published in *Kladderadatsch* in March 1866, depicts a game of chess between a temperamental 'Grand Vizier' and a sturdy man of the people (Bürgersmann); seeing that the game is lost, the Vizier sweeps the pieces from the board and throws them at the head of his opponent, crying, 'Now I have won the game!'—the poem was an encoded reference to the bitter conflict between Bismarck and the progressive movement in parliament.[23] Paul Kayser, head of the Colonial Department in the Foreign Office, observed that Bismarck's threat, during the conflict with Kaiser Wilhelm II that brought an end to his career, to trigger a crisis and then abolish the Reichstag in its current form was 'the most masterful move in the whole game of chess; it means checkmate for the king'.[24]

Bismarck, whose mother Wilhelmine Mencken was reputedly an outstanding chess player, frequently applied the analogy to himself and to the situations he faced as a statesman. He spoke in his memoirs of the 'political chess moves' of Russian diplomacy during his posting in Saint Petersburg.[25] The Alvensleben Convention of 1863, in which Prussia and Russia agreed to cooperate in the suppression of Polish insurrectionary activity, was 'a successful chess move', by which Bismarck was able to 'decide the [chess] match that the monarchical anti-Polish and the polonophile, pan-Slav elements within the Russian Cabinet were playing with each other at that time'.[26] Other passages distinguished between 'serious' initiatives and 'mere diplomatic chess moves', deployed the term neutrally to refer to domestic or external political initiatives of any kind, or used it to characterise tactical manoeuvres designed to place himself or an opponent at a disadvantage.[27]

These occurrences reflected the conventional valences of the metaphor, but there were also other passages in which Bismarck mined the chess analogy more deeply to expose the inner structure of his political reasoning. In one of the famous sequence of letters he exchanged with his old friend and patron, the conservative Leopold von Gerlach, Bismarck insisted that in external relations, it was crucial always to keep all options open, even if these included an alliance or an understanding of some kind with the French usurper Napoleon III: 'I must keep this possibility open', he wrote, 'because one cannot play chess if 16 of the 64 squares are forbidden from the very beginning'.[28] He drew on the same analogy in the memoirs when he defended the policy of rapprochement with Austria after the victory of 1866. To seriously damage Austria, he argued, would have produced a spirit of *revanche* in the conquered foe: it was far wiser to 'preserve the possibility of making friends with our current opponent', to 'view the Austrian state as a piece on the European chessboard and a renewal of good relations with it as a move to be kept in reserve'.[29]

Nowhere in the *Thoughts and Memoirs* does Bismarck set out exactly what he meant when he deployed the metaphor of chess to communicate his understanding of politics. But he comes close to making his sense explicit in an interesting passage of the 1857 correspondence with Leopold von Gerlach. In this exchange of letters, Gerlach protests against a policy that makes no distinction between powers legitimated by inheritance and tradition and those confected sovereignties, such as the imperial throne of Louis Napoleon III, forged in the satanic fires of revolution. Bismarck replies with a fascinating *tour d'horizon* of contemporary political cultures: which state, he asks, is not anchored in a revolutionary upheaval? The United States? Britain, which owes its modern form to the revolutions of 1641 and 1688? The root of Gerlach's error, he goes on to say, lies not in his having failed to recognise these features of the modern world, but rather in his deluded understanding of that world's underlying logic: 'I, too, acknowledge the struggle against the Revolution as my principle, but I do not take it to be correct to view Louis Napoleon as the only representative of the Revolution, or even as its representative *par excellence*, and I do not believe it is possible to apply this principle *as such* in policy, in such a way that even its remotest consequences override any other consideration, that it represents in a sense the sole trump suit in the game, whose lowest cards can win a trick over any card of another suit'.[30] What is interesting here is the implicit contrast with chess. In the card game referred to in this letter—Bismarck is probably referring to whist—the luck of the game determines that one suit be trumps, knocking out the cards of any other suit, regardless of their value. Chess is precisely not like that. The pieces on the chessboard do not cancel each other out, they hold each other in balance. And each is a force to be reckoned with: even a pawn can kill a king.

The Meaning of 1848

The force whose cards Leopold von Gerlach would have liked to see trumped out of the game was the revolution. Gerlach was a subtle and intelligent conservative, but in the face of the events of 1848 he responded as a reactionary who imagined that the spool of history could be rewound and the revolution made to unhappen. Bismarck saw the matter differently: for him, the changes wrought by the revolution of 1848 were irreversible. They had to be accepted. It is true that Bismarck had no sympathy for the proponents of revolution. His attitude to the events unfolding in Berlin during the March days of 1848 is captured in an emblematic and possibly apocryphal scene from the memoirs. In it, Bismarck proposes to the peasants on his estate—to general applause—that they arm themselves, march to Berlin, and 'free the king' from the insurrectionaries in the capital city.[31] In another scene from the memoirs, Bismarck recalled sitting in Berlin at the height of the March days with Generals Prittwitz and Möllendorf. When the question was raised of what should be done, Bismarck supposedly sat at a piano, naughtily picking out the notes of the infantry's attack march.[32]

Yet for all his contempt for the authors of the tumult on the streets of the German cities in 1848 and his undeniable attachment to the monarchical political culture of the 'old Prussia', Bismarck was quick to adapt to the new conditions created by the March events. In a speech delivered in Berlin to the reconvened United Diet on 2 April 1848, Bismarck spoke to a motion proposing that the chamber thank the revolutionaries for their achievements in March 1848. Naturally he was unable to support this motion, he declared. He was appalled by the assault on the monarchical order. But this was not tantamount to refusing to accept the authority of the new government. On the contrary, Bismarck made it quite clear that he accepted the new government's programme as 'a programme of the future'. He did so, he added, not because he wanted to, but because he was obliged to do so by what he called the 'force of circumstances' (*Drang der Umstände*). Yet he also conceded that 'this ministry is the only one which can lead us out of the current situation into an ordered and law abiding state of affairs'.[33] The theatrical effect of these words was heightened, if we are to believe the memoirs, by the fact that he left the podium sobbing. The historian Heinz Wolter rightly described this speech as Bismarck's 'funeral song for the old Prussia'.[34] In a letter he wrote for a Brandenburg newspaper late in April, Bismarck nailed the message home again. No one, he insisted, need fear that the East Elbian landowning elite would oppose the onwards march of events in the name of a restoration of the old regime: 'Like every sensible person, the landowner will acknowledge that it is pointless and impossible to halt the flow of time or to dam it up'.[35]

In other words, Bismarck was quick to recognise the new political order inaugurated by the revolution. But what exactly did that mean? The legacy of the revolution in Prussia was complex. On the one hand, the political reforms enacted during and after the revolutionary upheaval—most importantly a constitution and a parliament, national elections, and a relatively free and critical press, at least by the standards of the old pre-march censorship regime—created a new Prussia, in which political life widened to incorporate an unprecedented range of forces. On the other hand, the counterrevolution of the autumn and winter 1848 halted the process of democratisation started by the uprisings of the previous spring and consolidated the power of the monarchical executive. In order to understand the impact of 1848 on Bismarck's historicity, we need to look at both features of the transformation effected in that year: the consolidation of state power and the opening of politics to the interplay of interests in parliament and society.

The defining fact about the Prussian constitution of 5 December 1848, the first in the kingdom's history, was that it was not forced upon the government by an elected assembly, but granted or 'imposed' (oktroyiert) by the crown. The new constitution had much in common, to be sure, with the drafts drawn up by the Prussian liberals of the revolutionary National Assembly in Berlin during the spring and summer, but it was not issued under their authority. By the time it appeared, the Assembly had been forcibly dissolved by troops of the king's army and the deputies sent home. 'When a constitution is unilaterally issued by a prince', the constitutional lawyer Carl Schmitt would later argue, 'it rests beyond all doubt on the constituent power of the prince. . . . Either the prince, acting on the basis of the monarchical principle, issues a constitution out of the plenitude of his state power, or the constitution rests on a constitutive act of the people, i.e. on the democratic principle. Since they are fundamentally opposed, these two principles cannot be mixed with each other'.[36] The problem was neatly captured by a contemporary political caricature bearing the title 'The Prussian Way of Issuing a Constitution'; it showed the king and his ministers firing the constitution into a crowd with a cannon.

The Prussian crown (meaning the king and the conservative camarilla that gathered around the throne during the revolution) could have given the lie to Schmitt's axiom by conceding a constitution that really did endow the parliament with a share of sovereignty. Instead, they placed at the heart of the constitution an article that permitted the executive to issue emergency decrees (Verordnungen) with the force of law without the involvement of parliament. Clause 2 of article 105 stated that 'in urgent cases, when the chambers [of parliament] are not in session, decrees can be issued that have force of law'. As Günther Grünthal has shown, this provision was not included as a mere failsafe to ensure the continuity of government at times when parliament was not in session. Rather, it was intended from the start to provide the crown with a means of revising the constitution in a conservative sense. It was used on 30 May 1849 to replace the democratic electoral law conceded in 1848 with a plutocratic three-class franchise designed to cripple the efforts of the left to apply pressure on the government through parliament.[37] In the sphere of taxation, too, the December constitution tilted the playing field in favour of the monarchical executive. Article 98 stipulated that all state revenues and expenditures must be applied for in advance to parliament and approved by means of a budget law, and article 60 stated that king and parliament were partners in wielding the legislative power—so far, so good.[38] But article 108 stipulated that the taxes and expenditures agreed for any given year would *continue indefinitely* until they were amended by a new law—a provision that, in theory, gave the government the power to bypass parliament in the event of a failure to reach an agreement on the budget.[39]

As Hans-Christof Kraus has shown, this was exactly in accordance with the conservative view, which was that a monarchy that endowed parliament with the power to grant *and* to refuse taxation would be a monarchy in name only. When the chamber debated the issue on 24 and 25 September 1849, the conservatives lined up to defend article 108. Among them was a young Otto von Bismarck, who argued that the Prussian crown was under no obligation to place itself in the position of impotence occupied by the British monarchy: 'The British crown appears really just to be a decorative ornament on the dome that sits atop the building of the state', he declared, 'whereas I see our [Prussian crown] as its central, load-bearing column'.[40] This commitment to the constitutionally preeminent status of the monarchical state executive remained a central feature of Bismarck's politics. Amidst the shifting constellations of public life, it was something that abided, a source of cohesion through time.[41]

None of this meant that the revolution could be reversed or undone. The forces unleashed by 1848 continued to flow through the public life of the Prussian state, even if the channels that connected them to the political executive were narrow. A statesman hoping to make his way in the Prussian *Nachmärz* had to familiarise himself with a new world of parliamentary fractions and elections, campaigns, political scandals, and often bitter public debate.[42] The central figure in managing the new dispensation was Otto von Manteuffel, a sturdy and unexcitable career bureaucrat and Minister-President of Prussia from 1850 until 1858. Bismarck was rather dismissive of Manteuffel in the memoirs and in his contemporary correspondence with close associates, but the Minister-President's impact on Bismarck's evolving political outlook and technique may have been deeper than he was willing to acknowledge. More than anyone else, it was Manteuffel who accommodated the political culture of Prussia to the realities of the post-revolutionary situation. Manteuffel took the view that the purpose of government was to mediate among the conflicting forces of the organised interests that constituted civil society. He rebalanced the fiscal policy of the government, filing away at the privileges enjoyed by the East Elbian landed elite. It was unthinkable, he pointed out to the conservative rural opponents of fiscal reform, that the Prussian state should

continue to be run 'like the landed estate of a nobleman'.[43] As
Anna Ross has shown, Manteuffel consistently headed off attempts by the romantic-corporate aristocratic far right to engi-
neer a 'reaction' that would unmake the events of 1848.[44]

Manteuffel also took steps to secure the unity and cohesion
of the central administration. In 1852, he requested a cabinet order from the king establishing the Minister-President
as the sole conduit for formal communications between the
ministry and the monarch. This important document sig-
nalled an attempt to realise at last the unity of administration that the reformers of the Napoleonic era had struggled
for in the 1810s.[45] In later years, under the premiership of
the far more ruthless and ambitious Otto von Bismarck, the
cabinet order of 1852 would provide a mechanism for a concentration of power sufficient to ensure a measure of unity
across cabinet and administration; and it would play a key
role in the terminal crisis of Bismarck's political career—I return to it below.

Far from seeing the turbulence of the new parliamentary
politics as an argument for a coup d'état, Manteuffel saw it
as the anchor of his own authority, for what better argument could there be for the indispensability of the Minister-
President than his ability to manage the conflicting forces of
the Landtag? Indeed, one of Manteuffel's ultra-conservative
critics, Leopold von Gerlach, accused the Minister-President in 1853 of deliberately engineering crises in the Prussian
Landtag in order to convince the king of his indispensability—a charge that would later be levelled (with more justice)
at Bismarck.[46]

The underlying point is that Manteuffel accepted the
dynamics of the post-revolutionary situation and focused on
developing the tools to manage them successfully. Among
these, the most important was the management of public

opinion. Manteuffel believed that it was time to move beyond the traditionally confrontational relationship between press and government that had been the norm before 1848. This aspiration bore fruit in the creation, in December 1850, of the 'Central Agency for Press Affairs' (Zentralstelle für Pressangelegenheiten), whose responsibilities included the administration of funds set aside for the purpose of subsidizing the press and the cultivation of 'relationships' with domestic and foreign papers.[47] During the early 1850s, the Central Agency succeeded in building up a network of press contacts that penetrated deep into the provincial press.

Manteuffel's innovation thus heralded the transition from a form of control based on the filtering of press material through a cumbersome apparatus of censorship to a more nuanced system of news and information management.[48] All this was persuasive testimony to the irreversibility of the changes wrought by 1848. 'Every century has seen new cultural forces enter into the sphere of traditional life, forces which were not to be destroyed but to be incorporated', Manteuffel wrote in July 1851. 'Our generation recognizes the press as such a force. Its significance has grown with the expanded participation of the people in public affairs, a participation that is partly expressed, partly fed and directed by the press'.[49] Manteuffel captured the historicity of his form of post-revolutionary politics in a speech he gave on the occasion of his election to the Prussian parliament in early 1849: 'the old times are gone and cannot return! . . . It was popular in those days to speak of reaction. He is short-sighted who would think of an establishment of the old times. To return to the decaying conditions of the past would be like scooping water with a sieve'.[50] The resonance with Bismarck's speech to the Second United Diet on 2 April 1848 to the Berlin Constituent Assembly is impossible to miss.

This post-revolutionary order was the world in which Bismarck learned his craft. He took up his post—his first salaried post—as Prussia's representative at the Frankfurt Confederal Diet in 1851, where his most important duty was to bribe pro-Prussian journalists and newspaper editors with Manteuffel's government cash. He would later be famous for his management of an immense network of friendly journalists and newspapers, in whose service he recruited many lapsed 1848 radicals.[51] There was also a subjective and personal dimension to Bismarck's relationship with 1848. Only during the revolutions did he begin to align his political imagination with the destiny of the monarchy and of the state itself. He acknowledged throughout his life that the revolution was the enabling condition on which his own career in public life was founded. In transforming and opening the structures of political power, the revolution had created new opportunities for someone like himself. He could never, he conceded in the memoirs he wrote after his retirement, have embarked on a political career in 'the time before 1848'. The young Bismarck had lacked the social connections that would have put him on the fast track to high political office, and for the long, slow road up the ranks of the bureaucracy he lacked the patience and *Sitzfleisch*.[52]

Underlying this reluctant concession of the revolution's importance was a broader process of rhetorical inflation that transformed the term 'revolution' from a word denoting a specific event in the past, such as the storm on the Bastille or the fall of Robespierre, into an unsteerable and all-encompassing process, a world-historical principle whose impact zone included the entirety of humanity.[53] The conservative political theorist Friedrich Julius Stahl, an influential figure in Bismarck's milieu in and after 1848, captured this semantic transition in a talk given at the University of Berlin in 1852 and subsequently published as a pamphlet. In *What Is the Revolution?*, Stahl distinguished between mere tumults and 'Revolution': 'Does Revolution mean the people taking the initiative and wielding violence against the authorities? Is it the same as uprising? Not at all! The Revolution is not a single, unique act; it is a continuing condition, a new order of things. Uprising, the expulsion of the dynasty, overturning the constitution—these have happened in all ages. But the Revolution is the authentic, world-historical signature of our era'.[54] Expanding the concept in this way did not *necessarily* imply an acceptance of the legitimacy of the 1848 revolutions. Stahl's lecture urged listeners and readers to see contemporary politics in the light of a stark moral choice between reverence for God's ordinances and submission to the pride and desire of mere humans. But for those of a less theocratic bent, like Bismarck, the semantic inflation of 'revolution' made it easier to conflate the events of 1848 with the workings of history. However contemptible the actual enactors of revolution might be (in Bismarck's eyes), they were the executors of a historical transformation whose finality could not be denied.

Nowhere did Bismarck articulate his insistence on the watershed status of the 1848 revolution more forcefully than in his terminal dispute with Kaiser Wilhelm II. Determined to break the power of his chancellor, the impetuous new monarch demanded in early 1890 that Bismarck return to him the Cabinet Order of 1852, the order issued to Manteuffel assigning to the Minister-President authority over his fellow ministers. In his letter of resignation, dated—oddly enough—18 March, the day on which the 1848 revolutions had broken out in Berlin, Bismarck replied to this demand with a sophisticated historical genealogy of his own post, grounded in an account of 'the genesis and significance' of the Cabinet Order of 1852. It had been *proposed*, he noted, in the First United Diet of 1847 by the Liberal deputy Mevissen. It had actually been introduced in the spring of 1848, as a means of 'securing that degree of unity and stability' without which 'ministerial responsibility' as implied by 'the essence of constitutional life cannot be practised'. Abandoning the concentration of ministerial power conceded by the sovereign in the order of 1852 would be possible only if one returned to the era of absolutism, without ministerial responsibility. 'But under the constitutional arrangements that now prevail—and rightly so—a presiding authority over the college of ministers on the basis of the principle of the Order of 1852 is indispensable'.[55] This may appear a merely opportunistic appeal to history—after all, its purpose was to defend his own post as chancellor against a curtailment of his powers. But there was more to it than that. Bismarck had understood since the 1850s that the lofty structures of the once absolutist state were mired in a turbulent environment where everything was in motion.

The Flux of Politics

For Bismarck, wrote Helmuth Wolff, 'all the forces of the contemporary world had their pre-histories, each of which afforded a deeper insight into their character'. Bismarck's reasoning was 'genetic' in character, in the sense that it focused attention on 'processes of historical becoming that were to be traced continually in their constant fluctuations'.[56] He saw the European powers as embarked on journeys whose character could be elucidated by reference to their past. Modern England was growing in the soil of the 'Glorious Revolution' of 1688 and the industrial revolution of the late eighteenth and early nineteenth centuries; France was still struggling to come to terms with the forces released by the great revolution of 1789. Russian tsarist autocracy was the consequence of a journey into modernity that had begun with Peter the Great and Catherine II, but the movement of liberal dissent that was infiltrating Russian political society was also anchored in a deep history. The Polish nation had never accepted the verdict of the partitions of 1772, 1793, and 1795 and would never cease striving for the reestablishment of Polish statehood.[57]

This mode of historical reasoning left its mark on Bismarck's practice as a politician. We have seen that he claimed, like Manteuffel, to accept the transformative impact of the revolution of 1848. He understood, as Manteuffel did, that new forces had entered political life, forces whose interaction had to be carefully managed in the face of an unknown and unknowable future. Liberalism in its various manifestations, political Catholicism, the nationalist movement, parliamentary fractions and coalitions, the press and public opinion— these were tools with which the statesman had no choice but to work. They were not under his direct control. Even the conservatives were perfectly capable of going their own way— Bismarck repeatedly complained of the tendency of people in public life to overestimate his control over the conservative faction—supposedly his ideological allies—in the first chamber of the Prussian parliament.[58] But even if the forces could not be led or controlled, they could be held in balance or played off against each other. And new forces could be introduced to balance the old.

Playing the system in this way demanded extreme flexibility of the decision maker. Hence the need, at home and abroad, for rapidly shifting alliances and combinations—as in the game of chess. The historicity of his understanding of power is articulated as starkly in his techniques and praxis as in his utterances. Bismarck self-consciously distanced himself from the ideological prescriptions of any single interest—no chess player who felt a special sympathy for one of his pieces, he intimated to Gerlach, could hope to play the game effectively.[59] Though he counted many 'old conservatives' (Gerlach included) among his friends, he never adopted their nostalgic, corporatist politics. Nor, on the other hand, was he or could he be a liberal. And though he revered the monarchical state as an executive with the capacity for autonomous action, he was unimpressed by the 'fourth estate' of the civil servants (throughout his life he regarded the 'pen-pushers'— *Federfuchser*—of the administration with a certain disdain).

The result of all these nonalignments was a remarkable freedom from ideological constraint, an ability to spring from one camp to the other, wrong-footing his opponents or exploiting the differences between them. Scarcely had he humiliated the liberals in the constitutional crisis of 1862, but he was offering them a parliamentary indemnity, to the chagrin of his conservative allies. He collaborated with the forces of liberalism against the Catholics and conservatives (in the 1870s) and vice versa (in the 1880s); he brandished the democratic franchise as a weapon against elitist liberalism, consulted socialists on the social question, and then attempted to undermine their standing with the armature of social insurance legislation; he punctured the oppositional pretensions of the nationalists by seeming to align himself with the nationalist cause. 'There are times when one must govern in a liberal way and times when one must govern in a dictatorial way', he declared before the Reichstag in 1883.[60] His career was punctuated with the astonished gasps of those who, having enlisted Bismarck for their cause one day, found him bombarding them from an enemy position on the next. The protean nature of his politics infuriated his allies and his enemies, who were sometimes the same people, but it kept them guessing. It was one of the keys to his success.

Among the most momentous of Bismarck's power plays was his decision to press for a German parliament elected by universal suffrage. On 10 June 1866, he proposed that the German Confederation be reorganised, without Austria, around a national and democratically elected parliament. Justifying his decision, which shocked friends and enemies alike, he expressed his confidence that 'in moments of decision the masses will always stand by the king', in other words, that an expansion of the franchise would counterbalance the liberals with the ballast of mass conservatism.[61] This assumption was not unreasonable: it appeared to be borne out by the success of conservative countermobilisation in 1848 and the election of Louis Napoleon III to the French presidency in December 1848 on the back of four million largely peasant votes.[62] The ploy backfired: the masses who now entered the political fold proved not to be the deferential rustics Bismarck had imagined. The first and most spectacular beneficiary of universal suffrage was the Centre Party, whose phenomenal success among Catholics in the south, west, and east created a formidable oppositional bloc in the Reichstag. Then came the Social Democrats, whose remarkable rise to electoral dominance not even draconian antisocialist laws could halt.

In his memoirs, written in the 1890s when the consequences of universal suffrage were fully apparent, Bismarck offered a curiously ambivalent account of this policy. 'The adoption of universal suffrage', he wrote, 'was a weapon in the struggle against Austria and other foreign states'. 'In a struggle of this kind, where it is a matter of life and death, one doesn't reflect on the weapons, or on the values that will be destroyed by their use'. But then came a more principled defence: 'even today I hold universal suffrage to be a justified principle, not only in theory, but also in practice'. This, he argued, was because modern politics was an exercise in the balancing of social forces.

The interests of the 'more intelligent classes', who tended also to be the better-off, had to be secured, but so did those of the 'desirous element' for whom property was an aspiration rather than a reality. Yet the interests of the latter must be accommodated without a 'dangerous acceleration' of political change or damage to the state structure. If the state failed in this balancing act, the result would be a 'return to absolutism'. And absolutism was unworkable in the modern world, because even the best-led executives needed the corrective of public 'criticism'. And this criticism could come only from 'a free press and from parliaments in the modern sense'. The function of government was thus to interpose itself between the sovereign and the legislature, protecting the political process *both* against the caprice of passing popular majorities *and* against the intrigues of camarillas and royal favourites. Nations, after all, were 'great masses' that were obliged to move with immense care, 'since the paths on which they travel into an unknown future have not been laid with level rails'.[63]

These reflections should not be read as a candid exposure of Bismarck's political motives—we are dealing rather with an elaborate exercise in retrospective self-vindication. What matters in the context of this discussion is the historicity of the rationalisation. A locomotive—we can probably call it history—was slowly moving on rails, but rails that were being laid over broken ground into an unknown and unknowable future. Its ponderous motion was determined by the constantly shifting balance of forces within it. Whichever direction this figurative locomotive happened to travel in, there could scarcely be a more perfect embodiment of linear time.[64]

Bismarck built this understanding of politics as the interplay of forces into the German national constitution whose emergence he oversaw between 1867 and 1871. This was an extraordinarily open-ended document. Above all, it made no

serious effort to create a federal government. Although it determined the rights and responsibilities of the different constitutional organs (Bundesrat, Reichstag, Emperor, Chancellor),
it said virtually nothing about who or what was to assume the
function of a government—in this respect it was quite unlike
the draft national constitution drawn up by the deputies of the
Frankfurt Parliament in 1848. The 1871 constitution was designed as the framework for an interplay of forces in which, as
in chess, nothing but the basic rules of the game were defined—
outcomes and the choice of play remained open. The German
federal constitution of 1871, moreover, by contrast with its earlier Swiss and American counterparts, made no provision for a
constitutional court. In Germany, as Oliver Haardt has shown,
the evolution of the federal system came rather to be driven
by a haphazard interaction among its parts.[65] The absence of
a constitutional court reflected Bismarck's understanding of
the constitution as an open-ended instrument of power—the
political power plays of the chancellor were not to be judged or
checked by an impartial nonexecutive adjudicator who could
determine the basic direction of constitutional evolution.

Bismarck's openness to the interplay of forces might suggest an affinity with the realist thinking of Ludwig Rochau,
an influential theorist of the post-revolutionary moment, who
proposed in 1853 that the foundations of all political understanding lay, or ought to lie, in the study of 'the forces that
shape, carry and transform the state'. Like Manteuffel and
Bismarck, Rochau saw that the revolution had released new
historical forces that could not be banished from the world:
'[In recent times] a rich new growth of youthful societal
forces has emerged, all of which demand acknowledgement
within the life of the state, either individually or in combination. Bourgeois self-awareness [das bürgerliche Bewußt-
sein], the idea of liberty, national sentiment, the idea of an

equality of human rights, partisan politics, the press: for many states today these are quite new factors of social life'.[66] Like Bismarck's, Rochau's realism was anchored in the 1848 revolution; it was at once an attempt to explain the failure of that revolution and to manage the consequences of its success. In the aftermath of that upheaval, Rochau argued, a realistic politics must possess a feeling for historical change and for the 'shifting constellations of opposed political and social forces'.[67] Bismarck might well have found these observations congenial (I don't know for sure, because to my knowledge he never passed judgement on Rochau's work). But there was a fundamental difference: Rochau, the theorist of *Realpolitik*, was a liberal with radical sympathies for whom the state was ultimately subordinate to the forces of society. The constitution of a state, he wrote, was 'determined by the relationship among the partly latent, partly active forces within it'. Every social force had a right to a level of official recognition congruent with its size 'and the state power itself consists exclusively of the sum of the societal forces that the state encloses within itself'.[68] Bismarck would have found this latter claim abhorrent. For the Prussian statesman, the monarchical state was not a manifestation or plaything of social or political forces, but the enduring structure that made it possible for them to play themselves out without collapsing the entire system into chaos.

Apotheosis of the Moment

In Jean-Léon Jérôme's *The Death of Caesar*, painted between 1859 and 1867, the senate of ancient Rome has become a crime scene. Upturned chairs bear witness to a recent struggle. A corpse lies in the foreground, draped in white fabric. In the middle ground, men in togas make their way out of the chamber; all have raised their swords, except for the last in

FIGURE 3.2. Jean-Léon Jérôme, *The Death of Caesar* (1867).
Source: By kind permission of The Walters Art Museum, Baltimore.

the group (Brutus?), who has not yet lifted his sword, but presumably soon will. In the deep background is an arch leading
out into daylight and onto the Forum. The eye's short journey
away from the murdered Caesar to the departing senators and
the light-filled arch is also a journey into the future: the news
of this momentous deed will pass from the chamber onto the
forum, enter public knowledge, and ultimately merge with
the history of Rome. Jérôme's painting is a scene dense with
narrative, strewn with clues to what has just transpired and
intimations of what will happen next. It is as if the painter
has tried to compress more time into the frame than a static
two-dimensional image can logically hold. *The Death of Caesar*
is typical of those 'plot-paintings', increasingly dominant in the
exhibitions of the European academies between the 1840s and
the 1880s, in which, as Nina Lübbren has argued, the traditions of history painting and genre painting merged to produce images saturated with the time of a particular moment.[69]
    It is a distinctive feature of chess that it is measured
out in moments, in each of which there inheres a new and

unforeseen array of opportunities and threats. The game flows diachronically, but it also evolves in moments where the balance of forces is temporarily frozen, moments in which decisions have to made about the next step. The same can be said of Bismarck's conception of politics—if statesmanship meant managing the relationship between forces whose relative strength and reciprocal relations were constantly in flux, then success depended upon acting at specific junctures when the current alignment happened, however briefly, to favour a specific course of action. 'Moments of decision' and 'decisive moments' (the two are not identical) were the joints from which his political ego-narratives were constructed. What point was there in seeking a military showdown with Austria over the creation of a Prussian-dominated German union, Bismarck asked a political associate in the autumn of 1850, if one could not be sure that the monarch's support would be forthcoming at '*the decisive moment*'?[70] The presentation of a new press law to the Reichstag should be delayed, he told William I in in May 1873, 'until the moment [Zeitpunkte] when the harmonisation of the German penal code would create a consistent basis for prosecution and condemnation of punishable actions by the press'.[71] In a letter of summer 1878 to the king of Bavaria, Bismarck acknowledged that if the new Reichstag failed to support measures against the Social Democrats, it might be necessary to consider a dissolution: 'But I do not believe that *the correct moment* for such a decision will arise this autumn'.[72] In a chapter on the German 'dynasties and tribes', Bismarck observed that he had always succeeded in winning the support of the Prussian monarch (Wilhelm I) for 'the German side of our development', because '*in decisive moments*' Wilhelm had always leaned towards the national cause.[73] In November 1870, 'at the moment when the question of the imperial title was critical', it was Bismarck's fancy footwork, he recalled in the memoirs, that had reconciled the king of Bavaria with the plan to proclaim a 'German Kaiser'. In this case, the window of opportunity had been so narrow that Bismarck scribbled the decisive letter on a dining table using 'flimsy paper and uncooperative ink' and sent it by hand at the greatest possible speed from war-torn France to Hohenschwangau, where the Bavarian monarch was confined to bed with a toothache.[74] The implication here was that even the slightest delay might have changed the course of history. The idea that the time of political decision making was punctuated by situations that created certain constraints and opportunities was not new, of course. Pleading with his Estates for money, the Great Elector had cited the exigencies of 'current constellations' (gegenwär-tigen Conjuncturen). The difference was that in Bismarck's time, the constellation of current affairs appeared both to be much harder to read or decipher and to change much more rapidly, so that the pressure to intervene, choose, and decide became an existential condition.

In structuring his narratives and his self-understanding in this way, Bismarck was articulating a period sensibility marked by the ascendency of the moment as an experiential and her-meneutic category. The revolutions of 1848 had something to do with this: by unleashing the masses as a factor of unpre-dictability in public life, the historian Johann Gustav Droysen suggested in 1851, the revolutions had burdened European politics with a 'fear of the moment' from which there was no longer any escape.[75] Far from abolishing time, as has sometime been claimed, the revolutionary transformation in midcentury telecommunications charged ever smaller units of time with ever greater value, especially in market environments such as stock exchanges, where the speed of access to information could bestow a commercial advantage.[76] Over the course of the nineteenth century, Sue Zemka has argued, the penetration of all domains of life by industrial and clock time 'set the stage for a hyperawareness of the momentary'; the moment came to perform a heightened interpretative function as a window onto hidden sources of meaning.[77] Ulrich Raulff has traced the proliferation of moments (of coincidence, creation, insight, decision, illumination, and so on) as attributes of modern temporal awareness.[78]

An analysis of Bismarck's fictional reading lies outside the compass of this study, but it is worth noting that *History of the United Netherlands* (1860), by John Lothrop Motley, his lifelong and closest friend, was a book thickly saturated with moments of decision, danger, opportunity, destiny, and revelation. In every chapter of this work, which Bismarck knew well, Motley situated the actions of his protagonists within unique envelopes of time. The effect was to sharpen awareness of the contingent quality of every historical situation, the time-limited character of opportunities, the suddenness of threats, the simultaneities, often hidden from the protagonists, that reveal the true meaning of events.[79] It was Motley who could see and make sense of these moments, not the actors in his story—in this sense they were artefacts of the historian's hermeneutic mastery.

This was the elevated standpoint to which Bismarck also aspired. In his speech of 3 December 1850 to the Prussian parliament, Bismarck defended the Prussian decision to abandon the (Prussian-dominated) Erfurt Union and to accept the revival of the German Confederation under Austrian leadership, laid down in the Punctation of Olmütz only four days earlier. Bismarck rejected the arguments of those national-minded parliamentarians who denounced Olmütz as a humiliation for Prussia. In such weighty matters, he argued, the decisions of the Prussian government should be swayed not by public emotion but by the cool and precise evaluation of the threats and exigencies of a specific and contingent moment. Why should Prussia risk the recourse to war at '*a moment when* our neighbours will stand in arms against us if we hasten in arms to our borders, . . . *a moment when* a spirit of trust [in the Prussian authorities] can be found in those who usually eschew it, *a moment when* every question . . . touching on foreign policy could carry war or peace in its belly?'

Bismarck's purpose was not to win friends in the legislature (the speech had rather the opposite effect), but rather to commend himself to the court as a candidate for future high office. What is interesting is that Bismarck did this by identifying himself not as the advocate of a tendency or principle, but rather as a uniquely skilled reader of the historical moment for action.[80] The same idea lay at the heart of his protests against the efforts of the military command to exclude him from decision-making processes during the war of 1870. There was more to the successful waging of war than victory in the field, he remarked. Managing the larger consequences of armed conflict required political skills: 'After all, to judge when *the correct moment has arisen* to commence the transition from war to peace, a knowledge of the European situation is necessary, a knowledge that military commanders do not usually possess'.[81]

One could greatly extend this list of pivotal *Momente, Zeitpunkte,* and *Augenblicke*—today, the existence of searchable digital versions of the memoirs and much of the correspondence makes it beguilingly easy to track them. The underlying point is simply that these references to decisive moments—the entire oeuvre is peppered with them—are not a stylistic feature or a metaphor. They take us to the heart of Bismarck's understanding of the time of politics. If politics, at home and abroad, meant trying to manage the interactions of numerous domestic and international variables whose mutual relations were constantly changing, then it followed that high office and the power that came with it belonged by rights to him who could anticipate, read, and exploit the conjunctures that provided opportunities for decisive action.

In a mental world where political life unfolded as a sequence of critical moments charged with the potential for decisive action, it made sense to speculate about counterfactual scenarios, in which a different path was chosen or no decision offered at all. In the course of discussing the events of 1848, for example, Bismarck pondered in the memoirs on what might have happened if the Prussian government had succeeded, through energetic and unconditional action, in securing German unity immediately, rather than waiting for the opportunities that opened up in the 1860s. Perhaps unsurprisingly, he concluded that it was just as well that things took the course they did.[82] But it is interesting all the same that 1848 served as the fulcrum for this speculative modulation of the historical narrative.

In another interesting passage, Bismarck explains the lateness of German unification by postulating a *proton pseudós*, a term from Aristotelian logic denoting the point at which a false premise is inserted into a deduction, rendering its conclusion false, even though the procedure is correct in formal terms.[83] In other words, Bismarck combed back through the history of the Prussian state, imagined as a decision tree in which each step created a new point of departure, in search of the original 'wrong turn' (*die Gabelung auf den unrichtigen Weg*)—a quest that would have seemed meaningless to Frederick II (except of course in the context of a battle, where he acknowledged that there were moments of high-risk decision that could be crucial to determining the outcome),[84] but also to Pufendorf, who, for all his interest in the choice-making situations that confront the sovereign actor, never assigned the 'moment of decision' the load-bearing role it plays in Bismarck's narratives. The difference between Bismarck and the statesmen of earlier eras, he argued, in a characteristically self-aggrandising (and anachronistic) flourish, was that they (unlike Bismarck) had failed to see and make sense of moments of historical possibility as they arose.[85]

By the end of his career, Bismarck had come to see his career as a chain of epoch-making moments of decision—and the elderly monarch who had shared so many of them with him clearly agreed. In a letter of 23 September 1887, the twenty-fifth anniversary of Bismarck's appointment as Minister-President of Prussia, the ninety-year-old William I thanked him for elevating Prussia to a 'rank in fame and honour unprecedented in world history' and added, 'I am sending to you in memory of the last 25 years this image of the building in which we had to discuss and implement so many crucial decisions—may they always resound to the honour and benefit of Prussia and hopefully of Germany'.[86] History flowed, but it was also portioned out in stark moments of decision. The stop-start texture of the decision tree and the continuous motion of time's stream were two ways of understanding the same process, just as the logic of chess can be exposed both through the reconstruction of play-sequences extending through time and through 'problems' in which the player is presented with a postulated moment in a game that may have no concrete history. Helmuth Wolff came close to capturing this tension when he distinguished between the 'genetic' and the 'comparative' dimensions of Bismarck's historical thinking.[87] Genetic trains of thought worked cumulatively, diachronically, and metonymically: nations and movements, for example, accrued attributes over time, gradually becoming what they now were; comparative ones balanced options and possibilities against each other in synchronic array. The two were only notionally separate, of course, because if everything really was evolving and becoming at a range of speeds, then good decision making demanded not just the weighing of different objectives and targets, but the capacity to work simultaneously in different time frames. Recalling his role in managing the twists and turns of the Schleswig-Holstein question in the early 1860s, Bismarck spoke of a hierarchy of different 'planes of action' (*Abstufungen*) that had to be kept in play—today we would call them 'options'—but whose relative risks and benefits were constantly in flux.[88] The same can be said of his handling of the crisis of 1870. Some form of German union was on Bismarck's wish list when a quarrel blew up between France and Prussia over the candidacy to the vacant Spanish throne, but the timing of that process remained open. A war with France could be welcomed as a catalyst for an accelerated resolution of the German question towards a union. But menaces from Paris without a declaration of war would also have been useful, since they would have reminded the southern German states of their precarious situation and therefore of the need to seek security in a closer relationship with Prussia. And there were also moments when Bismarck envisaged a longer-term, entirely war-free solution to the problem of Prussia's relationship with the German south.[89] In almost every major enterprise of his career, Bismarck entered the fray with a relatively open mind, with regard to not only methods and affiliations, but also the sequence and timing of objectives.

The Monarchical State and the Meaning of History

Bismarck could tolerate the domestic interplay of forces for only so long as he possessed the means to curb and channel the impact of their interactions. Of these means—aside from his own intellectual, political, and tactical superiority, a matter on which he never entertained any serious doubt—the most important was his elevated location within the structure of the Prussian monarchical state, and specifically his intimate link to the sovereign person.

There is a lot one could say about the place of the monarchy in Bismarck's imagination. He announced in the opening paragraph of the memoirs that the efforts of his primary school teachers to imbue him with German national sentiment had never dislodged his 'inborn Prussian-monarchical feeling'. 'My historical sympathies always remained on the side of authority'.[90] In the emotional economy of the memoirs, encounters with his various monarchs play a unique role, unlocking powerful waves of emotion that are found nowhere else. His interactions with the whiskery patriarch William I are a study in long-term codependency.[91]

'Managing up' was the chancellor's most pressing task, not just because he was an imperial appointee who might at times have to make do without a Reichstag majority, but also because Bismarck's historical imagination was framed by a certain view of the monarchical state as a privileged structure located above the political fray, above the interplay of forces. The constitutionally elevated role of the imperial-federal union, anchored in the prerogatives of the Prussian king, was not negotiable. It was the hard and unyielding node in the soft clay of politics. Hence Bismarck's strong retrospective attachment to the *Machtstaat* of Frederick II—Bismarck had no desire to return to the era of absolutism; he knew, as we have seen, that the past was 'dead and buried'. But he believed that the *essence* of the old state had survived in the form of the monarchical principal, meaning the inviolability of a monarch endowed with prerogatives that remained partially outside the purview of parliament. His first and chief concern when the news of 1848 reached him on his estate was that the king was 'unfree'—by which he meant not just that the king was a 'prisoner' in his capital city but also that the monarchical state had forfeited the political independence that made it a state. The monarchical person was mortal (Bismarck saw three Prussian kings—two of them emperors—to their graves during his career), but the state was a piece of eternity. 'The turnover of individuals', he wrote in 1882, 'is irrelevant. . . . The state and its institutions are only possible if they are imagined as permanent-identical personalities'.[92]

Whereas the state as an agency wielding power (*Machtstaat*) was permanent and unalterable, the specific constitutional arrangements sustaining its political life were contingent and negotiable. How Bismarck thought about the relationship between the two is revealed by an episode from 1858. A stroke had incapacitated King Frederick William IV and since the stricken king was childless, the accession of his younger brother, Prince William, appeared imminent. William glimpsed the possibility of using the accession to claw back a small part of the constitutional ground that had been ceded by the monarchy in the aftermath of the revolution. He raised with Bismarck the possibility of demanding a revision of the constitution as a condition for his acceding to the throne. Why, after all, should he accept unconditionally an agreement to which he had not himself been a party?

Before we come to Bismarck's reply, we should recall that in the March days of 1848, Prince William of Prussia had emerged as one of the most vehement reactionaries in the circles close to the king, insisting that infantry charges and grapeshot were the best answer to political agitation on the streets. Indeed, he was so outspoken in his demands for a crackdown that the king sent him off to England to cool down. Yet once the shock of the initial uprising had subsided, the prince had been quick to adapt to the demands of the new situation. 'What is past is past!' he wrote in a remarkable letter to the new liberal Berlin government of Ludolf Camphausen only three weeks after the March events. 'Nothing can be brought back; may every attempt to do so be abandoned!' It was now the 'duty of every patriot' to 'help build the new Prussia'.[93] The former 'grape shot prince' returned from Britain in the summer of 1848 ready to work within the post-revolutionary order.

By the mid-1850s the Crown Prince had affiliated himself with the liberal faction at court. One of his first actions on taking power would be to dismiss Manteuffel and his conservative ministers and replace them with liberal substitutes, ushering in what came to be known as the 'New Era'. And yet, as the moment for the establishment of a regency neared in 1858, the Prince was drawn to the idea of using the transition to reinforce his own constitutional primacy through a coerced revision of the constitution. Asked for his advice, Bismarck counselled against this move, on the grounds that this was not just a matter of dynastic family law, but a question of politics and the stability of the state. But his rejection of the Prince's proposal was purely tactical, a function of the current political situation:

I said that the rejection of the constitution could be justified if this were a case in which feudal law applied, according to which a legatee is bounds by the stipulations of the father, but not by those of the brother. But for political reasons I advised him to leave the matter untouched and not to bring about the uncertainty in the condition of our state that would result even from a partial rejection. It would be wrong to awaken fears of a change of system every time a new monarch acceded to the throne. . . . I proceeded from the premise that constitutional questions were subordinate to the needs of the country and its political position in Germany, and that there was *for the present* no pressing need to tamper with our [constitution], that *for now* the question of power and inner cohesion was the main consideration.[94]

Whenever he believed the power and autonomy of the monarchical state to be under threat, on the other hand, Bismarck was prepared to override the constitution, or reboot it along lines more favourable to the untrammelled exercise of the monarchical prerogative. This way of thinking dated back to the inception of the Prussian constitution of 1848, into which, as we saw, the conservatives implanted provisions that would allow the constitution to be used against itself. In the crisis of 1862–63, when the Prussian government clashed with the Liberal majority in the Landtag over the funding of military reform, Bismarck invoked the 'gap theory' contending that in the absence of any contrary provision, the government could continue to tax and govern with sanction if no budget were agreed with parliament—this line of argument had first been formulated by the conservatives in the context of the constitutional debates of 1849–51.[95] After failing to rally the chamber to the government's cause, Bismarck enacted military reforms and collected taxes without parliamentary approval. Measures of dubious constitutionality were employed to suppress dissent, including reprisals against liberal deputies (in contravention of article 84 granting parliamentary immunity) and repressive measures against the opposition press, launched under the flimsy cover of an article (63) granting the king the power to issue decrees when 'urgently' required to do so 'for the preservation of public safety or the settlement of an unusual emergency'. In 1863, Bismarck spoke repeatedly of abolishing the electoral law and even of launching a coup d'état.[96] If, as he told the Minister of the Royal Household, Alexander von Schleinitz, the present constitution and the Prussian monarchy were 'irreconcilable', then it followed that the former must be sacrificed to protect the latter. It was the unexpected triumphs of the Danish War of 1864 that saved Bismarck from the incalculable risks of such a course and rescued both his career and his historical reputation.

After 1867–71, the new imperial constitution was Bismarck's own creation, rather than an arrangement inherited from his predecessors. And yet in 1889–90, during the terminal crisis of his career, Bismarck once again contemplated restoring the independence of the executive (and particularly of his own position) by shutting down the parliament and unilaterally altering the electoral law. He justified himself this time by invoking the theory that since the constitution was founded upon an agreement among the various rulers, rather than upon the actions of the state governments, it was perfectly permissible to revise it with the agreement of the princes alone.[97]

This was the theory of the 'legal coup d'état'. It was never actuated in a political assault on the constitution, but it casts in stark relief the limits of what might otherwise appear a benign Bismarckian vision of history unfolding through the interplay of forces. At moments of crisis he was prepared, like the Grand Vizier in Horst Kohl's poem, to tip over the chess board and throw the pieces at his adversary. So much for his pious sermonising to the young Kaiser William II on the impossibility of a return to 'absolutism'. Bismarck's vision of the contending forces that shaped the historical life of a modern constitutional state was ideologically narrow. He easily and often conflated opposition to his own policies with a fundamental threat to the system as a whole. The Catholics were denounced as the 'fatherlandless' agents of a foreign sovereignty. The forces united around the Centre Party might appear to be fighting under the standards of the Papacy, he declared in a hallucinatory letter to King Ludwig of Bavaria, 'but they were all enemies of the state, even if the flag of Catholicity ceased to cover them; [the Centre's] association with the Progressives and the Socialists was founded on hostility to the state'.[98]

Bismarck never conceded the Social Democrats a legitimate place on the political stage. The dramatic growth in support for Social Democracy, despite the drastic measures enacted against the party and its personnel, prompted him to look to the emergency powers sanctioned under article 28 of the constitution to establish a permanent state of exception, in the course of which the Social Democrats would be definitively cut off from the body politic.[99] 'To a greater extent at present than any foreign country', Bismarck wrote in the controversial 'suppressed' third volume of his memoirs, not published until 1922, 'Social Democracy [represented] a war-threat for monarchy and state and should be viewed as an internal question of war and power, not as a legal issue'.[100] It is doubtful, given the state of public opinion, the scepticism of the new Kaiser, and the increasingly robust structures of the German *Rechtsstaat*, that Bismarck could ever have put this line of thought into political effect; he was dismissed from office before he could try.

These desperate manoeuvres to protect his creation suggest an aporia at the heart of Bismarck's historicity. Bismarck's history was developmental, but not progressive. The idea of progress, Ernst Troeltsch wrote, was 'a secularisation of Christian eschatology, the idea of a universal ultimate goal to be reached by all humankind, transferred from the sphere of miracle and transcendence into that of natural explanation and immanence. The concept of historical development, by contrast, refers merely to the quality of historical movement and flux in itself'.[101] Bismarck's historical thinking lacked this kind of futurity. And it was not secularised in Troeltsch's sense. Bismarck's God-belief was real and psychologically important. It dates back to his contacts in the late 1830s with the politically conservative Pomeranian pietist milieu in which he met his wife Johanna von Puttkamer, and it remained an inner refuge and support throughout his life. 'I cannot understand', he wrote to Johanna in 1851, 'how a reflective person who knows or wants to know nothing of God could bear the contempt and boredom of life. . . . I don't know how I used to get by; if I lived now as I did then, without God, without you, without the children, I really wouldn't know why I shouldn't cast aside this life like a dirty shirt'.[102] Bismarck took comfort in the thought that the events of his career were sanctioned by God; there were times when he expressed an almost ecstatic sense of the harmony between his own life and the intentions of the deity. Articulations of this kind occur with sufficient regularity over the span of his life to suggest that this dependence on belief was a permanent feature of his personality, though it tended to manifest itself most intensely at moments of stress, frustration, anger, and despair.

There is no reason, however, to believe that this providential awareness endowed the history of events or even his own role in them with ultimate meaning. Bismarck did not share Friedrich Julius Stahl's belief that the purpose of the state was to propagate Christianity or to prepare the world for salvation in accordance with a divine plan. He retained a belief in providence, but it was a providence external to the workings of the world. Faith was Bismarck's *personal* protection against the perversity of events, not the key to their meaning. It was a dependent variable of his experience of power, not a force capable of shaping or justifying action.[103]

During the turbulent 1860s, the intermittent synergy between Bismarck's political achievements, his quest to

maximise the power and security of Prussia, and the aspirations of the national movement endowed his leadership with
a sense of direction and futurity. But since Bismarck did not
and could not sincerely embrace the teleologies of national-
ism, liberalism, or socialism, his history remained goalless,
churning and fluxing, but without the futurity of an anticipated state of affairs. By the 1880s at the latest, his approach
both to foreign and to domestic policy was oriented towards
the preservation of what was already there. 'Bismarck's system', the historian Otto Hintze would write in 1926, was 'allied more with the powers of the past than with those of the
future'. There was no linkage with the 'national strivings' of
the population, and he failed to capture the aspirations of the
'rising masses'.[104] Bismarck depended, politically and intellec-
tually, on the monarchical state as the only agency capable of
endowing the interplay of forces that was 'history' with coherence. But coherence is not the same as significance. Once he
had achieved German unification under terms advantageous
to Prussia, Bismarck's political enterprise suffered from a critical insufficiency of meaning.

1918 and the End of History

It was the monarchical state that had allowed Bismarck to
entertain the illusion that he was looking 'down' on the parties, managing or at least overseeing their interactions from
above. Bismarck's understanding of politics assumed a degree of complexity reminiscent of Clausewitz's understanding
of battle as a space in which planning and rational cognition
counted for less than an immersed, 'world-oriented' form
of action 'based on subconscious processing of the situated
body'.[105] But there was a crucial difference. For Clausewitz, the
stresses and unpredictability of battle obliged the theorist of

war to think immersively, from the ground up.[106] Bismarck, by contrast, surveyed politics from the elevated vantage point of the monarchical state. His was a vision of complexity without immersion.

Bismarck's esteem for the transcendent political agency of the state was widely shared in nineteenth-century Germany. Like the word 'history', the word 'state' had undergone an unprecedented discursive escalation. Indeed, the two ideas existed in a relationship of interdependence with each other. It is a familiar but remarkable fact that modern Germany's most significant theorist of the modern state also happened to formulate the most influential nineteenth-century German philosophy of history. More than anyone else, the philosopher Georg Wilhelm Friedrich Hegel helped to establish the modern state as a privileged object of enquiry and reflection. It was not just the site of sovereignty and power; it was the engine that makes history, or even the embodiment of history itself. This distinctively Prussian intimacy between the idea of the state and the idea of history left abiding traces on the emergent cultural disciplines of the universities. So powerful was this nexus that it infiltrated the thinking even of those who viewed themselves as opponents of Hegelian philosophy. The young Leopold von Ranke, a Saxon who came to Prussia in 1818 at the age of twenty-three and was appointed to an academic post at the University of Berlin in 1825, did not escape the contagion of Hegel's statist idealism. The state, Ranke declared, was more than a political institution; it was a 'moral good', and an 'idea of God', an organic being with its 'own original life', which 'penetrates its entire environment, identical only with itself'. Throughout the nineteenth and well into the twentieth century, the 'Prussian school' of history would remain overwhelmingly focused on the state as the vehicle and agent of historical change.[107]

The influence of this exalted conception of the state was felt so widely that it bestowed a distinctive flavour on Prussian political and social thought. In his *Proletariat and Society* (1848), Lorenz Stein, a pupil of Hegel, observed that Prussia, unlike either France or Britain, possessed a state that was sufficiently independent and authoritative to intervene in the interest conflicts of civil society, thereby preventing revolution and safeguarding all members of society from the 'dictatorship' of any one interest. It was thus incumbent upon Prussia to fulfil its mission as a 'monarchy of social reform'. A closely affiliated position was that of the influential conservative 'state socialist' Carl Rodbertus, who argued in the 1830s and 1840s that a society based upon the property principle alone would always exclude the propertyless from true membership—only a collectivised authoritarian state could weld the members of society into an inclusive and meaningful whole.[108] Rodbertus's arguments influenced in turn the thinking of Hermann Wagener, editor of the ultra-conservative *Neue Preußische Zeitung* (known as the *Kreuzzeitung* because it bore a large black iron cross on its banner). Even that most romantic of conservatives, Ludwig von Gerlach (brother of the Leopold who argued with Bismarck over the satanic illegitimacy of the revolution), viewed the state as the only institution capable of bestowing a sense of purpose and identity upon the masses of the population.[109] Among the most influential later nineteenth-century readers of Lorenz Stein was the historian Gustav Schmoller, who coined the term 'social policy' (*Socialpolitik*) to convey the right and obligation of the state to intervene in support of the most vulnerable members of society; to leave society to regulate its own affairs, Schmoller argued, was to invite chaos.[110] Schmoller's appeal to the idea of a neutral but interventionist state standing above the struggle of classes and parties did not go unchallenged. At the turn of the twentieth century, 'agonistic' theorists, like Werner Sombart and Max Weber demanded that the social and sciences shift their attention from the state to the competitive dynamism of civil society. But their campaigning was itself an expression of frustration at the state-centred orientation of German social and political thought.[111] The state remained a crucial anchor and point of reference.

What if the waters of society were to rise, submerging the high ground of the monarchical state? To travel on the swollen river of history, a boat was necessary, a permanent (or at least stable) structure that sat atop the currents of change. But what if the boat capsized, or what if there were no boat at all? What if one were not borne along *on* the flood but *in* it, caught up and overwhelmed by forces beyond one's control? Might the state not then become a mere effect of history, its political existence marked by radical heteronomy? And might not history, in turn, degenerate into mere tumult?

In the aftermath of the defeat and revolution of 1918–19, these seemed very pressing questions indeed to some German intellectuals. The war of 1914–18 had laid bare in a thousand ways the insufficiencies of the old monarchical state structure. As Jörn Leonhard observed, drawing on Reinhart Koselleck's thesis about the French Revolution, a drastically expanded space of experience exploded the horizons of historical expectation.[112] The collapse of the old order was dramatically enacted in the flight of the last Kaiser into exile and a helter-skelter cascade of German princely abdications.[113] And the result of these abdications was—in Prussia at least—the decapitation of the state. A peace settlement followed that—in the eyes of many educated Germans—indefinitely suspended the sovereign independence of the German state. And the new democratic state order of the Weimar Republic, founded in conditions of extreme political uncertainty, shed much of the authoritarian paraphernalia of its monarchical predecessor. The 'monarchical state of civil servants'—to borrow the formulation of Carl Schmitt—forfeited its privileged position; it 'got caught in the game of the pluralistic system'. It was forced to become 'the playmate and political accomplice in the traffic of mutual concessions and, as a result, to lose its essence'.[114]

The impact of these events on the historical imagination of Germans can hardly be overstated. 'We no longer theorise and construe under the protection of an all-sustaining order', Ernst Troeltsch wrote in 1922, 'but in the midst of the storm of a world remaking itself . . . where countless things that were once solemnly serious or seemed to be are today nothing but phrases and paper. The ground is shaking beneath our feet and the different possibilities of becoming are dancing around us'.[115] This was not, Troeltsch insisted, a crisis in historical disciplinary practice, in the sense of the things that happen in the history faculties of universities. The historians went on teaching, researching, and writing, as was their wont; the powerful conventions of their craft ensured that the discipline would change more slowly than the world around it. Rather it was a crisis in 'historical thinking', in the relationship between history and public life, its philosophical connections with political and ideological utterance, in short, in the historicity of politics.[116] Many writers and cultural figures saw in the events of 1918–19 something like a break in the fabric of historical experience. In a study of wartime 'intellectual mobilisation', Kurt Flasch has shown that by the end of the conflict the most important categories of conventional historical interpretation had suffered an irredeemable loss of credibility.[117] Lucian Hölscher has argued that for a generation of intellectuals, the First World War and particularly the tumults and political shocks that followed defeat were 'an existential thunderstorm that turned the experience of time upside down' and undermined faith in the 'very foundations of the concept of history'.[118]

Historians (when they were not writing history but 'thinking historically') drew a range of conclusions from this collapse of certainty. For Friedrich Meinecke, the reasons for the current crisis lay in the always-intimate relationship between historical awareness and the power of the state, a nexus that could be traced back as far as Machiavelli and Pufendorf. The early modern state, he suggested, had developed a form of 'reconnoitring and judgment that was already closely related to modern historical judgment'.[119] It followed that the exhaustion of that state structure must also disrupt the operations of history as a form of understanding. Meinecke wondered whether the war and the advent of what he imagined would prove a millennial era of Anglo-American supremacy might not mean that the history of Germany was simply over. On a pacified continent, the European states would eke out their post-historical retirements as 'burnt-out volcanoes'.[120] Julius Kaerst, historian of Hellenism at the University of Würzburg, pursued a similar line of argument. For historians, he wrote in 1928, the state as an agency of undiluted power had once been an axiomatic framing concept. Any threat to its autonomy was thus an assault on the movement of history itself, for there could be no history in a future in which states, submerged in the structures of 'global society', sank to the level of mere administrators of a 'humanitarian policy' focused exclusively on the management of resources and 'human economics', to the radical exclusion of the foreign policy and power projection that had once been the state's *ultima ratio*. 'I need hardly point out', Kaerst wrote, 'that under such circumstances, all historical life would cease'.[121]

For the Bismarck scholar Hans Rothfels, writing in the mid-1920s, the defeat and collapse of the empire in 1918–19 represented a traumatic break. Like many of his colleagues, Rothfels idealised the Bismarck era as 'a bygone age in which "the State" was thought to have stood incorruptibly "above the parties"'.[122] By identifying himself unconditionally with the 'traditions and interests of the state' and a 'suprapersonal and suprahistorical' entity, Rothfels argued, Bismarck had embodied more than any other individual the 'permanent and unchanging idea of the state'. The dissolution of that state in 1918–19 was the 'gravest physical collapse' in German history. It had severed the thread of historical continuity. The peace settlement imposed at Versailles was the expression of a 'historically unprecedented will to destroy', an attempt—otherwise unknown to history—to throw the historical evolution of a great nation back by two and a half centuries.[123]

Otto Hintze, celebrated historian of Prussia, was less histrionic, but he too saw the end of the war as a profound caesura. There was a world of difference, Hintze wrote, between the system that had sustained Bismarckian politics and 'the conditions governing our utterly sad and abnormal political existence today': 'Bismarck's system was that of a well-armed Great Power; it can hardly be applied to a forcibly disarmed, internationally dependent and thus unfree people, whose character as a state is confined to a degree of technical administrative autonomy in the spheres of economics and politics'.[124] These responses reflect the depth of the political crisis that beset Germany in the aftermath of the First World War, but they also remind us of what 'history' had come to mean to the intellectuals of the Wilhelmine Empire. It had acquired metaphysical authority as the field in which supposedly transcendent 'ideas' (like that of 'the state') interacted dynamically with the forces unleashed by a flawed humanity. The tendency to infuse history with (Protestant) theological presumptions and objectives helps to explain why the 'crisis of historicism' was so intensively experienced and suffered in Germany. If history had to some extent absorbed that elementary stabilising and orienting function we ascribe to religion, then it followed that the crisis in traditional historical thinking must present itself as 'a problem for life and culture of the greatest and most difficult kind'.[125]

Not everyone doubted history's future as a form of understanding—Ernst Troeltsch kept a cool head: he saw that what needed to be jettisoned was not history as such, but 'the specific notion of historicity which since the early modern period had been tied to the adventures of the state'. Dethroning the historiography of the nation-state and focusing instead on the cultural history of Europe might be a good start.[126] But in its most extreme manifestations, the twentieth-century crisis in 'historical thinking' could manifest itself in a global rejection of history in the sense of a progressive or even just a developmental narrative. The prophet and the historian were now indistinguishable, Paul Valéry, a keen French observer of German intellectual life, declared in 1919.[127] History, he remarked in a later essay, was 'the most dangerous product ever to have been concocted by the chemistry of the intellect'—it 'gives rise to dreams, intoxicates nations, engenders false memories, exaggerates their reflexes, keeps open their old wounds, torments them in their sleep'. Notwithstanding its obsession with 'events' and its claim to provide foresight, historical knowledge had done nothing to impede the outbreak of war in 1914.[128]

In a short treatise published in 1919, the German-Jewish philosopher Theodor Lessing went even further. History, he argued, had nothing whatsoever to do with objective reality, life, or truth. Born of myth, it was 'humanity's fabric of dreams' whose function was to endow an essentially meaningless and chaotic past with significance. What was most toxic about history's myth was its insistence on the progressive character of historical development, the notion that historical events in themselves revealed 'progressive gradations of value, such as the gradual ascent towards ever higher, ever better, ever more complete stages'.[129] Progressivism, Lessing argued, provided a 'seductive backdrop' for the 'soul-rotting mechanisation' of the 'culture disseminated by bourgeois-capitalist Europe, . . . because if history really does contain the promise of progress, then any force that happens to come to power can repose on the belief that it represents the current summit of a natural process and thereby enjoy its power as if by right'.[130]

The early twentieth-century crisis of historicism is a large and complex problem, whose ramifications lie beyond the scope of this book. Suffice it to say that in its most extreme manifestations, it could manifest itself in a global rejection of history, understood in its modern and 'temporalised' sense as a developmental unfolding of change through the continual disruption of prior states of affairs. There are circumstances, the Romanian scholar of religion and myth Mircea Eliade observed, in which humans may 'revolt against the nightmare of history' and seek refuge 'outside the boundaries of profane time'.[131] There is nothing exclusively German about this reflex. We can discern it in many times and places where political upheaval and trauma produce deep temporal realignments. What was special about the German case was the profundity of the revolt and the fact that its most influential subject would not be an individual, but a regime of immense power.

CHAPTER FOUR

Time of the Nazis

IN THE SPRING OF 1935, the Swiss writer and journalist Max Frisch visited the National Socialist mega-exhibition 'Miracle of Life' in Berlin. Frisch was fascinated by the technical perfection of the exhibits: in the vestibule he marvelled at a 'glass human being whose internal organs are shown by a system of internal lighting, a work of cutting-edge German technology'. There were flawless models demonstrating the circulatory system and the workings of the heart, so that one was 'constantly astonished at the way in which the gifted exhibitors managed to render almost unimaginable concepts visible'. A room adorned with slogans displayed huge images of 'blond young men with spades' and 'girls with long hair'. Only when one moved beyond the opening halls did the underlying political purpose of the exhibition become manifest: idealised images and supersized models of the perfect Nordic body were juxtaposed with degrading depictions of the congenitally ill, Jews, and other 'non-Aryans'. This was a celebration not of the human being as such, but of the 'Nordic human being'.

Strangest of all was the massive 'bell of life' in the main hall. Four times the size of a human being, the bell dominated a central court dedicated to 'Family, People, Nation', chiming once every five minutes to announce that nine new Germans had been born. Beneath the tower in which the bell was suspended, sand poured through an oversized hourglass, signifying that over the same five-minute interval, only *seven* Germans had *died*—a net gain of two. One's thoughts, Frisch recalled, were constantly being interrupted by the clang of the bell. Its purpose was obvious enough: to demonstrate the inescapability of biological time.[1]

This chapter builds a case for the distinctiveness of National Socialist temporality. It swims against the current of those recent studies that have viewed the German and Italian regimes as expressions of a generic 'fascist' temporality or have bracketed the three totalitarian dictatorships together as 'political religions'.[2] The political religion literature on National Socialism and its totalitarian contemporaries is now vast. Studies of this kind have done much to illuminate family resemblances among the totalitarian regimes by highlighting the liturgical character of public ceremonial or focusing on common themes, such as rebirth, acceleration, the glorification of an idealised past, and the appeal to myth and ideas of eternity. This chapter does not deny these commonalities, but it is concerned with what was distinctive in the National Socialist regime's intuition of its place in time.

Extrapolating a timescape from the cultural practices and public utterances of the Hitler regime is not a straightforward enterprise. We cannot speak, in the case of the 'Third Reich', of a conscious or coordinated effort to restructure formal temporal frameworks. There was no attempt to redesign the calendar, as occurred under the French Republic, and the aspiration to replace Judaeo-Christian liturgical calendars with 'pagan' or 'Germanic' substitutes remained confined to marginal groups.[3] Nor was there a single coherent 'temporal dogma'. This is not a unique difficulty; none of the regimes examined in this book produced such a thing. I will try to work around the absence of a coherent programme by tracing influential tropes through a variety of sources ranging from speeches, printed texts, images, and the built environment to relevant strands of regime practice, and inferring from these a collective awareness. But proceeding in this way is particularly problematic for the Hitler era because it raises further questions about which sources and utterances should be regarded as characteristic of a power structure marked by the competition between different agencies. And yet, tracking the temporal textures of political and cultural utterances from across the range of the movement's public activity does allow us to assay the 'imagination of time and history' that endowed the policies of a uniquely destructive regime with 'meaning and legitimacy'.[4] This chapter explores a range of public utterances and installations, but it opens with the modest and improvised museums with which parts of the Nazi movement sought both to celebrate and to commemorate the recent seizure of power.

Museums of Revolution

On 15 September 1933, a new museum opened in Berlin. Its purpose was to mark the events that had recently transformed the German political landscape. The main exhibition chamber displayed piles of weapons confiscated from communist street fighters and objects stolen from the Communist Party offices at the Karl-Liebknecht-Haus. A life-sized male fashion mannequin with rouged cheeks and a fey expression stood incongruously decked in the uniform of a fighter of the communist paramilitary organisation Rotfront, a knife, a pistol, and a dagger stuck under its belt and a cosh of twisted metal cable tied to its right hand. Next to it was a tall glass cabinet bearing the label 'Murder weapons from the Fischerkietz' (a poor area, formerly controlled by the communists, on the southern end of the Spree Island that is now part of central Berlin) and containing piles of hand grenades, clubs, knives, daggers, pistols, cartridges, and peaked caps bearing communist insignia. The walls were a chaos of political posters from the 'years of struggle'. An adjacent room was set aside as a 'Hall of Honour': here, party banners framed neoclassical memorial arches and plaques bearing the names of fallen Nazi comrades.

The Berlin Revolutionsmuseum was initially housed in one of the new regime's *lieux de mémoire*, the apartment block of the fallen Nazi activist and SA-Mann Horst Wessel on the corner of Jüden- and Parochialstraße, though it later relocated to a more impressive venue, on the Neue Friedrichstraße.[5] Its founder was Willi Markus (1907–69), a friend and sometime comrade of Horst Wessel and commanding officer of the Sixth Regiment of the Berlin SA. Guests at the modest opening ceremony included friends of the Wessel family and a gathering of the local SA, including Brigadeführer August Wilhelm, fourth son of Germany's last Kaiser, Wilhelm II. In time, the museum established itself as one of the cultural fixtures of an emerging 'National Socialist Berlin'.[6]

The Revolutionsmuseum in Berlin was not the only institution of its type. There were similar foundations in Halle, Kassel, and Düsseldorf—not to mention *Ehrenhallen* (halls of honour) established in various other locations to commemorate the 'achievements' and 'sacrifice' of the National Socialist movement. These were not the consequence of directives from the regime, but local initiatives driven by regional or district SA leaderships, often in collaboration with the Gau authorities.[7] The SA appears to have founded these institutions as a means of advertising its role in the Nazi seizure of power. Local SA leaderships were also involved in the Museum der

FIGURE 4.1. The entrance to the Berlin Revolutionsmuseum.
Photograph by the British Archaeologist O.G.S. Crawford.
Source: Photo archive of O.G.S. Crawford. By kind permission
of the Institute of Archaeology, Oxford University.

Deutschen Erhebung in Halle, figured prominently in the
Revolutionsschau in Düsseldorf, and collaborated in the establishment of Ehrenhallen. The area around the Revolutionsmuseum in Berlin was one in which SA units had faced
especially determined resistance from the communists. At
Parochialstraße 29, just around the corner, were the premises of what had once been the Berlin Anti-Kriegs-Museum,
a crowded and rather shambolic installation founded by the
pacifist Ernst Friedrich (1894–1967) that used images and objects—including photographs of maimed invalids—to invoke
the horror of military violence; in March 1933, the local SA
had seized and ransacked the museum, before transforming it
into an SA leisure facility and torture chamber.[8]

The choice of the name Revolutionsmuseum is note-
worthy, reflecting as it does the SA's preoccupation with the

revolutionary character of the takeover and the imminence of a 'second revolution', in which the political achievements of January 1933 would be followed up with a far-reaching social transformation. The choice of objects and the mode of their exhibition reflected the petty resentments and hatred fanned by the 'years of struggle' for the German capital. Among the exhibits was a framed photograph from an illustrated supplement of 1932, showing the spacious apartment of the Jewish former Vice President of Berlin's police department, Bernhard Weiß (1880–1951), onto which has been mashed a pair of broken spectacles. Weiß had been a determined defender of the Weimar republican order and—under the mocking sobriquet 'Isidor Weiß'—the foremost hate figure of the Goebbels press in the capital. Nazi caricatures regularly focused their loathing on the police chief's round, 'Jewish' spectacles.[9] A review of the exhibition written by Joseph Goebbels and published in the party daily *Völkischer Beobachter* described this item as 'a cheerful and tragic-comical reminder: Herr Isidor Weiß in person, [in the form of] the spectacles he left behind as he fled in the greatest haste [from his home]'.[10]

Clearly, one of the objectives of the Revolutionsmuseum was to advertise the victory of the regime (or at least of its armed shock troops) over the forces that had opposed its coming into existence. A 'rote Ecke' (red corner), in which captured communist weapons and insignia were displayed, was a feature common to several exhibitions of this type.[11] This flaunting of trophies was not insignificant at a time when the danger of a communist retaliation was still presented in official propaganda as a genuine threat—throughout the autumn of 1933 and the spring and summer of 1934, the party press continued to cover alleged 'red plots' and incidents of 'red terror' against policemen, Nazi officials, and members of the Hitler Youth, and there were widely publicised trials against

supposed communist rings, in which the description of confiscated weapons played a prominent role.[12] The museum
was, one commentator put it, a 'chamber of horrors' (*Schreckenskammer*) whose purpose was to impart a frisson of dread
at the thought of what might have been if the National Socialists had not come to power. 'It's hot at the moment in Berlin', wrote the conservative satirist Adolf Stein in the summer
of 1935, 'but an ice-cold shudder runs down one's back in the
Revolutionsmuseum'.[13]

To the student of political temporalities, these institutions
are of interest above all because the museum as an institution
was (and is), among other things, an instrument for the manipulation of temporal awareness.[14] The apparatus of the museum could be used both to distance the viewer from the epoch
or phenomena on display and to establish a sense of immediacy. As Martin Roth has shown, the years 1924 to 1932 saw a
massive growth in museum foundations, an elevation in the
cultural authority of the institution, and a dramatic 'actualisa-
tion' of museum content—several features of the Revolutionsmuseum were borrowed from the left-leaning 'social museums'
of the early Weimar Republic, whose exhibits were almost entirely contemporary in orientation.[15] In deploying the idiom of
the museum—with its labelled exhibits and glass cabinets—
the makers of the Revolutionsmuseum aimed to connect the
visitor with the actuality of the National Socialist transformation, while confining the Weimar Republic, whose history extended to within nine months of the moment at which the
exhibition was opened, to a bygone past. 'The Revolutionsmuseum', said the posters on the newspaper columns in central
Berlin, 'shows the symbols of a superseded era'.[16] In his commentary on the exhibition, Goebbels observed that the objects
on display were mere remnants, reminders of a bygone epoch.
'Only in the memory', he wrote, 'do those days of bloodthirsty

[communist] terror once again rise up'.[17] The purpose of these 'symbols' of the conquered left, another party journalist observed in 1937, was to serve as a reminder of 'times that will never return'. The leftist posters that hung from the walls were 'dead rags, as dead as the mottos they were emblazoned with'.[18] Laid out and labelled in their glass cases, the paraphernalia of the Weimar communists resembled the mute pottery shards and metal ornaments that adorned so many museums of ethnography and Germanic prehistory.

This effort to confine the Weimar years to the past and to posit a fundamental rupture between the events of the Weimar era and those of the Nazi present was entirely in accordance with the priorities set by the public utterances of a regime that defined itself as marking a caesura between ages and inaugurating a new epoch.[19] 'It is not merely that a new government was constituted on the 30 January 1933', Hitler declared in a speech of July 1934. 'Rather, a new regime extirpated an old and sickly era'. The transition between the political history of Weimar and the Nazi seizure of power was to be seen as a radical temporal disconnect: 'We National Socialists have the right to refuse that we be integrated into that line', Hitler insisted, referring to the 'miserable' sequence of Weimar Chancellors between 1919 and 1932.[20] Restructuring the relationship between the present and the past in this way allowed the vanquished 'system' of the recent past to be evacuated from the present.

This denial of continuity between the present and recent past was not unique to the National Socialist regime. We find it in the early years of the French Revolution, and the same reflex can be discerned in those Soviet museums that marked the victory of communism and modern science over the faith and superstition of the past, such as the 'Antireligious Museum' housed in Saint Isaac's Cathedral, Saint Petersburg, between 1930 and 1936.[21] Saint Isaac's was stripped of all its

FIGURE 4.2. Newspaper column advertising the Berlin
Revolutionsmuseum. *Source*: Photo archive of O.G.S. Crawford.
By kind permission of the Institute of Archaeology, Oxford University.

religious effects, some of which were assembled for an exhibition on the history of superstition and religious belief. In 1931 a Foucault pendulum was installed; a fifty-six-pound ball of lead clad with bronze hung from ninety-three metres of wire suspended from the apex of the main dome, the slowly rotating plane of its swing registering the motion of the earth. The purpose was to demonstrate the displacement of faith and revelation by the experimental observation of scientifically verifiable truth. But what is striking about the National Socialist museums is the sense that what had been accomplished was not merely a break with the immediate past, but the inauguration of a new kind of time.

We can see this more clearly if we examine another National Socialist museum in the city of Halle, a much more imposing foundation than its Berlin counterpart, which opened on 14 June 1934 before formations of SA, SS, Reichswehr, and Police, flanked by members of the public and local party officials. The Halle 'Museum of the National Socialist Uprising' (Museum der Nationalsozialistischen Erhebung) was a foundation of the Gau leadership and was intended to project the regional identity of the party in the Halle-Merseburg region. Situated in a converted water tower, it was divided into two parts. A lower section offered a spectacle similar to the one on show in Berlin: this was, as one press commentator put it, 'no paper museum with bare statistical tables', but a collection of 'tangible pieces from the days of most bitter struggle', including 'political stickers, armbands, membership books, clubs of iron and wood'.[22]

Here one wandered through a disorienting space densely packed with posters, documents, photographs, and telling objects, such as a *Litfaßsäule* peppered with bullet holes, or caches of confiscated weapons and bombs. The upper storey, by contrast, housed a Hall of Honour (Ehrenhalle) for fallen

FIGURE 4.3. Museum of the National Sozialistischen Uprising in
Halle. Photograph from the official guidebook. *Source*: Kreisleitung
der NSDAP Halle (ed.), *Führer durch das NS-Museum des Gaues
Halle-Merseburg der NSDAP. Ehrenhalle der Nationalsozialistischen
Erhebung, Revolutionsmuseum, NS-Archiv* (Halle, 1934).

FIGURE 4.4. Ground floor of the Museum of the National Socialist Uprising in Halle. Photograph from the official guidebook. *Source*: Kreisleitung der NSDAP Halle (ed.), *Führer durch das NS-Museum des Gaues Halle-Merseburg der NSDAP. Ehrenhalle der Nationalsozialistischen Erhebung, Revolutionsmuseum, NS-Archiv* (Halle, 1934).

Nazis from the region. This was—in the words of the official guide to the museum—'a place of memory for the blood witnesses of the national and National Socialist revolution, a place of meditation to celebrate the new Germany'.[23] Here there were no exhibits, just a large darkened space occupying the entire upper floor of the building and lined with 'memorial niches and windows' bearing the names of fallen comrades and of units that had distinguished themselves in the struggle. This juxtaposition of remembrance on the one hand and the turmoil of history on the other was entirely deliberate. On the one hand, as Gauleiter Rudolf Jordan put it in a speech for the opening of the museum, there was the 'timeless struggle' (*der zeitlose Kampf*) of the National Socialist movement; on the other, the 'parliaments, with all the blabbering of day-to-day politics'.[24]

FIGURE 4.5. Upper Floor of the Museum of the National Socialist Uprising in Halle. Photograph from the official guidebook. *Source*: Kreisleitung der NSDAP Halle (ed.), *Führer durch das NS-Museum des Gaues Halle-Merseburg der NSDAP. Ehrenhalle der Nationalsozialistischen Erhebung, Revolutionsmuseum, NS-Archiv* (Halle, 1934).

A number of the revolution museums combined memory and remembrance in this way. Even the relatively modest Berlin museum incorporated a simple shrine room with inscriptions, insignia and lists of names. The Revolution Show (Revolutions-schau) at Düsseldorf combined a triumphal process of party flags and side galleries exhibiting objects from the Weimar years with a large chamber for the purpose of meditation and remembrance, in which the lights were dimmed and the Horst Wessel Song could perpetually be heard at low volume in the background. But nowhere was this juxtaposition more starkly articulated than in Halle, where the visitor could ascend directly from the chaos of the lower story into the stillness of the memorial chamber above.

In his speech at the opening ceremony, the director and creator of the Halle Museum, Professor Hans Hahne (1875–1935), gave an account of the thinking behind the dual structure of the installation. The museum, he wrote, had been planned not as a 'depot for more or less valuable objects', but rather as 'a visible extension of the Hall of Honour using the medium of the museum' (*ins Museale*). The museum, Hahne suggested, served two kinds of memory. On the one hand, the exhibits downstairs would awaken many 'inconspicuous "recollections" of the time of struggle and victory', restoring the totality of a past experience. 'Holes in letter boxes and poster columns once again become whistling gunshots, garish colours become highpitched screams'. But in its 'formal totality' (*Gesamtformung*), Hahne explained, 'our museum is also a memorial for the dead'. The roots of this form of remembrance, he claimed, lay deep in the past of Nordic man. And it was a feature of Nordic memorials for the dead that they did not confine the deceased to a world beyond or below, but integrated them into the world of the living: 'The kingdom of the dead is part of the total domain of existence (*Gesamt-Daseinsbereiches*) of the human community to which the dead continue to belong'.[25] In short, the upstairs-downstairs structure of the Halle Museum invoked two kinds of temporality: the history of events, of conflict, disruption, and discontinuity on the one hand, and the *longue durée* of Germanic memory on the other.

Totalitarian Contrasts

A comparison of these exhibitions with analogous efforts by the Italian fascists to celebrate the establishment of their regime reveals a suggestive contrast. The fascist super-exhibition La Mostra della Rivoluzione Fascista, which went on show in Rome from 1932 to 1934 and attracted over three and a half million visitors, was no conventional exhibition, but rather a highly charged space in which one could experience 'history in action'. A vast complex of carefully sequenced halls and rooms instilled a sense of 'perpetual movement and instability', of 'agitation, compression and disorientation'.[26]

The contrast with Nazi temporal sensibilities is best captured in Giuseppe Terragni's spectacular 'Room O', an immense chamber on the left side of the exhibition. This space was dominated by a vast photo montage extending high into an asymmetrical space. On the bottom right of the image could be seen thronging crowds of individual heads surging wavelike towards two immense turbines; rushing away from the turbines towards the upper left were masses of stylised hands outstretched as if in the fascist salute, a feature that may have been borrowed from a 1927 Soviet poster by the Bolshevik constructivist Gustav Klutsis.[27] The turbines collaged along the fault line between the massed heads and the massed hands rendered explicit the historical dynamism suggested by the composition. They were aligned with the image of a letter written by Mussolini to the mother of a fascist martyr, as if Terragni wanted the viewer to understand not just that it was the party (and above all the *Duce*) that transformed masses of individuals into fascists animated by a collective will, but also that this transformation was achieved through a process of turbine-like acceleration.[28]

There was, to be sure, a memorial chamber in the Mostra, the 'shrine of the martyrs' (sacrario dei martiri), a darkened space centred on a simple cross inscribed with the words 'For the Immortal Fatherland!' and ringed by bands of dark metal into which was cut, thousands of times over, the luminous word 'Presente!' Here, as in the 'memorial niches' of the Nazi revolution museums, the dead were remembered within a perpetual present. But the structural relationship between

FIGURE 4.6. Giuseppe Terragni, Room "O" of the Mostra della Rivoluzione Fascista (1932–34). *Source*: Dino Alfieri and Luigi Freddi, *Mostra della Rivoluzione Fascista* (Rome, 1933), 189.

the memorial chamber and the rest of the exhibition was fundamentally different. The visitor to the Mostra had no choice but to approach the shrine chamber through a 'gallery of fasci' lined with stone columns bearing a sequence of dates: 1918, 1919, 1920, and so forth; and the only way out of the sacrario led back down the gallery of the years and into the kinetic historical trajectory of the museum. There was a tension between the cool modernism of the memorial chambers and the hot modernism of the other rooms, but their purpose was above all to 'reinscribe' the diachronic sequence of history 'within a ritual order', and to present the fascist seizure of power as the completion of a historical process, not to undermine the legitimacy of history as such.[29] The imposing modernist armature of the exhibition, as a reviewer in the weekly magazine *Il Popolo d'Italia* put it, 'signified the enormous weight of fascism, which throws itself onto the paths of history'.[30] To put it another way, in the fascist museum, history in the form of a chronological sequence surrounds and incorporates the space of memory; in the National Socialist 'revolution-museum', the continuum time of memory trumps and stifles history.

This helps to explain the curious remark by a French visitor that the Mostra was 'so thoroughly Bolshevist' in spirit that 'with a change of emblems, the piece would bring applauses in Moscow'.[31] For all the differences between them, both the fascist and the Soviet revolutionary temporalities were based upon a kind of turbo-charged Hegelianism. As Stephen E. Hanson has suggested, Marxism-Leninism was based on the Marxist idea that 'effective revolutionary praxis depends upon utilising rational time discipline to master time itself'. What resulted was an amalgam that Hanson describes as a 'charismatic-rational conception of time'.[32] And Francine Hirsch has shown that Soviet ethnographers responded to the essentialism of Nazi race theory with an insistence that 'national cultures' did not express primordial traits, but were rather artefacts of a 'sociohistorical process' that could be accelerated by the intervention of the vanguard party. The notion that the Tajiks, for example, should be musealised by means of displays highlighting the abiding and timeless strands of Tajik culture—the Tajik tea ceremony, for example—fell swiftly from favour, to be replaced by exhibitions depicting Tajiks on the historical road towards Soviet peoplehood, their progress accelerated by the interventions of the communist party.[33]

Soviet thinking on time was founded upon a collapsing of theory and praxis into a model in which progress and history were essentially the same thing. The Soviet 'anti-religious museums' did not simply contrast the present and the past as a binary ontological opposition. Rather, they imagined the demise of religion as the consequence of a developmental process that was still under way. Two French scientists who visited the Moscow Museum of Atheism in 1934 reported that they were first shown 'the evolution of religion through the centuries', from the earliest human communities to the intertwining of religion and temporal power in the great empires, and then taken on a tour from ancient Egypt to tsarist autocracy. As they left the museum, their guide explained that if religious faith was defunct in the Soviet Union, this was because in an age of science 'we don't need religion to accomplish miracles'.[34] For both the Soviet and fascist regimes, it was the party that represented the apotheosis of history, a history still conceived as a forwards-driving machine of progress.[35]

For the National Socialists, by contrast, the idea of history as an unstoppable forwards career of transformation had much less appeal. 'Every people has its own rhythm' wrote the poet and publicist Carl Maria Holzapfel (1890–1945) in an op-ed reflection on 'The Rhythm of Time' for the *Völkischer Beobachter*, a newspaper in which reflections on the nature of time are surprisingly frequent. For the German people, it was the pattern of seasonal renewal and death, 'the polarities of the solstice in nature', that set the 'pulse-beat' of existence. Time, in this sense, was just 'a portion of eternity'; the great revolutions—including the putative revolution of 1933—were not just moments in high politics, but 'hours of renewal' for all members of the ethnic community, 'hours in which every one of us experiences God in the most extraordinary way'.[36] The National Socialist regime did not seek to revolutionise the paradigm of linear history from within, powering it up for the needs of an all-transforming party, but rather sought to evade history altogether, to slip out of it into the racial continuum-time of a transhistorical memory. In this, it resembled Mircea Eliade's archaic man, who 'sets himself in opposition to history, regarded as a succession of events that are irreversible, unforeseeable, possessed of no autonomous value' and can apprehend past events and individuals only in the form of timeless archetypes.[37]

Among those who propagated this rejection of history in its conventional form was Adolf Hitler himself. In *Mein Kampf,* the future dictator argued for a break with the state-focused historicism of the old German Empire. At the core of the old historicism had been a bogus legal theory whose core axiom was 'preservation at any price of the current monster of human mechanism, called State'. The problem with the classical concept of the state, he argued, was its elevation of the state to an end in itself. But this doctrine, he suggested, was an inversion of the true order of priorities: 'The State is a means to an end. Its end is the preservation and the promotion of a community of physically and psychically equal living beings. This very preservation comprises first the racial stock and thereby it permits the free development of all the forces slumbering in this race. . . . States that do not serve this purpose are faulty specimens, even miscarriages. . . . We must sharply distinguish between the State as a vessel and the race as the content. This vessel has meaning only if it is able to preserve and to protect the contents; in the reverse case it is useless'.[38] By 'severing' the state from 'racial obligations', he asserted, the 'bourgeois world' had emptied the state of its meaning. And the chief beneficiary of this de-ethnicisation of the state was 'the Jew, Karl Marx', who 'was able to draw the ultimate conclusion from those erroneous conceptions and opinions about the nature and the purpose of a State'.[39] What had once been understood as the driver and focal point of historical change was here demoted to the tool of an alien power and the negation of history's truly central actor—the *Volk*. In *Mein Kampf*, Hitler associated the very idea of history-as-progress with 'the Jew' who first establishes himself as the supposed 'benefactor and friend of mankind', then 'suddenly also becomes "liberal" and begins to rave of the necessary "progress" of mankind'. By this means, Hitler went on, 'the Jew' had made himself 'the spokesman of a new time'; 'praising all progress, but most of all, of course, that progress which leads others to destruction'.[40]

From all of this it followed that the forms of historical education inherited from the old empire were poor nourishment for the youth of the German nation. The current condition of historical education was such, Hitler wrote, that it would have been 'much better and of greater benefit to the nation' if the Germans 'had not studied history at all'. 'For one does not learn history merely in order to know what has been, but one learns history in order to make it a teacher for the future and for the continued existence of one's own nationality. This is the end, and the history lessons are only a means to it'.[41] The task of the future must therefore be—if one took such utterances seriously—to establish an ever more perfect identity with the remote past, out of whose still uncontaminated timbers the house of the future would have to be built. In the 'longing for a common [German] fatherland', Hitler wrote, there lies 'a well that never dries; especially in times of forgetfulness and of temporary well-being, it will again and again forecast the future in recalling the past'.[42]

Such was the redemptive power of race that it could suspend the linearity of history. No event need be irreversible if the charisma and force of the race remained intact: 'Any defeat can become the father of a later victory. Any lost war can become the cause of a later rise, every distress the fertilization of human energy, and from every suppression can come the forces of a new spiritual rebirth, as long as the blood remains preserved in purity'.[43]

We find a similar re-patterning of time in the major German mass-audience mega-exhibitions of the 1930s. There was, to be sure, no systematic regime-driven policy on museums and exhibitions, and such efforts as there were to align all museums with the regime's priorities foundered in the face of local and regional rivalries.[44] Even among and within those institutions committed to placing their research in the service of the regime, there were bitter factional struggles driven by vanity, envy, and professional competition.[45] And yet a survey of major exhibitions reveals a common underlying template. Ewiges Deutschland, for example, curated in Berlin by the Reichsstelle zur Förderung des deutschen Schrifttums and the Prussian State Library in 1934, aimed to awaken in the minds of visitors an awareness of 'the eternal' (*das Unvergängliche*) in German literature, in order to 'bring German present and German future into new relationships with German ethnicity (*Volkstum*) in the past'.[46] Das deutsche Antlitz im Spiegel der Jahrhunderte, which opened in Frankfurt in 1937 under the curatorship of the City of Frankfurt and the Rassenpolitisches Amt of the NSDAP, argued that the foundations of all culture lay in the 'inherited powers of race'; it aspired to expose 'the unchangeable and constant blood-values of our people' that had been obscured by the 'vicissitudes of its history' (*Wechselfälle seiner Geschichte*).[47] Here, too, history was mere contingency, a sequence of more or less random divergences from an underlying pattern that bestowed meaning on the past, the present, and the future. The mega-exhibition Deutsche Größe, which opened in Munich on 8 November 1940 and then toured the country attracting a total of 657,000 visitors, was more emphatically historical in its content and far less focused on racial themes. But even here, the linear sequences of 'history' were folded into a millennial chronoscape. The Germans of 1940 appeared in this exhibition as the direct heirs and executors of the Ur-Germans of prehistory, so that the re-energised 'history' of the present culminated in an encounter with the distant past.[48] 'Eventually the steel arch of the German armies [in the First World War] extended from the Baltic to Alsace, from Flanders to the Crimea', the Munich historian Karl Alexander von Müller declared in the catalogue of the exhibition. 'And in almost every place where their boots struck the ground, old memories rang like echoes of our past'.[49] What struck and moved the visitor to this exhibition, one anonymous reviewer observed, was not the momentum of history unfolding, but 'a frisson of awe at the prospect of that which is immortal and transcends the centuries'.[50]

Even the exhibition Gebt mir vier Jahre Zeit, which opened amidst a storm of publicity on 30 April 1937 and was intended to advertise the transformation of Germany over the four years since the seizure of power, subordinated the developmental logic of history to a temporally flat ontological opposition between the new time and the old. As Joseph Goebbels reminded visitors in his opening speech, the only way to show what the National Socialists had achieved since the seizure of power was to juxtapose the present with the 'hopelessly devastated time' whose legacy the Nazis had inherited in 1933. This exhibition, he announced, would take the form of a 'spectacle of oppositions' (Schau der Gegensätze), for the contrasts between then and now were as profound as 'between day and night'.[51] There was no attempt here to 're-actualise history' or to 'involve the observer in a sequence of actions'; this was revelation, not history.[52]

None of this is to suggest that the museums of the National Socialist era were in some categorical sense 'unmodern'. No one who visited the German museum exhibits at the Paris World Expo of 1937 could be in any doubt about the aesthetic and technical modernity of many German museums. And Hall 2 of the Berlin exhibition Gebt mir vier Jahre Zeit (Give Me Four Years' Time, 1937), designed by Egon Eiermann, was a brilliant and formally innovative example of a space designed to immerse the visitor in a dynamic and overwhelming experience.[53] Its most striking feature was the drastic variation of scale: at the heart of the space was a machine so immense that it dwarfed the crowds milling around it. Only a few steps away was a long tract of miniature railways showing freight cars being loaded with raw materials by tiny human figures. The argument seemed to be about the immense multiplier effect of industry, with its capacity to translate the work of individual humans into achievements stunning in their power and scale. Yet the claims made for the dynamism and modernity of industry were not translated into claims about the regime itself. By contrast with Room O of the Roman Mostra, the depiction of productive power and accelerated effort served not as a metaphor for the political transformation of Germany by the National Socialist movement, but rather as a spectacular demonstration of the raw power at the disposal of the new regime.

The Nearness of the Remote Past

Germanic prehistory was an area of special interest to the temporal activists of the regime. The Reichsbund für deutsche Vorzeit, a pressure group with close links to the Amt Rosenberg, coordinated efforts to raise the profile of Germanic archaeology by developing a more attractive, informative, and accessible mode of exhibition.[54] The aim was to depict the millennial evolution of Germanic life both as a self-enclosed and autochthonous phenomenon capable of warding off alien influences and as something vivid and proximate to contemporary experience.[55] The early years of the Nazi dictatorship witnessed a sharp growth in archaeology and prehistory at the universities and the subject expanded dramatically across research institutes and in the teaching training sector as well, encouraged by a public endorsements from Hermann Goering.[56] Archaeological and prehistorical themes were prominent in schoolbooks and attracted much attention in novels, cinema, collecting cards to the extent that one could speak of prehistory as a propagandistic 'advertisement' for the regime.[57]

Not everyone in the regime shared this enthusiasm for Germanic prehistory. Hitler at times expressed scepticism about Himmler's enthusiasm for Germanic archaeology. 'It's bad enough', Alfred Speer recalled him saying, 'that the Romans were erecting great buildings when our forefathers were still living in mud huts; now Himmler is starting to dig up these villages of mud huts and enthusing over every potsherd and stone axe he finds'.[58] Hitler's own awareness of Germanic racial continuity was less geographically specific than Himmler's. His racial history was a millennial narrative in which the achievements of the Third Reich were bound to 're-enact' those of the Roman Empire at the height of its power, a viewpoint reflected in his strong preference for neoclassical forms in the public architecture built and planned for the present and future National Socialist Germany. In this respect Hitler differed from those enthusiasts of *deutsche Vorgeschichte* (such as Hahne) who celebrated the Nordic and the Germanic in opposition to Rome. But whichever of these variations one adopted, the novelty of the resulting chronoscape was evident: the recent political history of Weimar would become astronomically remote, while the millennial antecedents of the new regime—either Greek and Roman antiquity or the long and obscure history of Germanic settlement in Central and Northern Europe, or both—came to seem (or were supposed to seem) very near.

This was the vision that was institutionalised in the cultural work of the SS-Ahnenerbe (Ancestral Heritage).[59] But it also shaped the agenda of many local actors. In a speech of February 1937, Gerhard Körner, director of the Lüneburg Museum, declared that the new racial laws issued in the previous year were the 'boundary stones' of the latest research in prehistory and that the principal objective of this discipline must be the 'rediscovery of Ahnenerbe'. Research, he went on, must meet the needs of the present: 'The service consists in this: to explore the history of our forefathers in such a way that political insights can be drawn from research: to use the cultural legacy in order to extend research into customs and belief, to explore that which is unique to our people and specific to the thinking and feeling of our race'.[60]

There was a direct connection between this reorientation and the efforts to musealise the Nazi seizure of power, because the director and designer of the Museum of the German Uprising in Halle, Professor Hans Hahne, had been a prominent exponent of a new discipline in which the study of prehistoric Germanic settlement and the methodology of ethnography blended with *völkisch* racial ideas to produce an ultra-essentialist and biologistic account of the genesis and evolution of German life in Europe. For this method of studying the remote past, Hahne popularised the term *Volkheitskunde*. In 1912, he was appointed director of the Provinzialmuseum zu Halle, a rather dusty institution founded in 1884 that housed the collection of the 'Thuringian-Saxon Association for History and Antiquities'. Under Hahne's supervision, the provincial museum was transformed: under its new name, the Landesanstalt für Volkheitskunde acquired a large main building for the purpose of exhibiting the collection and hosting conferences and colloquia.

Hahne took the lead in developing a mode of exhibition practice that would render visible the continuities between the present and the prehistoric past of the Germanic peoples. Maps, models, and illustrations were used to bring alive the scattered remnants of ancient settlements. The aim, Hahne wrote in 1914, was to 'lay bare the threads that connect us who live in the present with the [world] of prehistory . . . , for our culture of today and the culture of the prehistory of our country is linked above all by the identity of our blood with that of our forebears'.[61] This implied, among other things, working against the contemporary preeminence of *classical* archaeology, and against the tendency to ascribe the more sophisticated archaeological discoveries to Roman workmanship or influence—a number of Hahne's early works focused on refuting various 'Roman hypotheses' in defence of an autonomous 'German archaeology' concerned with 'self-contained existential groups and cultural circles' whose identity was shaped by a harmonious relationship with a specific natural landscape.[62]

Hahne's understanding of his discipline had always been *völkisch* in orientation, but it was only in the years following the end of the First World War that biological and racist perspectives began to dominate his thinking. It was in these years that he became an exponent of a 'politically applied biology' for which 'racial science is the foundation and key to world history'.[63] Hahne's idea of history was not about disruption, conflict, and change, but about the eternal return of a cyclical existence marked out by the seasons. He was enthralled by the various seasonal rituals that could still be observed in the rural and small-town communities of Thuringia—an example was the Questenfest, a communal ritual of allegedly ancient Germanic origin associated with the little town of Questenburg in the Harz mountains in which a wreath possibly signifying the sun was hung from a ten-meter-high pole, to be burnt and replaced amidst singing and celebrations on the Whit Monday of each year. Hahne and his collaborators became practitioners of *Brauchtumsforschung*—the study of custom—and documented a range of local seasonal rituals. So fond was Hahne of these observances that he invented sunfeasts and *Jahresspiele* of his own, scripted with passages from the Edda and performed by bands of local children and adolescents.

Hahne's deepening engagement with the traces of a cyclical time that possessed intimations of temporal depth and continuity was more than a merely intellectual preoccupation; it was a refuge from the predicaments of history. For Hahne personally, it was clearly connected with the trauma of the First World War—or more precisely of the war's traumatic close, amidst defeat, economic uncertainty, and political unrest. In a letter of May 1919 to his mother, Hahne gave expression to a sense of dislocation: 'The thoughts of every waking and sleeping hour, indeed of *every* hour, are a motley, wild confusion. These days, everything one "thinks" is built on mood, physical condition and random influences, in fact one doesn't really think any thought through to its conclusion, because everywhere there are barbed wires of ifs and buts. So one does, step by step, what the day, what the hour demands, absorbing nothing and hoping, as appearances warrant, for much, little or

nothing'. In a curious passage from this letter, Hahne fuses his
misery with the idea of history itself. The printing press, he
wrote, has turned out to be the work of the devil: 'I can't love
Gutenberg any more, I would almost like to erase him—was
[the invention of print] really a kind of progress? The whole
idea of progress seems more dubious to me than ever'.[64] There
are echoes here of what Mircea Eliade called the 'terror of history'—a condition of radical heteronomy, of exposure to the
random agitations of an environment rocked by upheavals
whose outcome is utterly unforeseeable. The historian Hans
Rothfels put the same point in a different way when he observed that the 'shock to German historical consciousness'
caused by the First World War launched historians on a quest
for 'the exemplary' in German history.[65] But the enthroning of
archetypes inevitably suppresses contingency, in the manner of
Eliade's 'man of archaic culture' who 'tolerates "history" with
difficulty and attempts periodically to abolish it'.[66]

The Triumph of Prophecy over Contingency

Once we become attuned to this re-patterning of temporality, we find it almost everywhere we look in the world fashioned by the National Socialists. It was already implicit in the
substitution of the *Volk* for the state as a central organising
concept in political and historical thought. In nineteenth- and
early twentieth-century Germany, the state had been a crucial
reference point in German historical and political awareness,
not just because it was believed to endow the unruly forces
of society with cohesion and significance, but also because it
was the agency through which, more than any other, history
was imagined. By contrast, as we have seen, the Hitler regime
emphatically rejected the state as the goal or focus of historical striving. Much that had once seemed integral to German

history now appeared as an alien intrusion. 'We now recognize', the National Socialist historian Adolf Helbok declared in 1936, 'that our past existence as a state was not always carried by the powers of our own race'. 'Over long stretches of our development', he added, 'we were led astray by alien forms'.[67] Hitler captured a similar intimation in *Mein Kampf* when he ascribed the phenomena of class-formation and 'progress' to the influence of Jewish agitators.[68] A temporality centred on the *Volk*—not as a population, but as a transhistorical racial essence—was likely by nature to be nonprogressive and non-developmental. The history of the *Volk* could ultimately only be a chronicle of its identity with itself, of its refusal to succumb to alien power and influence.

This had profound implications for the historicity of the National Socialist regime. Bismarck had prided himself on the statesman's skilful management of the historical forces whose contention generated the churn and motion that history was made of. Hitler offered a starker vision. In his universe, the interplay of forces took place under the iron rule of a struggle for existence. This was no chess game, but a battle to the death. Nature, Hitler wrote, 'does not know political frontiers. She first puts the living beings on this globe and watches the free game of energies. He who is strongest in courage and industry receives, as her favourite child, the right to be the master of existence'.[69] The fundamental choice in politics was always a binary one: to survive and triumph or to go under. Hitler knew only one future, the preordained victory of 'Aryan' forces over every opponent.[70] The interplay of forces possessed in itself no intrinsic legitimacy—it was a means to establishing the hegemony of one force over the others. The decisional structures of Bismarck's timescape were now obsolete, for this was a world where the defining task of politics was no longer to balance interests but to pursue a single foreordained goal.[71]

Adam Tooze's thought-provoking juxtaposition of Gustav Stresemann with Adolf Hitler illuminates how sharp the contrast between a conventionally 'historical' understanding of the past and one centred on racial destiny could be.[72] Hitler and Stresemann were exponents, as Tooze shows, of diametrically opposed understandings of what history, and specifically economic history, meant. Stresemann, the author of a doctoral dissertation on the Berlin retail business in beer, embraced the idea of an economic history driven by the heterogeneous stresses of an economy marked by internal stresses and the exposure to international pressures. Even an industry as localised in its sourcing as beer was susceptible, Stresemann argued, to the fluctuations of a modernising economy and the impact of disruptions emanating in dysfunctions of the global system. Mastering these challenges would thus require pragmatic adjustments to changing conditions.[73]

By contrast, Hitler envisioned an economy sufficient unto itself, securing by conquest the resources it needed, autarchic, centrally controlled, oriented towards shared goals, and immune to international pressures. Stresemann became an annexationist during the First World War, because he believed that Germany's interest lay in securing dependable access to continental markets large enough to allow it to compete in terms of economies of scale with the United States. But while Stresemann sought access to markets and consumers, in order, as it were, to insert Germany under the most advantageous terms possible into the 'economic history' of the future, Hitler eventually resolved to enslave or exterminate the consumers and people their evacuated lands with Germans. Far from being the objects (or even the subjects) of international market forces, the Germans would create a history-proof self-sustaining millennial production system of their own. The *völkisch* ideologue Hermann Wirth (1885–1981), founder of the Ahnenerbe-SS, wrote in 1928 of how a reawakening Nordic racial consciousness would lead to 'a redemption from the otherwise inexorably encroaching total mechanisation and materialisation, from the mammonism with its cult of the moment, which we know as "world economy"'.[74] This was a violent rejection of heteronomy, of an order in which the nation is forced to live within someone—or something—else's time. For the Germans under Hitler, the road out of history was to lie in the virtually limitless expansion of biological space, the conquest of *Lebensraum*. The *Volk* would flow out across the European plain, suspending the operations of *Weltwirtschafts- geschichte*, precipitating the Germans at the end of history and the beginning of the unruffled, ethnographic, millennial time of the Third Empire.[75]

The imprint of this historicity can be discerned in Hitler's modus operandi as a politician. Hitler was perfectly capable of working in an incremental and tactical way, in the manner of modern politicians. His manoeuvring among the partisan formations of the Weimar Republic, his negotiations with Hugenberg and the 'Harzburg Front', his management of opposition within the NSDAP, his dissimulation at the Ulm Reichswehr trial, and the brutal opportunism of his foreign policy after 1933 all reveal an operator of great tactical skill in the mould cast by Bismarck. Yet if Hitler expressly rejected the notion that politics was 'the art of the possible', this was not hypocrisy or self-delusion.[76] Rather it reflected the subordination of conventional means to unconventional ends. In formulating his *ultimate* political objectives, Hitler oriented himself towards end states, vanishing points at which all the demands of the present could be presumed to have resolved themselves. His political calculus was not founded on probabilistic predictions that incorporate an element of contingency and presume factors beyond the control of the calculator—rather, it was articulated under the rubric of will and prophecy. Whereas prediction represents the projection into the future of a non-cyclical historical time in which numerous possible risks and gains have to be weighed up, prophecy, as Reinhart Kosel-leck observed, draws no fundamental distinction between past, present, and future; it anticipates an end that is already given; it is posited upon the projection of millennial time into a promised future.[77]

Hitler often referred to himself as a prophet, most famously on 30 January 1939, when he 'prophesied' the extermination of European Jewry in the event that 'the Jews' were to 'succeed' in plunging the states of Europe into 'another world war', by which he meant a war involving the United States. This prom-ise, to which Hitler repeatedly returned, has drawn much at-tention from historians of the Holocaust, because it appears to set the scene for the escalation in mass murder from August 1941, when Churchill and Roosevelt signed the Atlantic Char-ter and the subsequent transition to a policy of continental ex-termination after December, when the United States entered the war.[78] There was an element of primitive blackmail in Hit-ler's formulation, in the sense that it identified the Jews as hos-tages, whose fate would be sealed as soon as America ventured to enter the conflict. But the fact that he chose to articulate the threat through prophecy is important, because it framed the future as something ordained and inherited: 'I have often been a prophet in my life and was generally laughed at. During my struggle for power, the Jews primarily received with laughter my prophecies that I would someday assume the leadership of the state and thereby of the entire *Volk* and then among many other things achieve a solution of the Jewish Question. . . . Today I will be a prophet again'.[79]

The 'redemptive antisemitism' of the Nazi regime was it-self a form of inverted prophecy operating in a millennial time frame.[80] The promise supposedly given in Paul's Letter to the Romans that the Jews would ultimately be restored to Christ, though its meaning had always been contested, was long taken to support the millenarian expectation that a Jewish conversion en masse would usher in the end of days for Christians and Jews alike. But this presumption of an intimacy between the Jews and salvation, an influential theme in seventeenth- and eighteenth-century German Lutheran and Pietist theology— was secularised and inverted in the nineteenth century, when the view gained ground that the Jews would bring about the end of days only in a secular and negative sense—hence Treitschke's inverted Pauline slogan: 'Die Juden sind unser Unglück'.

Two different chains of thought converged in the eschatology of Nazi anti-Semitism. One was the secularised form of the old eschatology, in which it was promised that the Jews would expedite the completion of Christian history, a tradition whose hermeneutical instability created space for the inversion of millennial hope. The other was its radically supersessionist elaboration, in which the logic of the eschaton, of a future accessible only through prophecy, remained, but the Jewish place in it did not. The old eschatology was still latent in the future visions of the nineteenth-century anti-Semites, in which Jews busied themselves accelerating processes of cultural and political fermentation and decay, severing the links between Christ and the nation and reversing the priority of the New Covenant over the Old. The new eschatology manifested itself in the Nazi vision of a future entirely purged of Jews, in which the redemptive agency of the Jews had been replaced by that of the German *Volk*, whose status as the new Chosen People had long been a central theme of the Protestant German national movement.

In a future emptied of Jews, the entire history and culture of the Jewish people would belong to a remote past. Nowhere was this idea more clearly articulated than in the efforts of the SS in Prague to establish a Jewish Central Museum, staffed by indentured Jewish experts pulled from the ghettos and brimfull of looted devotional and cultural objects, that would in the future recall the vanished religious, social, and cultural life of still-to-be-exterminated Jewry in Central Europe.[81] This was perhaps the single most perverse institutional articulation of the Nazi regime's eschatological timescape.

A similarly preemptive structure can be discerned in the urban transformations planned and sponsored by the National Socialist regime. The phenomenal scale of these plans is well known: over fifty city centres were to be completely reconstructed around an ensemble of immense north-south and east-west axes, gigantic halls and assembly areas, and domes and towers that dwarfed all nearby buildings, including the largest cathedrals. These projects were intended to send out signals internationally, proving that the German nation was 'not second-rate, but the equal of any other people on earth, even America'.[82] But they also served to anchor the regime in a millennial timescape. If the glory of ancient Greece and Rome could still be glimpsed in 'the wreckage and fields of ruins of the old world', this was because both of those ancient states had invested effort in the construction of splendid public buildings whose broken profiles still dominated contemporary memory of them. It was not the 'villas and the palaces of individual citizens' that communicated the splendour of ancient Rome, Hitler wrote in *Mein Kampf*, but rather 'the temples and the thermae, the stadia, circuses, aqueducts, basilicas, etc., of the State, which is to say: of the entire people'.[83] How crass, then, was the contrast with the Berlin of his own time: 'If Berlin were to meet the fate of Rome, then the coming generations could one day admire the department stores of some Jews and the hotels of some corporations, the most imposing works of our time, as the characteristic expression of the culture of our days'.[84] Viewed from this perspective, the neoclassical monuments and edifices planned by the regime were appeals to a millennial future, a future in which Germany, too, would be judged by its 'ruin value'. This was no passing fantasy, but a theme that appeared repeatedly in the dictator's speeches and conversations. Only a people capable of endowing a remote posterity with an enduring artistic heritage possessed a 'moral right to life', he declared in an 'Address on Art and Politics' of 1935; such an art must possess the power to express the greatness of the people, even if that people were itself to perish without trace.[85] In September 1941, Hitler imagined a future in which the Slavs of Eastern Europe would survive only as the helot inhabitants of reservations policed by the Germans: 'We shall be their masters. If there is a revolution, all we shall need to do is drop a few bombs on their towns and that's that. Then, once a year, a troop of Kirghiz will be led through the Reich capital in order that they may fill their minds with the power and grandeur of its stone monuments'.[86]

Common to these reflections (and one could cite many more) was the tendency to look back from the vantage point of an anterior posterity upon an already accomplished future. Future Kirghiz slaves gaze up in awe at monuments that have yet to be built. The ruins of great edifices speak to future humans of the achievements of a vanished people. 'Architecture', Eric Michaud remarks, in a formulation that neatly captures the weirdness of this vision, 'was to propel the German people to its common destiny by revealing its true grandeur in funeral monuments'.[87] The logic of prophecy, which frames the future as something inherited from the past, was at work here, just as it was in the efforts of the SS in Prague to establish a 'Jewish Central Museum'. In general, the Nazi movement exhibited prophecy's traditional preference for final states of affairs, for the painting and realisation of *Endzeit* scenarios—*Endkampf, Endlösung, Endsieg.*

Oddly enough, the books and articles produced by the professional historians of the Nazi era are the last place we should look for the traces of these manipulations.[88] Hitler's writings never became the template for a new historiography. The 'folk history' (*Volksgeschichte*) that flourished in the Weimar and Nazi years did idealise the rural past and stigmatise modernisation as a negative counterfoil to preindustrial harmony, but it also tended to merge the emphasis on racial continuity with other approaches, including progressive and developmentalist forms of social history, producing a range of hybrid historiographical modes that varied in the intensity of their commitment to racial thinking.[89] The regime never got around to prescribing a specific agreed mode of historical writing, beyond calls for an approach more firmly centred on race and *Volkstum*.[90] Even the Reich Institute for the History of the New Germany run by the historian Walter Frank (1905–45) was riven by professional rivalries and competence struggles within and between the Rosenberg office, the Interior Ministry, the SS-Ahnenerbe, and the education ministry of Bernhard Rust.[91] There was no shortage of historians willing to 'work towards' the regime, but the conventional practices of their craft proved resistant to swift and fundamental change. And in any case, this short-lived regime collapsed before the ideas of the new leadership could work their way with any consistency into historiographical practice.[92]

Conclusions

In a radio speech announcing the anti-Jewish boycott on 1 April 1933, Joseph Goebbels declared that 'the year 1789' could now be 'expunged from the history books'.[93] His confidence that one could empty out and substitute the meaning of a date, thereby unmaking the past, was characteristic of the supersessionist temporality of a regime obsessed with anniversaries, the recurring markers of its own brief history. By investing the red-letter day 14 July with new meanings, Goebbels implied, one could overcome, supersede, an abandoned past. And it is interesting in this connection to recall a remark from Goebbels's commentary on the Berlin Revolutionsmuseum. The 'most interesting and valuable object of all [those on display]', he observed, 'priceless for any collector, was a *laissez-passer* from Paris to Nice dated 25 Ventose of Year 5 (1794) of the French Republic and bearing the signature of Robespierre'.[94] This document had been pillaged by the SA from the communist headquarters at the Liebknecht House. The Revolutionsmuseum, Goebbels implied, had captured and neutralised the imagined future of the French Revolution, trapping it within its own very different timescape.

Overcoming the French Revolution meant not only breaking with the idea of rights, individual liberty, and political citizenship associated with the great Revolution in its opening phase, but also escaping from a *kind of time*—a *régime d'historicité*—that had been inaugurated, or at least whose advent had been accelerated, by the events in France. More than any other event in modern times, Peter Fritzsche has argued, drawing on the arguments of Reinhart Koselleck, the French Revolution made possible the idea of history as a 'continual iteration of the new', as a runaway train, as a sequence of 'moments' or 'events' that, because they are not anchored in a cyclical temporal structure, can play through at any speed.[95] History was no longer confined to the past; it was unfolding in the present and doing so with an unpredictable violence and destructive force that seemed unprecedented to contemporaries. One can argue about the extent to which the foundations for this transition had already been laid down before the revolution, but the place of the revolution in accelerating it seems beyond question.

In the context of the three totalitarian regimes, then, National Socialist temporal awareness appears rather distinctive. Underlying the dictatorship's vision of its place in time was a radical rejection of 'history' and a flight into deep continuity with a remote past and a remote future. It would be ludicrous to suggest that this amounted to a homogeneous period temporality or that the temporal awareness we have been exploring was equally valid at all times and for all groups and individuals. Recent research in this field has stressed the plurality of contemporaneous chronoscapes and the difficulties elites have always faced in attempting to suffuse societies with their own temporal awareness.[96] It may well be, moreover, that this regime's peculiar timescape was more forcefully articulated at some moments than at others (the opening phase of the Hitler dictatorship, for example, or the apocalyptic years after Stalingrad). Even within the regime's leadership, as Frank-Lothar Kroll has shown, a range of quite diverse 'philosophies of history' shaped the political thought and praxis of the leading National Socialists.[97] The same can be said of the 'racial science' of the Nazi era, which was riddled with inconsistencies and factional strife.[98]

But these ideological variations should not be allowed to obscure the contours of the intuitions that were common to them all. There were doubtless important differences between the blood-and-soil agrarianism of Richard Walter Darré, the biological ultra-racism of Himmler, and Rosenberg's weird amalgam of Aryanism, anti-Semitism, and Spenglerian cultural theory. But common to them all was a way of thinking about the past and the future that reflected an intuitive grasp of the same fundamental chronoscape.

Rosenberg found in the forms of the prehistoric German peasant house the 'prototype' (*Urtyp*) of the Greek temple that the Nordic tribes had once 'brought' to Greece. Himmler saw in the hardy Soviet resistance to the German invasion evidence of long-submerged Germanic hereditary material that could be salvaged for future generations. Darré dreamed that the future would bring a recursion to the pre-Christian, preindustrial life of the ancient Germans. All three held in contempt the kind of analytical and 'over-intellectual' history produced by history professors.[99]

To be sure, this regime derived some of its charisma from its ability to align itself with 'themes of modernization and industrial progress'—a feature exemplified in the person and career of the amoral technocrat Albert Speer.[100] But the question I have asked is not whether the regime was 'modern'; in many respects, it obviously was. My question is rather how we should conceptualise the relationship between its modernism and those attributes that suggested a fundamental disavowal of modernity. Which was the more fundamental? Which takes us deeper into the self-awareness of this regime, its capacity to make sense of itself? Important as the linear energies of productivisation and force maximisation were, they were embedded into a larger, nonlinear temporality. And this was the chronoscape that in turn endowed what came to be the ultimate and definitive objectives of the regime—the destruction of European Jewry, the murder and enslavement of Slavs, the biologisation of politics, the extirpation of the socially and sexually deviant, the construction of vast neoclassical edifices, and the acquisition of an immense continental *Lebensraum*—with 'meaning and legitimacy'.[101] Not everyone needed to inhabit the new timescape—Albert Speer, for example, did not. It sufficed that those who did not were willing to place themselves in the service of those who did.

Herein lies the difference between the German and the Italian dictatorships. Like National Socialism, Italian fascism aimed to transform the lived relationship between past and present. The excavation of ancient structures in the Italian capital was intended not to preserve a bygone past, but rather to 'blur the spatial and temporal boundaries between Roman antiquity and fascist modernity'. The ancient and renaissance pasts were to be mobilised in the service of fascist counter-modernism, with ancient Rome as 'a dynamic vital force, to be enacted in the present'.[102] The commonalities between the 'hybrid' temporalities of National Socialism and Italian Fascism are undeniable, but the difference is equally important, namely, that whereas the fascist regime projected these chronopolitical manipulations onto a temporality whose logic remained essentially historical, linear, and modernist, the German regime adorned itself with modern attributes but articulated its ultimate and defining claims in terms of an ahistorical, racial continuum.[103]

Conclusion and Epilogue

With Bismarck's departure, a lot changed. . . .
If before 19 March 1890 you set your clock to the
Wilhelmsstraße, you always knew what time it was.
With Bismarck's resignation, the normal time expired.
There were many clocks now. They often went at
different speeds, and you had to keep your ears open
in order to know how late it was.[1]

NONE OF THE REGIMES discussed in these pages made formal alterations to the calendar. None imposed a new form of
time discipline. But each possessed a distinctive temporal signature. Each moved to a different temporal music. The Elector
Frederick William's embryonic state executive leaned into the
future and away from the past; it was a history machine that
steered its course and charted its own story by positing and
then choosing among possible futures. Frederick II's world
hovered in philosophical stasis, centred on a king who com-
muned with the ancients. Bismarck's historicity grew out of

the tension between the torrential momentum of political and social change and the supposedly permanent and autonomous structures of the monarchical state. And the regime of the National Socialists anchored itself not in history, but in the non-linear time of racial identity.

These ways of imagining time had in part a legitimating function. For Elector Frederick William, invoking the 'imminent dangers' stored in the future was one way of undermining the standing of those who rooted their authority in the claim to continuity with the past. For Frederick II, the rejection of that conflictual and kinetic understanding of the state's progress through history served restorative aims, such as the stabilisation of the nobility in the face of socioeconomic change. In claiming that history unfolded in unforeseeable and fleeting moments of opportunity, Bismarck made the case for his own preeminence as the supremely skilled decision maker. And the flight of the Nazi regime from linear history endowed its pursuit of an apocalyptic project of racial self-realisation with coherence. If 'modernity', as a timescape, justified some forms of political behaviour and constrained or delegitimised others, the same applied to each of the timescapes sketched in this book.

In focusing the enquiry so firmly on the shapers of power in a sequence of governmental regimes, this book steps away from the currently prevalent emphasis in temporality studies on diffused processes of agentless change. What we see instead is the warping of temporality by power, the appropriation of historicity by the claimers of sovereignty, a process that may be consciously and even aggressively directed at the alternative historicity of an adversary. And the sequential, episodic approach adopted in this book also has the advantage that it captures the cumulative, reflexive quality of the relationship between one era and the next: Frederick II of Prussia knew, but chose to dismiss or ignore, the historical templates of Pufendorf and Hartknoch. Bismarck admired the political autonomy of Frederick's *Machtstaat*, but Hegel's dialectical teleology was alien to him. The Nazis celebrated Bismarck as the personification of a Germanic archetype, but their racist, pseudo-biological political vision was the absolute negation of Bismarck's intuition that history unfolded in the field of tension between the monarchical state and the forces of civil society. Neither civil society nor the state commanded the respect of the Hitler movement—both were denounced as the 'Jewish' inventions of liberal political theory. And the weight and depth of the Nazi rejection of history make sense only against the background of the debacle of the old state-centred historicism, whose hold on the political culture of the German-speaking lands had once seemed so deep and secure.

In many of the most important recent studies of temporality, the narrative has tended to be engineered from within by a more or less explicit theory of modernisation. The problem to be accounted for is the transition from 'premodern' cyclical or recursive to 'modern' linear orders of time. The soundings I have taken of regime temporality across three centuries complicate this narrative. Instead of a linear advance towards modernity, we see something more oscillatory; changes in the intellectual climate fuse with a process of trans-generational reflection in which prior forms of regime historicity are rejected, emulated, or modified. Frederick II's historicity was not unequivocally more *modern* than that of Pufendorf, it was just different. This does not mean that modernisation was not taking place in some form in the societies that generated these regimes. But it does suggest that the relationship between societal modernisation and regimes of historicity may be more oblique than is implied by the binary opposition between premodern and modern forms of temporality.

Does this book describe a specifically German trajectory? The structuring presence of the state in modern German historical sensibility may be a distinctive feature. The fact that nineteenth-century Germany's most influential philosopher of history and its most significant theorist of the state are the same person (Hegel) is remarkable, even if it is familiar. In an article published in the 1960s, Helmut Koenigsberger, a distinguished early modernist at the University of London, observed a deep contrast between German and British grand narratives in political history. At the heart of the British *grand récit* was a story (sometimes described as whiggish) about how society emancipated itself from the monarchical state. At the core of many German historical narratives was a story (sometimes called Borussian) about how the modern state emancipated itself from the feudal structures of traditional society.[2] The Nazi rejection of the state as a way of thinking about history could resonate as it did only in a world whose intellectuals had been raised on such state-centred narratives.

It would be a mistake to push these observations in the direction of an exceptionalist claim. The Great Elector stands out in some respects among his contemporaries, but the arguments he advanced from the 1650s to the 1680s can also be situated within a broad spectrum of seventeenth-century discourses of state power. Frederick II's historicity was more distinctive in embracing an aestheticised stasis without appealing to the idea of continuity or inheritance, though it retained the rhetorical trappings of an enlightened historical sensibility. Bismarck's sense of history's movement placed him at the centre of the European mainstream; it was just one distinctive variation on a broader nineteenth-century theme. Germany was not the only country to witness a crisis of historicism in the early twentieth century, and Eliade's 'terror of history' never referred to a specifically German malaise. The Nazi flight from history exemplified a turn in temporal awareness that can also be discerned in other settings in Europe and beyond.

Indeed, there may be a generic dimension to the relationship between trauma and temporality, especially when the trauma in question involves a violent disruption of the structures of power. Literary scholars have identified a tendency in postcolonial writing to structure narratives around a recursive 'temporality of trauma'.[3] We can discern signs of an analogous linkage in the work of Fernand Braudel, the historian associated with the ascendancy of the *longue durée* in postwar French historical studies.[4] The *longue durée* was imagined in contrast to an event-based or political history that privileges a short time span. But it was also a refuge from the agitations of history. Without the *longue durée*, Braudel observed, the contemporary individuals would be trapped in a 'brief living moment' in which they were 'cloistered, a prisoner' and unable to 'make use of the past or be nourished by it'.[5] The insistence on continuity thus possessed therapeutic potential, for the traumatic events of (French) history, recalled as a list of calendrical markers signifying defeat and invasion—1815, 1871, 1914, 1940—merely signified a sequence of 'monstrous wounds'. The quest for continuity was a flight from history: 'Rejecting events and the time in which events take place', he wrote, 'was a way of placing oneself to one side, sheltered, so as to get some sort of perspective, to be able to evaluate them better, and not wholly to believe in them'.[6]

Mahatma Gandhi's *Hind Swaraj*, written in 1910 to counter the terrorist politics of expatriate Indian radicals, exposes a similar nexus. In this key text, Gandhi dismissed history as a mere 'record of the wars of the world' in which there could be no place for the trans-generational continuity of soul-force. History, by this reading, was 'a record of every interruption of the even working of the force of love' and thus of the 'force of nature'. It was the instrument with which the English sought to maintain the Indians in an awareness of their own cultural inferiority.[7]

Just to be clear, this is not to suggest that the nonviolent antinationalist Gandhi or the scrupulous democrat Braudel should be placed in proximity to the Nazi movement! Gandhi's soul-force was universal and human, not racist, and Braudel's *longue durée* was not a flight into irrationalism but a carefully controlled hermeneutic tool. The Indian leader's deprecation of history in *Hind Swaraj* was limited and instrumental: it pertained to a specific modern and Western understanding of what history is, an understanding deeply interwoven with the disruptive structures of colonial power. Like Walter Benjamin's 'Angel of History', who can see only catastrophe where we see history's narrative unfolding, Gandhi's eyes were fixed, for the moment at least, on the turbulence and ruin of history.[8] Nevertheless, these two cases do illuminate some of the ways in which political disruption or trauma can trigger a reorientation away from contingency and towards continuity in one form or another.

Perhaps it is not the specific content of the oscillations as such but their amplitude that is distinctive in the German case. Three of the eras examined in this book were marked by the recent experience of war and/or political turbulence: the Thirty Years' War, the revolutions of 1848 and the Wars of Unification, and the double crisis of defeat and political revolution in 1918–20. There was an experiential and psychic dimension to each of the constellations we have explored, at least if we view them from the perspective of the persons who did most to shape them. The Elector's reign was a flight forwards away from the chaos of the Thirty Years' War. Frederick II's quest for stasis was partly rooted in sexuality and youthful experience. Bismarck's bipolar historicity drew on his ambivalent understanding of the revolutions of 1848. And the millennial temporality of Nazism represented one uniquely brutal articulation of the 'terror of history' triggered by the crisis of 1918–19 and sympathetically diagnosed by Eliade.

We might thus expand the scope of Troeltsch's insight into the crisis of German 'historical thinking' at the end of the First World War by noting that since our temporal and historical imagination is more deeply structured by relations of power than most of us suspect, disruptions in the flow or structure of power can produce corresponding realignments in historicity. We can acknowledge this without presuming that there is anything predictable or automatic about this causal nexus: in China, the immense upheavals of the great nineteenth-century revolutions produced a precipitation towards 'modern', Western-style linear time; in Germany, political trauma produced a realignment in the opposite direction, away from developmental, linear historical narratives towards a millennial time posited on the triumph of Being over Becoming.

A cursory look at the two postwar German states suggests that this pattern of oscillation continued after 1945, though the emancipation of civil society (in West Germany at least), the proliferation of parallel historicities, and the accelerated pace of temporal change make overarching patterns harder to discern. The two German states were founded under quite different temporal dispensations. The Federal Republic acknowledged its responsibilities as the 'successor' state of the German Reich and the 'continuator' (Fortsetzer) of 'that same state . . . that was founded in 1867 as the North German Federation and enlarged in 1871 by the addition of the south German states'.[9] The GDR announced itself as a new antifascist entity, purged—at least from 1952, when the regime officially declared itself 'socialist'[10]—of structural continuities with the capitalist past. At the same time, the German revolutions of 1848 reemerged in the eastern zone as an unfinished experiment in 'democratisation' in urgent need of present-day completion.[11]

Yet the early postwar years were also imprinted in both states by inherited interwar social models of futurity, such as the creation of a Western *Kulturstaat* in the Federal Republic, or of a proletarian people's state in the GDR.[12] In the 1960s, these older templates were partially displaced by a boom in speculation about the future.[13] The new science of 'futurology' secured funding from government and industry in the West. There was intense interest in long-term planning and a revival of socialist utopianism in academic circles.[14] This was a 'decade of the future' marked by a sense of accelerated change, in which philosophical and historically inspired models of the future were replaced by scientific and cybernetic projections.[15] After the construction of the Berlin Wall in 1961, the East German leader Walter Ulbricht began to emphasise technology as the key to the future economic and political power of the GDR, which would soon outperform the capitalist West and even the Soviet Union.[16] As this example suggests, futurological visions were in essence mostly tools for valorising and achieving certain kinds of change in the present.[17] The futurology boom of the 1960s stimulated a wave of publications on the future by West German historians; among these was Koselleck's foundational foray into the history of past futures.[18]

The optimism of early futurology was short-lived. Confidence in the continued progress of a virtuous 'modernisation' alternated with unease about the current direction of travel.[19] In 1972, the Club of Rome published a study called *The Limits to Growth*, which concluded that 'if the present growth trends in world population, industrialization, pollution, food production, and resource depletion' continued unchanged, the limits to growth on this planet would be reached sometime within the next one hundred years, and that this would be accompanied by a 'rather sudden and uncontrollable decline in both population and industrial capacity'.[20] In West Germany, exponents of an emancipatory 'human future' critiqued the technocratic, system-stabilizing planning of government agencies.[21] There was a deepening awareness of the link between economic progress and prosperity and the destruction of the physical environment, expressed in a sequence of moral panics around pollution and smog, acid rain, the death of the forests, the hole in the ozone layer, the 'death of the Rhine'. From the early 1980s, in the shadow of the NATO double-track strategy and the neutron-bomb scare, these concerns were over-layered by visions of an imminent self-extermination of humankind and the irreversible destruction of life on earth. These visions tended to dissolve the outlines of the nation-state in a panorama of global dysfunction.

In the East, too, one could speak of an 'exhaustion of the future'.[22] References to the future became less frequent in official publications, and with the appointment of Erich Honecker as First Secretary of the Central Committee in 1971, the regime began to focus its public communications less on sacrificing the present to the future and more on the status of the GDR in its current form as a mature socialist nation. The year 2000, once an important vanishing point, disappeared (literally) from regime propaganda.[23] And as the future began to shed political weight, the regime invested more in the past, encouraging its citizens to engage (through TV and radio programmes, popular books, and exhibitions) with the history of—among other things—Prussia. The high point of the resulting *Preussenwelle* was the 1980 reinstallation of Christian Daniel Rauch's equestrian statue of Frederick II on Unter den Linden.[24]

In view of the proliferation of parallel historicities (facilitated in the West by the diminished role of the state in establishing the contours of prevalent temporalities) and the accelerated fragmentation and alternation of horizons of expectation, Jenny Andersson has suggested that the 'large changes' mapped for the modern period by Koselleck 'do not make much sense' after the caesura of 1945.[25] Yet the truly astonishing thing about this period is surely the durability of the modernist paradigm as such. The *idea* that history could still be accommodated within a linear narrative of 'modernisation' survived the disenchantment with modernisation's societal and ecological effects. The ascendancy of the term 'postmodern' was in some ways an acknowledgement that no better way had yet been found of thinking about our position in the expanse of historical time. In historiographical terms, the persistence of the German *Sonderweg* thesis as a master narrative and an organising principle in research was symptomatic of the desire to insulate the idea of modernity as such from the disasters that had befallen Germany. By positing that Germany had failed to 'modernise', or at least to modernise in a properly balanced way, instead pursuing an aberrant path that led to war, dictatorship, and genocide, historians found a way of preventing Nazism from contaminating modernity as a project under whose rubric the chastened German state could now be readmitted to the world community of civilised nations. The monumental efforts of Heinrich August Winkler to chart the history of modern Germany as a 'long road to the West' are among the most powerful recent articulations of this idea.[26]

What happens if, instead of critiquing the dark side of modernity, we simply cast modernity aside altogether as a way of situating ourselves in history? This was the unsettling question posed in the early 1990s by the French sociologist Bruno Latour. Writing in the aftermath of what he called 'the miraculous year 1989', and specifically of the fall of the Berlin Wall, Latour proposed that we abandon altogether the notion that we are or ever have been 'modern', jettisoning with it the entire progressive phantasmagoria of rationalisation, acceleration, and control that has guided Western elites since the nineteenth century. In this 'non-modern world that we are entering . . . without ever having really left it', Latour suggests, we will have to find new (or perhaps old) ways of imagining our place in time and sanctioning our collective enterprises.[27]

Whether or not one agrees with Latour, he and today's 'temporal turn' more generally are symptomatic of a widely felt sense that the present is in transit from the futurities of the modern to something more recursive, chastened by the collapse of past human projects and deferential to the voices of 'elders'.[28] Both state-oriented communist forms of progressivism and neoliberal, free-market visions of the future have undergone a crisis of legitimacy. The 'hopes of socialism', Perry Anderson has written, have been 'struck off the agenda' of the left.[29] In postcommunist Russia, the collapse of the Soviet regime has inaugurated a 'time out of time' in which politics has been severed from any kind of ultimate objective. Rather than discrediting the deposed Soviet order and replacing it with an alternative, the anticommunist revolution has decorated itself with the paraphernalia of the imperial past while instituting a 'deactivated' form of politics whose purpose is to impede the emergence of autonomous formations within civil society and deny them the possibility of historically consequential political action. Against those forces in society—the radical left, for example, or pro-Western liberal groups, who do still situate themselves in a progressive historical narrative—the Putin regime deploys the tools of 'bureaucratic suppression', suspending the legitimacy of alternative political options 'without itself occupying a substantive ideological locus'.[30]

Liberal democracy is founded, no less than communism, on a linear understanding of history. For all the differences between them, Riszard Legutko has observed, both systems are founded on the intention to change reality for the better; at the heart of both is an idea of modernisation that requires 'breaking from the old and initiating the new'; both claim to unfold historically in accordance with a 'linear pattern'; and both confront intellectuals with a stark choice between supporting and opposing progressive change.[31] Hence the strong attachment of recent Democratic presidents in the United States to the notion that there is a 'right' and a 'wrong' side of history.[32] But the collapse of expectations that has transformed the former Soviet empire has not left 'the West' unscathed. The abysmal failure of liberal democratic 'nation-building' projects in the wake of the Iraq and Afghanistan wars discredited the pretensions both of 'democratic peace theory' and of the political culture that gave rise to it. The global financial crisis of 2007–8 and the European debt crisis that followed cast a deep shadow over the 'neoliberal' economic governance of the Western capitalist states. Deepening social inequality and the hyper-concentration of new capital at the very uppermost tip of the income pyramid have made it harder to plead for the progressive societal benefits of capitalism. The promise that each generation will be better off than its predecessor no longer appears credible. And at the same time, regimes have emerged within the community of modern 'Western' states that have found ways of using democracy as an instrument of authoritarian rule while evacuating the liberal substance from their political systems. Here, as in postcommunist Russia, it is argued, politics exhausts itself in 'ceaseless activity deprived of any telos'.[33]

Terminal scenarios are in vogue, from 'The Stunning End of the Left and the Right' and 'The End of the Left and the Right as We Knew Them', to 'The End of Politics as We Know It' and 'The End of Neoliberalism'.[34] 'How Will Capitalism End?', Wolfgang Streeck has asked, a question that would have seemed meaningless in the late 1980s or early 1990s, when it was the endlessness of capitalism that appeared obvious.[35] 'Is this how democracy ends?' asked David Runciman in a piece for the *London Review of Books*, reflecting on the meaning of the Trump election victory.[36] Is this the 'end of history' diagnosed by Francis Fukuyama? Fukuyama's famous article (and later book) of that name referred to the arrival of history's Hegelian locomotive at its terminal station, the fulfilment of a linear progression towards liberty and plenitude, marked by the 'universalization of Western liberal democracy as the final form of human government'.[37] But today's 'end of history' is different. It is about the moment when 'the very presupposition of such an end-state is terminated'.[38]

The simultaneity of temporal uncertainty in liberal democratic and leftist politics is suggestive. It may reflect a latent codependency between the two, meaning that the demise of socialist promise necessarily entailed the collapse of liberal hope—this was the deeper meaning Perry Anderson discerned in Fukuyama's essay. But it may also direct our attention to those historical pressures that bear equally on left and right, giving rise to predicaments that neither seems well placed to resolve. In *The Great Derangement: Climate Change and the Unthinkable*, Amitav Ghosh reflects on the impact of climate change on temporal awareness, suggesting that the true significance of the ecological threat we now face lies in its cumulative and terminal quality: 'The events of today's changing climate, in that they represent the totality of human actions over time, represent also the terminus of history. For if the entirety of our past is contained within the present, then temporality itself is drained of significance'.[39]

In the era of the Great Elector, the appeal to future danger had been part of an argument for the concentration of power. But the circuitry that made such arguments effective is lacking in the domain of climate change, because there is no single state structure with the competence to address issues of such immense scope and gravity, but only a plethora of states whose pursuit of individual interest impedes progress towards a systemic solution. Instead of enabling politics as an argument for empowering the state in its pursuit of transcendent ends, the 'great derangement' holds up to the structures of territorial state authority a mirror of their impotence. If states can no longer generate plausible futures and civil society lacks the means to do so, then we truly are imprisoned in the present.

There was a time when the European Union seemed to offer the best hope of confronting those issues—on the European continent, at least—that the nation-states had failed to resolve. The union was founded as a progressive enterprise oriented towards a better future. The preamble to the Rome Treaties of 25 March 1957 stated that the common purpose of the signatories was to 'lay the foundations of an ever closer union among the peoples of Europe' in order to achieve 'the constant improvement of the living and working conditions of their peoples' and to 'preserve and strengthen [their] peace and liberty'.[40] Today, progress towards these objectives is faltering. The Greek financial crisis of 2009–16, the Ukraine crisis of 2013, and the European migrant crisis of 2015–17 all cast a harsh light on the deep structural flaws that impede collective action. The economic distress generated by the global financial crisis, especially in Southern Europe, and the stresses of globalisation have fuelled the growth of nationalist and populist movements offering a range of visions whose common theme is an appeal to an idealised past.

It was in order to counter these recursive visions that Emmanuel Macron, President of the French Republic, spoke in a speech delivered at the Sorbonne on 26 September 2017 of Europe as 'our horizon, that which protects us and gives us a future'. Macron went on to propose many things, but his central theme recalled the arguments of the Great Elector and his administration against the holders of provincial privilege: in order to prepare proactively for the challenges of the future—ecological transition, globalisation, migration, security threats—Europe must end the 'civil war' over budgetary, financial, and political differences to 'construct' a 'genuine sovereignty'. The member states must learn the virtues of 'solidarity'—an injunction that recalls the Elector's reminder to his Estates that the provinces, for all their distinctive privileges and traditions, were 'limbs of one head', *membra unius capitis*. If the nation-states failed to rise to this challenge, Macron warned, the present, and with it the future, would be submerged by the past: 'For too long we were sure in our belief that the past would not come back, we thought that the lessons had been learned, we thought that we could settle into inertia, habit, putting our ambition somewhat to one side, this hope that Europe had to carry because we took it for granted and risked losing it from sight'.[41]

Whether Macron will succeed in restarting the European 'motor' and aligning all or part of the union with these objectives remains unclear at the time of writing. For the moment, the current wave of temporal uncertainty and disorientation—itself a cultural phenomenon of great historical interest—continues to deepen.[42] Its traces can be detected in the retro feel of contemporary political rhetoric, the ubiquity of 'presentism' and nostalgia,[43] in the collaged or palimpsestic timescapes of contemporary fiction,[44] and in those works of art that have focused attention in recent years on time as a destabilising dimension of experience. Anselm Kiefer's vast north German canvasses depict the present as a condition of depleted anticipation, 'radically permeated with meaning from the past'.[45] The Berlin-based artist Jorinde Voigt's large works on paper, annotated like musical scores, swarm with temporal vectors and markers—'now', 'today', 'tomorrow', 'process', 'frequency'.[46]

We are at the end of this book. The image below, from the series *Captured on Paper* by the Austrian artist Sonja Gangl, may *look* like a still from the closing credits of a Hollywood movie—in fact it is painstakingly hand-worked in hundreds of thousands of tiny pencil-strokes of graphite, the incremental slowness of the process proposing an uncomfortable tension with the illusion of photography's instant capture.

FIGURE 5.1. Sonja Gangl, from the series *Captured on Paper*, THE END_1100101 (2014). *Source*: Courtesy of Sonja Gangl.

NOTES

Introduction

1. François Hartog, *Régimes d'Historicité, Présentisme et Expériences du Temps* (Paris, 2003).

2. On time regimes as structures of perception, rather than semantic phenomena, see Cornel Zwierlein, 'Frühe Neuzeit, Multiple Modernities, Globale Sattelzeit', in Achim Landwehr (ed.), *Frühe NeueZeiten. Zeitwissen zwischen Reformation und Revolution* (Bielefeld, 2012), 389–405.

3. Cornel Zwierlein, *Discorso und Lex Dei. Die Entstehung neuer Denkrahmen im 16. Jahrhundert und die Wahrnehmung der französischen Religionskriege in Italien und Deutschland* (Göttingen, 2006).

4. Thus Niklas Luhmann on the temporalities generated by different 'social systems'; see Luhmann, 'Weltzeit und Systemgeschichte. Über Beziehungen zwischen Zeithorizonten und sozialen Strukturen gesellschaftlicher Systeme', in Luhmann, *Soziologische Aufklärung II. Aufsätze zur Theorie der Gesellschaft* (Opladen, 1986), 103–33, here 103–4; see also Luhmann, 'Temporalisierung von Komplexität. Zur Semantik neuzeitlicher Zeitbegriffe', in Luhmann, *Gesellschaftsstruktur und Semantik. Studien zur Wissenssoziologie der modernen Gesellschaft*, vol. 1 (Frankfurt/Main, 1980), 235–300.

5. On historical 'distance' as constructed and manipulable, see Mark Salber Phillips, 'Rethinking Historical Distance. From Doctrine to Heuristic', in *History and Theory* 50 (2011), 11–23.

6. On the 'temporal turn' in the human sciences generally, see Robert Hassan, 'Globalization and the "Temporal Turn". Recent Trends and Issues in Time Studies', *Korean Journal of Policy Studies* 25 (2010), 83–102. On the temporal turn in history, see Alexander Geppert and Till Kössler, 'Zeit-Geschichte als Aufgabe', in Geppert and Kössler (eds.), *Obsession der Gegenwart. Zeit im 20. Jahrhundert* (=Geschichte und Gesellschaft, Sonderheft 25) (Göttingen, 2015), 7–36. There are some conceptual parallels with the 'spatial turn', in which space is understood not as a 'passive backdrop upon which history plays out', but as a 'socio-spatial dialectic'; see Eli Rubin, 'From the *Grünen Wiesen* to the Urban Space: Berlin, Expansion, and the *Longue Durée*. Introduction', *Central European History* 47 (2014, special edition), 221–44, here 233.

7. Thomas Henri Bergson, *Time and Free Will: An Essay on the Immediate Data of Consciousness*, trans. F. L. Pogson ([Paris, 1889] London, 1910); Werner Bergmann, 'The Problem of Time in Sociology: An Overview of the Literature on the State of Theory of Theory and Research on the "Sociology of Time,'' 1900–1982', *Time and Society* 1 (1992), 81–143; Martin Heidegger, *Sein und Zeit*

(= F.-W. von Herrmann (ed.), Gesamtausgabe, vol. 2; Frankfurt/Main, 1977), 437; for literary theorists and narratologists, see Mikhail Bakhtin, 'Forms of Time and of the Chronotope in the Novel. Notes toward a Historical Poetics', in *The Dialogic Imagination. Four Essays* ([1975] Austin, 1988), 84–258; Gérard Genette, *Narrative Discourse*, trans. Jane E. Lewin (Oxford, 1986); John Bender and David E. Welberry (eds.), *Chronotypes. The Construction of Time* (Stanford, CA, 1991); Mark Currie, *About Time. Narrative, Fiction and the Philosophy of Time* (Edinburgh, 2007); J. Ch. Meister and W. Schernus (eds.), *Time. From Concept to Narrative Construct. A Reader* (Berlin, 2011); A. A. Mendilow, *Time and the Novel* ([1952] New York, 1972); M. Middeke (ed.), *Zeit und Roman. Zeiterfahrung im historischen Wandel und ästhetischer Paradigmenwechsel vom sechzehnten Jahrhundert bis zur Postmoderne* (Würzburg, 2002); Paul Ricoeur, *Time and Narrative* (3 vols.; Chicago, 1984, 1985, and 1988).

8. Marc Bloch, *The Historian's Craft*, trans. Peter Putnam (Manchester, 2004), 23–24; on time and the *Annales* school, see Thomas Loué, 'Du present au passé: le temps des historiens', *Temporalités. Revue de sciences sociales et humaines* 8 (2008), http://temporalites.revues.org/60.

9. Fernand Braudel, 'Histoire et Sciences sociales: La longue durée', *Annales E.S.C.* 13.4 (1958), 725–53; on Braudel as the exponent of 'multiple social times', see Immanuel Wallerstein, *World-Systems Analysis: An Introduction* (Durham, NC, 2004), 18; Jacques Le Goff, *À la recherche du temps sacré, Jacques de Voragine et la Légende dorée* (Paris, 2011); Le Goff, 'Au Moyen Âge: temps de l'Église et temps du marchand', *Annales E.S.C.* 15.3 (1960), 417–33.

10. The classical essay collection is Reinhart Koselleck, *Vergangene Zukunft. Zur Semantik geschichtlicher Zeiten* (Frankfurt/Main, 1979), but see also the essays in Koselleck, *Vom Sinn und Unsinn der Geschichte. Aufsätze und Vorträge aus vier Jahrzehnten*, ed. Carsten Dutt (Berlin, 2014); Koselleck, *Zeitschichten: Studien zur Historik* (Frankfurt/Main, 2000); Koselleck and Reinhart Herzog (eds.), *Epochenschwelle und Epochenbewusstsein* (Munich, 1987); Koselleck, Heinrich Lutz, and Jörn Rüsen (eds.), *Formen der Geschichtsschreibung* (Munich, 1982); Koselleck (ed.), *Historische Semantik und Begriffsgeschichte* (Stuttgart, 1978); see also the articles by Koselleck in Otto Brunner, Werner Conze, and Koselleck (eds.), *Geschichtliche Grundbegriffe: Historisches Lexikon zur politisch-sozialen Sprache in Deutschland*, 9 vols. (Stuttgart, 1972–97). On history as the 'relentless iteration of the new', see Peter Fritzsche, *Stranded in the Present. Modern Time and the Melancholy of History* (Cambridge, MA, 2010), 8.

11. Reinhart Koselleck, 'Modernity and the Planes of Historicity', in Koselleck, *Futures Past. On the Semantics of Historical Time* (New York, 2004), 9–25.

12. This sense of separateness does not, of course, in itself undermine intertemporal allegory as a modern historical practice—on its persistence, see Peter Burke, 'History as Allegory', *INTI, Revista de literatura hispánica* 45 (1997), 337–51.

13. Hans Robert Jauss, 'Literaturgeschichte als Provokation der Literaturwissenschaft', in Rainer Warning (ed.), *Rezeptionsästhetik* (Munich, 1979),

126–62; *Zeitlichkeit* is a central motif in Heidegger; for thematic discussions of the concept, see his *Sein und Zeit* (Tübingen, 1953), 334–438; 'temporalization': Arthur O. Lovejoy, *Great Chain of Being. A Study of the History of an Idea* (Cambridge, MA, 1936), esp. chap. 9 on 'The Temporalizing of the Chain of Being', 242–88; Nietzsche and acceleration: Nietzsche, *Vom Nutzen und Nachteil der Historie für das Leben*, ed. M. Landmann (Basel, 1949), which speaks of the 'thoughtless, hurrying fragmentation and fraying of the fundamentals, their dissolution into a becoming that is always flowing and dissipating, the tireless unravelling and historicizing by the modern human of everything that has come into existence'. On 'Verzeitlichung', see also Theo Jung, 'Das Neue der Neuzeit ist ihre Zeit. Reinhart Kosellecks Theorie der Verzeitlichung und ihre Kritiker', *Moderne: kulturwissenschaftliches Jahrbuch* 6 (2010–11), 172–84; for a critical discussion of Koselleck's method with pointers to the Koselleck literature, see Daniel Fulda, 'Wann begann die "offene Zukunft"? Ein Versuch, die Koselleck'sche Fixierung auf die "Sattelzeit" zu lösen', in Wolfgang Breul and Jan Carsten Schnurr (eds.), *Geschichtsbewusstsein und Zukunftserwartung in Pietismus und Erweckungsbewegung* (Göttingen, 2013), 141–72.

14. On Koselleck as a theorist of modernisation, see, for example, Jörn Leonhard, 'Erfahrungsgeschichten der Moderne: Von der komparativen Semantik zur Temporalisierung europäischer Sattelzeiten', in Hans Joas and Peter Vogt (eds.), *Begriffene Geschichte. Beiträge zum Werk Reinhart Kosellecks* (Berlin, 2011), 423–49; on Koselleck's embeddedness in preexisting discourses of modernisation, see Britta Hermann and Barbara Thums, 'Einleitung', in Hermann and Thums (eds.), *Ästhetische Erfindung der Moderne? Perspektiven und Modelle 1750–1850* (Würzburg, 2003), 7–28, here 9–10; on the links between temporalisation and modernisation, see Jung, 'Das Neue der Neuzeit ist ihre Zeit', esp. 172–75.

15. On the temporality of nostalgia, see Svetlana Boym, *The Future of Nostalgia* (New York, 2001), esp. 19–32.

16. On 'acceleration', see, above all, Hartmut Rosa, *Beschleunigung. Die Veränderung der Zeitstrukturen in der Moderne* (Frankfurt/Main, 2005); also James A. Ward, 'On Time: Railroads and the Tempo of American Life', *Railroad History* 151 (1984), 87–95; Lothar Baier, *'Keine Zeit!' 18 Versuche über die Beschleunigung* (Munich, 2000); Ryan Anthony Vieira, 'Connecting the New Political History with Recent Theories of Temporal Acceleration: Speed, Politics and the Cultural Imagination of Fin de Siècle Britain', *History and Theory* 50 (2011), 373–89; on the 'emptying' of time and 'time-space distanciation', see Anthony Giddens, *Consequences of Modernity* (Stanford, CA, 1990), 37–40; and Giddens, *A Contemporary Critique of Historical Materialism* (Berkeley, CA, 1981), 90–97; on splitting and fracturing, see David Harvey, *The Condition of Postmodernity. An Enquiry into the Origins of Cultural Change* (London, 1989), 260–307, and Richard Terdiman, *Present Past. Modernity and the Memory Crisis* (Ithaca, NY, 1993), 9, 23; on the 'annihilation' of time (and space), see Stephen Kern, *The Culture of Time and Space, 1880–1918* (Cambridge, MA, 2003), xiii; Wolfgang

Schivelbusch, *Geschichte der Eisenbahnreise. Zur Industrialisierung von Raum und Zeit im 19. Jahrhundert* (Munich 1977), 36; Iwan R. Morus, 'The Nervous System of Britain. Space, Time and the Electric Telegraph in the Victorian Age', *British Journal for the History of Science* 33 (2000), 455–75; Jeremy Stein, 'Annihilating Time and Space. The Modernization of Firefighting in Late Nineteenth-Century Cornwall, Ontario', *Urban History Review* 24 (1996), 3–11; on 'compression', see Jeremy Stein, 'Reflections on Time, Time-Space Compression and Technology in the Nineteenth Century', in Jon May and Nigel Thrift (eds.), *Timespace. Geographies of Temporality* (London, 2001), 106–19; for a critique of the annihilation metaphor, see Roland Wenzlhuemer, '"Less Than No Time". Zum Verhältnis von Telegrafie und Zeit', *Geschichte und Gesellschaft* 37 (2011), 592–613; on 'intensification', see Alf Lüdtke, 'Writing Time—Using Space. The Notebook of a Worker at Krupp's Steel Mill and Manufacturing—An Example from the 1920s', *Historical Social Research* 38 (2013), 216–28; on 'liquefaction', see Roger Griffin, 'Fixing Solutions: Fascist Temporalities as Remedies for Liquid Modernity', *Journal of Modern European History* 13 (2015), 5–23.

17. On the experience of time as 'simultaneous', 'atomistic', and 'heterogeneous', see Kern, *Culture of Time and Space*, 20, 68–70; on the psychology of time as experienced through memory, see Terdiman, *Present Past*, esp. 344–59; for a study that combines philosophical, experiential and psychological approaches, see Charles M. Sherover, *Are We in Time? And Other Essays on Time and Temporality* (Evanston, IL, 2003); on the Durkheimian roots of temporal studies that focus on patterns of social action and interaction, see Michael A. Katovich, 'Durkheim's Macrofoundations of Time. An Assessment and Critique', *Sociological Quarterly* 28 (1987), 367–85; on methodological and conceptual problems more generally, see Nancy Munn, 'The Cultural Anthropology of Time. A Critical Essay', *Annual Review of Anthropology* 21 (1992), 93–123. On the temporality of specific occupational and institutional cultures, see Jacques Le Goff, *Time, Work and Culture in the Middle Ages*, trans. Arthur Goldhammer (Chicago, 1980), esp. part 1 on 'Time and Labour'; E. P. Thompson, 'Time, Work-Discipline, and Industrial Capitalism', *Past and Present* 38 (1967), 56–97; Peter Clark, 'American Corporate Timetabling: Its Past, Present and Future', *Time & Society* 6 (1997), 261–85; Thomas C. Smith, 'Peasant Time and Factory Time in Japan', *Past & Present* 111 (1986), 165–97; J. Stein, 'Time Space and Social Discipline: Factory Life in Cornwall, Ontario, 1867–1893', *Journal of Historical Geography* 21 (1995), 278–99; Michael G. Flaherty, *The Textures of Time: Agency and Temporal Experience* (Philadelphia, 2011).

18. For chronosophically focused studies, see Charles M. Sherover, *The Human Experience of Time. The Development of Its Philosophic Meaning* (New York, 1975) and Kern, *Culture of Time and Space*, esp. chap. 3; Krzysztof Pomian, *L'Ordre du temps* (Paris, 1984); for studies that focus on terminology, see Penelope Corfield, *Time and the Shape of History* (New Haven, CT, 2007); Lucian Hölscher, 'Time Gardens: Historical Concepts in Modern Historiography', *History and Theory* 53 (2014), 577–91; Anthony Abbott, *Time Matters:*

On Theory and Method (Chicago, 2001); on the relationship between narrative, time, and historical experience, see David Carr, *Time, Narrative and History* (Bloomington, IN, 1991); Currie, *About Time*.

19. See the essays in Wolfgang Küttler, Jörn Rüsen, and Ernst Schulin (eds.), *Geschichtsdiskurs*, 5 vols. (Frankfurt/Main: Fischer Taschenbuch Verlag, 1993–1999), vol. 2, *Anfänge modernen historischen Denkens*, many of which explicitly embed their discussions of eighteenth-century historical thought and practice in a narrative of 'modernisation'.

20. See Jennifer Power McNutt, 'Hesitant Steps. Acceptance of the Gregorian Calendar in Eighteenth-Century Geneva', *Church History* 75 (2006), 544–64. On the confessional dimension of calendar reform, see Robert Poole, *Time's Alteration: Calendar Reform in Early Modern England* (London, 1998); on calendars as instruments of power more generally, see Ho Kai-Lung, 'The Political Power and the Mongolian Translation of the Chinese Calendar during the Yuan Dynasty', *Central Asiatic Journal* 50 (2006), 57–99; Clare Oxby, 'The Manipulation of Time: Calendars and Power in the Sahara', *Nomadic Peoples*, New Series 2: *Savoirs et Pouvoirs au Sahara* (1998), 137–49.

21. Jeroen Duindam, *Vienna and Versailles. The Courts of Europe's Dynastic Rivals, 1550-1780* (Cambridge, 2003), 143.

22. The ten-day week was abandoned in April 1802 and the calendar as a whole in 1805. See Reinhart Koselleck, 'Anmerkungen zum Revolutionskalender und zur "Neuen Zeit"', in Koselleck and Rolf Reichardt (eds.), *Die französische Revolution als Bruch des gesellschaftlichen Bewußtseins* (Munich, 1988), 61–64; Michael Meinzer, *Der französische Revolutionskalender (1792-1805). Planung, Durchführung und Scheitern einer politischen Zeitrechnung* (Munich, 1992); Noah Shusterman, *Religion and the Politics of Time. Holidays in France from Louis XIV through Napoleon* (Washington, DC, 2010); Sonja Perovic, *The Calendar in Revolutionary France. Perceptions of Time in Literature, Culture, Politics* (Cambridge, 2012); Matthew Shaw, *Time and the French Revolution. The Republican Calendar, 1789-Year XIV* (Woodbridge, 2011).

23. This is now a huge literature, but the classic study is Thompson, 'Time, Work-Discipline, and Industrial Capitalism', which focuses on time discipline both in metropolitan Europe and in a range of colonial contexts; see also Frederick Cooper, 'Colonizing Time. Work Rhythms and Labour Conflict in Colonial Mombasa', in Nicholas B. Dirks (ed.), *Colonialism and Culture* (Ann Arbor, MI, 1992), 209–45; Keletso E. Atkins, '"Kafir Time". Preindustrial Temporal Concepts and Labour Discipline in Nineteenth-Century Colonial Natal', *Journal of African History* 29 (1988), 229–44; Mark M. Smith, *Mastered by the Clock. Time, Slavery and Freedom in the American South* (Chapel Hill, NC, 1997); U. Kalpagam, 'Temporalities, History and Routines of Rule in Colonial India', *Time & Society* 8 (1999), 141–59; Mike Donaldson, 'The End of Time? Aboriginal Temporality and the British Invasion of Australia', *Time & Society* 5 (1996), 187–207; Alamin Mazrui and Lupenga Mphande, 'Time and Labour in Colonial Africa. The Case of Kenya and Malawi', in Joseph K. Adjaye (ed.), *Time*

in the Black Experience (Westport, CT, 1994), 97–120; Dan Thu Nguyen, 'The Spatialization of Metric Time. The Conquest of Land and Labour in Europe and the United States', *Time & Society* 1 (1992), 29–50; Anthony Aveni, 'Circling the Square: How the Conquest Altered the Shape of Time in Mesoamerica', *Transactions of the American Philosophical Society*, New Series 102 (2012). On modern temporality as a tool of domination over colonial others supposedly trapped in a prior epoch, see Kathleen Frederickson, 'Liberalism and the Time of Instinct', *Victorian Studies* 49 (2007), 302–12; Johannes Fabian, *Time and the Other: How Anthropology Makes Its Object* (New York, 1991).

24. See, for example, Donaldson, 'End of Time?' For a paradigmatic debate on the relationship between traditional, cyclical 'indigenous time' and its linear 'western' counterpart, see Marshall Sahlins, *Islands of History* (Chicago, 1985) and Sahlins, *How "Natives" Think, about Captain Cook, for Example* (Chicago, 1995), which proposes a stark binary opposition, and Gananath Obyesekere, *The Apotheosis of Captain Cook. European Mythmaking in the Pacific* (Princeton, NJ, 1992), which debunks the binary opposition, describing it as the artefact of European 'mythmaking'.

25. Vanessa Ogle, *The Global Transformation of Time, 1870–1950* (Cambridge, MA, 2015), 204, 208.

26. Sebastian Conrad, '"Nothing Is the Way It Should Be": Global Transformations of the Time Regime in the Nineteenth Century', *Modern Intellectual History* (2017), doi:10.1017/S1479244316000391.

27. Particularly interesting work has been done on the impact of political upheaval on the fracturing of traditional time orders. See esp. Luke S. K. Kwong, 'The Rise of the Linear Perspective on History and Time in Late Qing China c. 1860–1911', *Past & Present* 173 (2001), 157–90; Chang-tze Hu, 'Historical Time Pressure. An Analysis of Min Pao (1905–1908)', in Chun-chieh Huang and Erik Zürcher (eds.), *Time and Space in Chinese Culture* (Leiden, 1995), 329–31; Chang-tze Hu, 'Exemplarisches und fortschrittliches Geschichtsdenken in China', in Küttler, Rüsen, and Schulin, *Geschichtsdiskurs:* , vol. 2, *Anfänge modernen historischen Denkens*, 180–83; Q. Edward Wang, *Modernity inside Tradition. The Transformation of Historical Consciousness in Modern China* (Bloomington, IN, 1996). For a dissenting view stressing early 'modernising' developments in Chinese historiography, see Helwig Schmidt-Glintzer, 'Die Modernisierung des historischen Denkens im China des 16. Und 18. Jahrhunderts und seine Grenzen', in Küttler, Rüsen, and Schulin, *Geschichtsdiskurs*, 165–79.

28. Kwong, 'Rise of the Linear Perspective', 160, 163, 164, 166, 172, 176–80, 189–90.

29. The introduction of a five-day week triggered chaos; in 1932, it was replaced by a six-day week. In 1940, the Soviet Union reverted to the seven-day week and the Gregorian calendar. On Soviet calendar reform and its failure, see Robert C. Williams, 'The Russian Revolution and the End of Time', *Jahrbücher für Geschichte Osteuropas*, New Series 43 (1995), 364–401, here 365–69.

30. Stephen E. Hanson, *Time and Revolution. Marxism and the Design of Soviet Institutions* (Chapel Hill, NC, 1997), viii–ix, 180–99. On the stark linearity of Marxist-Leninist time and its relationship with Stalinist praxis, see also Stefan Plaggenborg, *Experiment Moderne. Der sowjetische Weg* (Frankfurt/Main, 2006), esp. 80–105; on the transition from the Taylorist romanticism of the early Soviet Union to the 'machine utopia' of the Stalinist era, see Richard Stites, *Revolutionary Dreams. Utopian Vision and Experimental Life in the Russian Revolution* (New York, 1989), 161–64.

31. Claudio Fogu, *The Historic Imaginary. The Politics of History in Fascist Italy* (Toronto, 2003), 34; Jeffrey T. Schnapp, 'Fascism's Museum in Motion', *Journal of Architecture Education* 45 (1992), 87–97; Schnapp, 'Fascinating Fascism', *Journal of Contemporary History* 31 (1996), 235–44; Marla Stone, 'Staging Fascism. The Exhibition of the Fascist Revolution', *Journal of Contemporary History* 28 (1993), 215–43.

32. Roger Griffin, 'Party Time. The Temporal Revolution of the Third Reich', *History Today* 49 (1999), 43–49; Griffin, '"I Am No Longer Human. I Am a Titan. A God!" The Fascist Quest to Regenerate Time', Electronic Seminars in History, Institute of Historical Research (May 1998), http://www.ihrinfo.ac.uk/esh/quest.html.

33. Eric Michaud, *The Cult of Art in Nazi Germany* (Stanford, CA, 2004), 184, 196, 202, 204; Michaud's concept of the 'Nazi myth' is inspired by the enigmatic reflections in Philippe Lacoue-Labarthe and Jean-Luc Nancy, 'The Nazi Myth', *Critical Inquiry* 16 (1990), 291–312.

34. Emilio Gentile, *Il culto del littorio. La sacralizzazione della politica nell'Italia fascista* (Rome, 1993).

35. On the 'denial of time' by the three totalitarian regimes, see Charles S. Maier, 'The Politics of Time. Changing Paradigms of Collective Time and Private Time in the Modern Era', in Maier (ed.), *Changing Boundaries of the Political. Essays on the Evolving Balance between the State and Society, Public and Private in Europe* (Cambridge, 1987), 151–75; on the 'eschatological self-image' that united the dictatorships of the left and right, notwithstanding differences in their 'temporal codes', see Martin Sabrow, *Die Zeit der Zeitgeschichte* (Göttingen, 2012), 21, 23.

36. See George W. Wallis, 'Chronopolitics: The Impact of Time Perspectives on the Dynamics of Change', *Social Forces* 49 (1970), 102–8.

37. This is the question Alon Confino asks of National Socialist anti-Semitism; see Alon Confino, 'Why Did the Nazis Burn the Hebrew Bible? Nazi Germany, Representations of the Past and the Holocaust', *Journal of Modern History* 84 (2012), 369–400, 381.

38. Maier, 'Politics of Time', 151.

39. See Achim Landwehr, 'Alte Zeiten, Neue Zeiten. Aussichten auf die Zeit-Geschichte', in Landwehr (ed.), *Frühe NeueZeiten*, 9–40.

40. For powerful articulations of this tendency, see Achim Landwehr, *Geburt der Gegenwart. Eine Geschichte der Zeit im 17. Jahrhundert* (Frankfurt/

Main, 2014); Zwierlein, *Discorso und Lex Dei*; Max Engammaire, *L'Ordre du temps. L'invention de la ponctualité au XVIe siècle* (Geneva, 2004).

41. For a discussion of this issue in Koselleck reception, see Helge Jordheim, 'Against Periodization: Koselleck's Theory of Multiple Temporalities', *History and Theory* 51 (2012), 151–71; Hans Joas and Peter Vogt, 'Jenseits von Determinismus und Teleologie: Koselleck und die Kontingenz von Geschichte', in Joas and Vogt (eds.), *Begriffene Geschichte*, 9–56, esp. 11–13; Fulda, 'Wann begann die "offene Zukunft"?'

42. On 'pluritemporality' as a feature of historical eras in general, see Landwehr, 'Alte Zeiten, Neue Zeiten', 25–29.

43. Duncan Bell, 'Empire of the Tongue', *Prospect*, February 2007, 42–45, here 45.

44. David Martosko, 'EXCLUSIVE: Trump Trademarked Slogan 'Make America Great Again' Just DAYS after the 2012 Election and Says Ted Cruz Has Agreed Not to Use It Again after Scott Walker Booms It TWICE in Speech', *Daily Mail*, 12 May 2016; Edward Wong, 'Trump Has Called Climate Change a Chinese Hoax. Beijing Says It Is Anything But', *New York Times*, 18 November 2016.

45. On these features of Trump's political rhetoric, see Stephen Wertheim, 'Donald Trump versus American Exceptionalism: Toward the Sources of Trumpian Conduct', H-Diplo ISSF, 1 February 2017, http://issforum.org/roundtables policy/1-5K-Trump-exceptionalism.

46. Cited in Mark Danner, 'The Real Trump. Review of Michael Kranish and Marc Fischer, *Trump Revealed: An American Journey of Ambition, Ego, Money, and Power* (New York, 2016)', *New York Review of Books*, 22 December 2016.

47. Marine Le Pen, interview with CNN, 28 November 2016, http://edition.cnn .com/2016/11/15/politics/marine-le-pen-interview-donald-trump/index.html.

Chapter 1. The History Machine

1. Helmut Börsch-Supan, 'Zeitgenössische Bildnisse des großen Kurfürsten', in Gerd Heinrich (ed.), *Ein Sonderbares Licht in Teutschland. Beiträge zur Geschichte des Großen Kurfürsten von Brandenburg (1640–1688)* (Berlin, 1990), 151–66.

2. Anselmus van Hulle, *Les hommes illustres qui ont vécu dans le XVII. siècle: les principaux potentats, princes, ambassadeurs et plénipotentiaires qui ont assisté aux conférences de Münster et Osnabrug avec leurs armes et devises* (Amsterdam, 1717).

3. The indispensable reference study is still Ernst Opgenoorth, *Friedrich Wilhelm. Der Große Kurfürst von Brandenburg. Eine politische Biographie*, 2 vols. (Göttingen, 1971/1978); articles on specific themes from a range of experts can be found in Heinrich (ed.), *Ein sonderbares Licht in Teutschland.*

4. Richard Dietrich (ed.), *Die Politischen Testamente der Hohenzollern* (Cologne, 1986), 189.

5. Ibid., 190.

6. Ernst Opgenoorth, 'Mehrfachherrschaft im Selbstverständnis Kurfürst Friedrich Wilhelms', in Heinrich, *Ein sonderbares Licht in Teutschland*, 35–52.

7. Reinhard Koselleck, 'Die Geschichte der Begriffe und Begriffe der Geschichte', in Koselleck, *Begriffsgeschichten*. *Studien der Semantik und Pragmatik der politischen und sozialen Sprache* (Suhrkamp: Frankfurt/Main, 2006) 56–76; on the temporalisation of concepts more generally, see Koselleck, 'Die Verzeitlichung der Begriffe', in the same volume, 77–85; for the classic account of the temporalisation of 'history', see Odilo Engels, Horst Günther, Christian Meier, and Reinhart Koselleck, 'Geschichte, Historie', in Brunner, Conze, and Koselleck, *Geschichtliche Grundbegriffe*, 2:593–798.

8. I use the term 'historicity' in the sense elaborated by François Hartog in his *Régimes d'historicité*—see the introduction to this book.

9. For an overview with literature, see Rudolf Endres, *Adel in der frühen Neuzeit* (Munich, 1993), esp. 23–30, 83–92.

10. Peter-Michael Hahn, 'Landesstaat und Ständetum im Kurfürstentum Brandenburg während des 16. und 17. Jahrhunderts', in Peter Baumgart (ed.), *Ständetum und Staatsbildung in Brandenburg-Preußen. Ergebnisse einer international Fachtagung* (Berlin, 1983), 41–79, here 42.

11. On the status of these principalities, see Rainer Walz, *Stände und frühmoderner Staat. Die Landstände von Jülich-Berg im 16. Und 17. Jahrhundert* (Neustadt, 1982), 50–52; for examples, see Frederick William to the cities of Wesel, Calcar, Düsseldorf, Xanten and Rees, Küstrin, 15 May 1643, and Cleve Estates to Dutch Estates General, Kleve, 2 April 1647, in August von Haeften (ed.), *Ständische Verhandlungen*, vol. 1 (Berlin, 1869), 205, 331–34.

12. Helmuth Croon, *Stände und Steuern in Jülich-Berg im 17. und vornehmlich im 18. Jahrhundert* (Bonn, 1929), 250; Walz, *Stände und frühmoderner Staat*, 74–77, 112–16; examples: Estates of County of Mark to Protesting Estates of Kleve, Unna, 10 August 1641, Estates of Mark to estates of Kleve, Unna, 10 December 1650, in Haeften, *Ständische Verhandlungen*, vol. 1 (=UuA, vol. 5), 182, 450; Michael Kaiser, 'Kleve und Mark als Komponenten einer Mehrfach herrschaft: Landesherrliche und landständische Entwürfe im Widerstreit', in Michael Kaiser and Michael Rohrschneider (eds.), *Membra unius capitis. Studien zu Herrschaftsauffassungen und Regierungspraxis in Kurbrandenburg (1640–1688)* (Berlin, 2005), 99–120.

13. Comment by the Viceroy of Ducal Prussia, Prince Boguslav Radziwiłł, cited in Derek McKay, *The Great Elector* (Harlow, 2001), 135.

14. Johann Gustav Droysen, *Der Staat des großen Kurfürsten* (Geschichte der preussischen Politik, pt. 3), 3 vols. (Leipzig, 1870–71), 1:31.

15. Christoph Fürbringer, *Necessitas und Libertas. Staatsbildung und Landstände im 17. Jahrhundert in Brandenburg* (Frankfurt/Main, 1985), 34.

16. Ibid., 54.

17. Ibid., 54–57; Otto Meinardus (ed.), *Protokolle und Relationen des Brandenburgischen geheimen Rates aus der Zeit des Kurfürsten Friedrich Wilhelm* (Leipzig, 1889), 1:xxxiv.

18. Meinardus, *Protokolle*, 1:xxxv; Haeften, *Ständische Verhandlungen*, vol. 1 (Kleve-Mark; =UuA, vol. 5), 58–82.

19. F. L. Carsten, 'The Resistance of Cleve and Mark to the Despotic Policy of the Great Elector', *English Historical Review* 66 (1951), 219–41.

20. Karl Spannagel, *Konrad von Burgsdorff. Ein brandenburgischer Kriegs- und Staatsmann aus der Zeit der Kurfürsten Georg Wilhelm und Friedrich Wilhelm* (Berlin, 1903), 265–67.

21. McKay, *Great Elector*, 21; Martin Philippson, *Der Große Kurfürst Friedrich Wilhelm von Brandenburg*, 3 vols. (Berlin, 1897–1903), 1:41–42.

22. Alexandra Richie, *Faust's Metropolis. A History of Berlin* (London, 1998), 44–45.

23. A. v. Haeften, 'Einleitung', in Haeften, *Ständische Verhandlungen*, 105.

24. Philippson, *Der Große Kurfürst*, 1:56–58.

25. M. F. Hirsch, 'Die Armee des grossen Kurfürsten und ihre Unterhaltung während der Jahre 1660–66', *Historische Zeitschrift* 17 (1885), 229–75; Charles Waddington, *Le Grand Électeur, Frédéric Guillaume de Brandebourg: sa politique extérieure, 1640–1688* (Paris, 1905–88), 89; McKay, *Great Elector*, 173–75.

26. Elector to the Clevischen Stände, Königsberg, 21 October 1645, in Haeften, *Ständische Verhandlungen*, 246–48.

27. Declaration by the Elector to the Deputies of the Kleve Estates, Königsberg, 7 December 1645, in Haeften, *Ständische Verhandlungen*, 252–54.

28. Elector to the Government [of Cleve], Königsberg, 8 November 1645, Elector to the Government [of Cleve], 14 March 1646, Elector to the Estates [of Cleve], Hervord, 5 October 1652, all in Haeften, *Ständische Verhandlungen*, 248–49, 259–60, 614–15.

29. The Northern War began when the Swedes invaded and occupied western Poland-Lithuania in 1655. Frederick William at first sided with Sweden in return for Swedish recognition of his full sovereignty over Ducal Prussia, fighting at the side of the Swedish army in the Polish campaign of 1656, but when the tide turned against Sweden, he first left the alliance and then, in 1657, joined forces with Sweden's enemies, in return for Polish ratification of his status as sole sovereign in Ducal Prussia, formalised in the Treaty of Wehlau (19 September 1657). These manoeuvres would have been impossible without an effective army with which to woo friends and intimidate potential enemies, hence the demand for more armed men and the money to support them.

30. Governor (Statthalter) John Moritz von Nassau-Siegen to Kleve Estates, Proposition of 3 March 1657, cited in Volker Seresse, 'Zur Bedeutung der "Necessitas" für den Wandel politischer Normen im 17. Jahrhundert', *Forschungen zur Brandenburgischen und Preussischen Geschichte* 11 (2001), 139–59, here 144–45. For the full text and the commentaries that followed, see Haeften, *Ständische Verhandlungen*, 1:888–92.

31. Reply of the Privy Councillors on behalf of the Elector, Cölln [Berlin], 2 December 1650, in Siegfried Isaacsohn (ed.), *Urkunden und Aktenstücke zur Geschichte des Großen Kurfürsten Friedrich Wilhelm von Brandenburg*, vol. 10, *Ständische Verhandlungen*, pt. 3 (Berlin, 1880), 193–94.

32. Patent of Contradiction by the Estates of Kleve, Jülich, Berg and Mark, Wesel, 14 July 1651; Union of the Estates of Kleve and Mark, Wesel, 8 August 1651, in Haeften, *Ständische Verhandlungen*, vol. 1 (=UuA, vol. 5), 509, 525–26; F. L. Carsten, 'The Resistance of Cleves and Mark to the Despotic Policy of the Great Elector', *English Historical Review* 66 (1951), 219 41, hcrc 224; McKay, *Great Elector*, 34; Waddington, *Grand Électeur*, 68–69.

33. Robert von Friedeburg, *Luther's Legacy. The Thirty Years War and the Modern Notion of 'State' in the Empire, 1530s to 1790s* (Cambridge, 2016), 240.

34. Kurt Breysig, 'Einleitung', in Breysig (ed.), *Urkunden und Actenstücke zur Geschichte des Kurfursten Friedrich Wilhelm von Brandenburg. Ständische Verhandlungen, Preussen*, vol. 1 (Berlin, 1894), 105, 114, 115–80.

35. See, for example, the pamphlet commissioned by the Elector in response to an appeal against him addressed to the Estates General of the United Netherlands on behalf of the Kleve Estates, *Cleefsche Patriot verthonende de Missive ghesonden aen H.H.M. de heeren staten general der vereigde nederlande van wegens de cleefsche landstenden grpresenteert d. 20 May 1647* (Wesel, 1647), which noted that terms such as 'immemorial liberty', 'Privileges', and 'Provence' were just 'windy words' designed to secure the interests of obstreperous nobles, see *Cleefsche Patriot* [n.p., 8 of the text].

36. Armand Maruhn, *Necessitäres Regiment und fundamentalgesetzlicher Ausgleich. Der hessische Ständekonflikt 1646–1655* (Darmstadt, 2004), 245, 276; cf. Seresse, 'Zur Bedeutung', which suggests that the old Normgefüge was 'exploded' by the emergence of the argument from necessity.

37. For an account stressing unitarisation, see Ludwig Tümpel, *Die Entstehung des Brandenburg-preußischen Einheitsstaates im Zeitalter des Absolutismus (1609–1806)* (Breslau, 1915); on the question of the extent to which the Elector was a unitarising monarch, see Michael Kaiser and Michael Rohrschneider, 'Einführung', in Kaiser and Rohrschneider, *Membra unius capitis*, 9–18; for a differentiated discussion of the problem of integration, see Wolfgang Neugebauer, 'Staatliche Einheit und politischer Regionalismus. Das Problem der Integration in der Brandenburg-preussischen Geschichte bis zum Jahre 1740', in Wilhelm Brauneder (ed.), *Staatliche Vereinigung: Fördernde und hemmende Elemente in der deutschen Geschichte* (=Der Staat, Beiheft 12; Berlin, 1998), 49–87.

38. Fürbringer, *Necessitas und Libertas*, 59; for examples of this mode of argument, see Supreme Councillors of Ducal Prussia to Frederick William, Königsberg, 12 September 1648, in ibid., 292–93.

39. On these debates, see Friedeburg, *Luther's Legacy*, esp. 168–236.

40. See Esther-Beate Körber, 'Ständische Positionen in Preußen zur Zeit des Großen Kurfürsten', in Kaiser and Rohrschneider, *Membra unius capitis*, 171–92, here 171.

41. Maruhn, *Necessitäres Regiment*, 242–45.

42. Ständisches Projekt einer Kurfürstlichen Assecuration, Bartenstein, 16 November 1661, in Breysig, *Ständische Verhandlungen (Preussen)*, 634–39, here 637.

43. Elector to the Clevischen Stände, Königsberg, 21 October 1645, in Haeften, *Ständische Verhandlungen*, 246–48.

44. Weimann to the Elector, Kleve, 14 March 1657, in Haeften, *Ständische Verhandlungen*, 889–92.

45. Weimann diary entry, 22 March 1657, cited in Haeften, *Ständische Verhandlungen*, 891–92.

46. Maruhn, *Necessitäres Regiment*, 106.

47. Declaration by the Elector to the Deputies of the Kleve Estates, Königsberg, 7 December 1645, in Haeften, *Ständische Verhandlungen*, 252–54.

48. 'Der Freien, Kölmer, Schultzen, Krüger und andern privilegirten Leuten theils Sambland undt ganz Nathangenschen und Oberländischen Kreises Beschwere', appended to Gravamina der gesammten Stände, 26 June 1640, in Breysig, *Ständische Verhandlungen (Preussen)*, 265–68.

49. Estates of Mark to the Government [of Mark], Unna, 19 April 1651, in Haeften, *Ständische Verhandlungen*, 486–88.

50. Elector to the Kleve Estates meeting in Xanten, Duisburg, 9 September 1651, in Haeften, *Ständische Verhandlungen*, 539.

51. Elector to the Estates of Kleve, 19 September 1651, in Haeften, *Ständische Verhandlungen*, 542–43.

52. Ibid.

53. On the access of the Elector and his officials to information networks, see Ralf Pröve, 'Herrschaft als kommunikativer Prozess: das Beispiel Brandenburg-Preußen', in Pröve and Norbert Winnige (eds.), *Wissen ist Macht. Herrschaft und Kommunikation in Brandenburg-Preussen 1600–1850* (Berlin, 2001), 11–21; Michael Rohrschneider, 'Die Statthalter des Großen Kurfürsten als außenpolitische Akteure', in Kaiser and Rohrschneider, *Membra unius capitis*, 213–34.

54. Cited from Montecuccoli's Treatise on War in Johannes Kunisch, 'Kurfürst Friedrich Wilhelm und die Großen Mächte', in Heinrich, *Ein Sonderbares Licht in Teutschland*, 9–32, here 30–31.

55. Memoir by Count Waldeck in Bernhard Erdmannsdörffer, *Graf Georg Friedrich von Waldeck. Ein preußischer Staatsmann im siebzehnten Jahrhundert* (Berlin, 1869), 361–62, also 354–55.

56. W. Troost, 'William III, Brandenburg, and the Construction of the Anti-French Coalition, 1672–88', in Jonathan I. Israel, *The Anglo-Dutch Moment: Essay on the Glorious Revolution and Its World Impact* (Cambridge, 1991), 299–334, here 322.

57. Kleve Estates to Elector [Kleve], 24 May 1657, in Haeften, *Ständische Verhandlungen*, 894–97.

58. See, for example, Estates deputies to Elector, Berlin, 30 November 1650, in Siegfried Isaacsohn (ed.), *Urkunden und Actenstücke zur Geschichte des Kurfursten Friedrich Wilhelm von Brandenburg. Ständische Verhandlungen*, vol. 2 (Mark-Brandenburg; Berlin, 1880), 191–92.

59. Elector to Cleve Estates, Richtenberg, Vorpommern 4 October 1659, in Haeften, *Ständische Verhandlungen*, 927–28.

60. Estates deputies to Elector, Berlin, 30 November 1650, in Isaacsohn, *Ständische Verhandlungen* (Mark-Brandenburg), 191–92.

61. Humble request of the Estates [of Ducal Prussia], 26 November 1661, in Breysig, *Ständische Verhandlungen (Preussen)*, 655.

62. Elector to the Privy Councillors, Potsdam, 2 April 1683 (replying to a letter of complaint from the Estates), in Isaacsohn, *Ständische Verhandlungen* (Mark-Brandenburg), 611–13.

63. Hirsch, 'Die Armee des grossen'; Waddington, *Grand Électeur*, 89; McKay, *Great Elector*, 173–75.

64. Bodo Nischan, *Prince, People and Confession. The Second Reformation in Brandenburg* (Philadelphia, 1994), 84, 111–14; Nischan, 'Reformation or Deformation? Lutheran and Reformed Views of Martin Luther in Brandenburg's "Second Reformation"', in Nischan, *Lutherans and Calvinists in the Age of Confessionalism* (Variorum repr.; Aldershot, 1999), 203–15, here 211.

65. Nischan, *Prince, People and Confession*, 217.

66. Johannes Schultze, *Die Mark Brandenburg*, 5 vols. (Berlin, 1961), 4:192.

67. J. T. McNeill, *The History and Character of Calvinism* (Oxford, 1967), 279.

68. Daniel Riches, *Protestant Cosmopolitanism and Diplomatic Culture: Brandenburg-Swedish Relations in the Seventeenth Century* (Leiden, 2013), 170–78.

69. Elector to his Councillors (Oberräthe), Königsberg, 26 April 1642, in B. Erdmannsdörffer (ed.), *Urkunden und Actenstücke zur Geschichte des Kurfürsten Friedrich Wilhelm von Brandenburg. Politische Verhandlungen*, vol. 1 (Berlin, 1864), 99–103.

70. 2 Kings 17:13, 15, New King James Version.

71. Königsberg Clergy to the Supreme Councillors of Ducal Prussia [n.d.; reply to the Elector's letter of 26 April], in Erdmannsdörffer, *Politische Verhandlungen*, 103–4.

72. On this meeting and its consequences, see Johannes Ruschke, *Paul Gerhardt und der Berliner Kirchenstreit. Eine Untersuchung der konfessionallen Auseinandersetzung über die kurfürstlich verordnete 'mutua tolerantia'* (Tübingen, 2012), 176–368.

73. See G. Heinrich, 'Religionstoleranz in Brandenburg-Preußen. Idee und Wirklichkeit', in M. Schlenke (ed.), *Preussen. Politik, Kultur, Gesellschaft* (Reinbek, 1986), 83–102, here 83; the classic exposition of this view, influential for generations thereafter, is Max Lehmann, *Preussen und die Katholische Kirche seit 1640. Nach den Acten des Geheimen Staatsarchives*, pt. 1: *Von 1640 bis 1740* (Leipzig, 1878), esp. 42–52.

74. An example is Johan Bergius, a clergyman close to the Great Elector, who took the view that the Lutheran and Reformed faiths were 'actually not two different religions, in spite of the fact that they are in disagreement on several doctrinal points'; see Bodo Nischan, 'Calvinism, the Thirty Years' War, and the Beginning of Absolutism in Brandenburg: The Political Thought of John

Bergius', *Central European History* 15.3 (1982), 203–23, 212–13; Calvinist-Lutheran irenicism was particularly pronounced among those who expounded the cause of closer relations between Brandenburg and Lutheran Sweden and saw inter-Protestant collaboration as crucial to mounting a successful opposition to Catholicism; see Riches, *Protestant Cosmopolitanism and Diplomatic Culture*, 170–78.

75. For a revisionist account, insisting on the actively confessionalist and pro-Reformed nature of the Elector's measures, on which the following discussion is based, see Jürgen Luh, 'Zur Konfessionspolitik der Kurfürsten von Brandenburg und Könige in Preußen 1640–1740', in Horst Lademacher, Renate Loos, and Simon Groenveld (eds.), *Ablehnung—Duldung—Anerkennung. Toleranz in den Niederlanden und in Deutschland. Ein historischer und aktueller Vergleich* (Münster, 2004), 306–24.

76. Walther Ribbeck, 'Aus Berichten des hessischen Sekretärs Lincker vom Berliner Hofe während der Jahre 1666–1669', *Forschungen zur brandenburgischen und Preussischen Geschichte* 12.2 (1899), 141–58.

77. Klaus Deppermann, 'Die Kirchenpolitik des Grossen Kurfürsten', *Pietismus und Neuzeit* 6 (1980), 99–114, 110–12; Ribbeck, 'Aus Berichten'.

78. Luh, 'Zur Konfessionspolitik'.

79. Dietrich, *Die politischen Testamente*, 182.

80. Cornel Zwierlein, *Discorso und Lex Dei. Die Entstehung neuer Denkrahmen im 16. Jahrhundert und die Wahrbehmung der französischen Religionskriege in Italien und Deutschland* (Göttingen, 2006), 790–92.

81. Ibid., 28, 64, 193, 791–92.

82. On the influence of neostoicism on the political thought and action of Elector Frederick William and of early modern sovereigns more generally, see esp. Gerhard Oestreich, *Neostoicism and the Early Modern State*, ed. B. Oestreich and H. G. Koenigsberger, trans. D. McLintock (Cambridge, 1982).

83. Johann Bergius, *Guter Bürger* (Danzig, 1656), cited in Nischan, 'Calvinism, the Thirty Years' War, and the Beginning of Absolutism in Brandenburg', 212.

84. Philippson, *Der Große Kurfürst*, 1:11.

85. McKay, *Great Elector*, 170–71.

86. Cited from an edict of 1686 in Philippson, *Der Große Kurfürst*, 3:91.

87. Peter Baumgart, 'Der Große Kurfürst. Staatsdenken und Staatsarbeit eines europäischen Dynasten', in Heinrich, *Ein Sonderbares Licht in Teutschland*, 33–57, here 42.

88. On the naval and colonial plans of the Elector, see Opgenoorth, *Friedrich Wilhelm*, 2:305–11; E. Schmitt, 'The Brandenburg Overseas Trading Companies in the 17th Century', in Leonard Blussé and Femme Gaastra (eds.), *Companies and Trade. Essays on European Trading Companies during the Ancien Regime* (Leiden, 1981), 159–76; Ludwig Hüttl, *Friedrich Wilhelm von Brandenburg, der Grosse Kurfürst 1620–1688: eine politische Biographie* (Munich, 1981), 445–46.

89. Peter Burke, 'Foreword', in Andrea Brady and Emily Butterworth (eds.), *The Uses of the Future in Early Modern Europe* (Routledge, 2010), ix–xx.

90. Pufendorf, *Rebus gestis*, VI, §§36–39; Leopold von Orlich, *Friedrich Wilhelm der Große Kurfürst. Nach bisher noch unbekannten Original-Handschriften* (Berlin, 1836), 79–81; the Elector's account is reprinted in the appendix, 139–42; on the reasons for publication, see August Riese, *Die dreitägige Schlacht bei Warschau 28., 29. Und 30. Juli 1656* (Breslau, 1870), 196.

91. Orlich, *Friedrich Wilhelm der Große Kurfürst*, 140–42.

92. 'Alles dahin zu deuten vnd zu dirigiren / daß gleich wie niemanden nichts zu Schmach vnd Vnehr / sondern allein die Historische Geschichte einfältig an Tag zu stellen'. See Merian's dedication to the government of Frankfurt in *Theatrum Europaeum 1617 biß 1629 excl. mit vieler fürnehmer Herrn und Potentaten Contrafacturen, wie auch berühmter Städten, Vestungen, Pässen, Schlachten und Belägerungen eygentlichen Delineationen und Abrissen gezieret* (Frankfurt, 1635).

93. This tendency can be discerned throughout the 1635 edition, but is more pronounced in the second edition of 1662, whose discussion of 1618 refers, for example, to the 'remarkable and great movement has made itself felt among us High Germans who live under the Holy Roman Empire since the year 1618, into which Fate hath for a time woven many other monarchies and kingdoms'. *Theatrum Europaeum 1617 biß 1629*, 1.

94. Ibid., 1. It is not clear who was responsible for rewriting this passage for the 1662 edition. The awareness of the years after 1618 as an epoch of unprecedented destruction must have been stronger after the Peace of Westphalia ended what later became known as the Thirty Years' War.

95. On the use of newspapers as sources, see Herbert Langer and János Dudás, 'Die Kämpfe in Ungarn 1684 bis 1686 und die Rückeroberung Budas im Spiegel des "Theatrum Europaeum"', *Acta Historica Academiae Scientiarum Hungaricae* 34.1 (1988), 17–25, here 18; Anna Schreurs-Morét, 'Der Vesuvausbruch von 1631, ein Spektakel auf der Weltbühne Europa: Anmerkugen zu Joachim von Sandrarts Beitrag zum Theatrum Europaeum von Matthäus Merian', in Flemming Schock, Ariane Koller, and Oswald Bauer (eds.), *Dimensionen der Theatrum-Metapher in der Frühen Neuzeit: Ordnung und Räpresentation von Wissen* (Hannover, 2009), 297–332; on the prevalence of the theatre metaphor in the seventeenth century, see Louis van Delft, 'L'idée de théâtre (XVIe–XVIIIe siècle)', *Revue d'Histoire littéraire de la France* 101.5 (2001), 1349–65; for an older general treatment: Hermann Bingel, *Das Theatrum Europraeum. Ein Beitrag zur Publizistik des 17. und 18. Jahrhunderts* (Berlin, 1909).

96. Cited in Peter Burke, *The Fabrication of Louis XIV* (New Haven, CT, 1992), 152.

97. E. Fischer, 'Die offizielle Brandenburgische Geschichtsschreibung zur Zeit Friedrich Wilhelms des Großen Kurfürst', *Zeitschrift für preussische Geschichte und Landeskunde* 15 (1878), 377–430, here 379–87.

98. Philippson, *Der Große Kurfürst*, 3:164–65.

99. Gregorio Leti, *Ritratti historici, politici, chronologici e genealogici della casa di Brandeburgo,* 2 vols. (Amsterdam, 1687); on the Elector's reward for Leti's efforts, see Orlich, *Friedrich Wilhelm der Große Kurfürst,* 313.

100. Leti discusses the critical reception of the first volume in the first pages of the second, acknowledging in characteristically excited prose that 'in this Battle, this most glorious hero performed one of his most glorious actions both through his leadership, and with sword in hand, . . . and having borne the greater burden of the assault on the main part of all the forces of the Poles', but stated in his own defence that 'since so much had already been written on this battle' it seemed unnecessary for him to enter into the details. Leti, *Ritratti historici,* Parte seconda, 2. Leti may have been thinking of the relevant volume of the *Theatrum,* published in 1685, which did indeed include a rather detailed account of the Battle of Warsaw, in which the Elector's role in supporting the Swedish attack was fully acknowledged; see J. G. Schleder, *Von den denckwürdigsten Geschichten, so sich hie und da in Europa, als in Hoch- und Nieder-Teutschland, Franckreich, Hispanien, Portugall, Italien, Dalmatia, Candia, England, Schott- und Irrland, Den[n]emarck, Norwegen, Schweden, Polen, Moscau, Schlesien, Böhmen, Ober- und Nieder-Oesterreich, Hungarn, Siebenbürgen, Wallachey, Moldau, Türck- und Barbarey, [et]c. Sowol im weltlichen Regiment, als Kriegswesen, vom Jahr Christi 1651. biß an [1658] bevorstehende Wahl . . . Leopolden dieses Namens deß Ersten, erwehlten Römischen Käisers, [et]c. Beydes zu Wasser und Land, begeben und zugetragen / So, Auß vielen glaubhafften Scripturen . . . zusammen getragen, und unpartheyisch beschrieben Johannes Georgius Schlederus, gebürtig in Regenspurg. Mit etlich hoher Potentaten . . . Bildnüssen außgezieret: Dabenebenst einige . . . Sachen in deutlichen Kupffern vor Augen gestellt* (Frankfurt/Main, 1685), 963–66.

101. Michael Seidler, 'Religion, Populism, and Patriarchy: Political Authority from Luther to Pufendorf', *Ethics* 103 (1993), 551–69.

102. On the differences between Hobbes's and Pufendorf's understandings of the state and the sovereign, see Ben Holland, *The Moral Person of the State. Pufendorf, Sovereignty and Composite Polities* (Cambridge, 2017), esp. 210–21, and Richard Tuck, *The Sleeping Sovereign. The Invention of Modern Democracy* (Cambridge, 2015), 96–116.

103. S. Pufendorf, *Elements of Universal Jurisprudence in Two Books* (1660), bk. 2, observation 5, in Craig L. Carr (ed.), *The Political Writings of Samuel Pufendorf,* trans. Michael J. Seidler (New York, 1994), 87.

104. S. Pufendorf, *On the Law of Nature and Nations in Eight Books* (1672), bk. 7, chap. 4, in Carr, *Political Writings,* 220.

105. Ibid., 221.

106. On the 'reasons which justify a person's claim to another obedience', see Samuel Pufendorf, *On the Duty of Man and the Citizen,* ed. James Tully, trans. Michael Silverthorne (Cambridge, 1991), esp. I.5–6, 28–29, also Tully's comments in the introduction, xiv–xliii.

107. Severinus de Monzambano (pseud.), *De statu imperii germanici liber unus* (Verona, 1668); for an English translation with an illuminating analysis of

the context, see Samuel Pufendorf, *The Present State of Germany*, ed. Michael J. Seidler, trans. Edmund Bohun ([1696] Indianapolis, 2007). It is not true that Monzambano supplied the inspiration for a plan to reform the Imperial constitution devised by the Elector in 1662, as Martin Philippson claims (Monzambano only appeared six years later), but the similarities between the Elector's and Pufendorf's thinking are striking nonetheless, as Droysen pointed out long ago; Philippson, *Der Große Kurfürst*, 2:205; Johann Gustav Droysen, 'Zur Kritik Pufendorfs', in Droysen, *Abhandlungen zur neueren Geschichte* (Leipzig, 1876), 309–86, here 339–40.

108. Samuel Pufendorf, 'Author's Preface', in *An Introduction to the History of the Principal Kingdoms and States of Europe* (London, 1719), 2–3; orig. (with the same preface): *Einleitung zu der Historie der vornehmsten Reiche und Staaten, so itziger Zeit in Europe sich befinden* (Frankfurt/Main, 1682).

109. Samuel Pufendorf, *De rebus gestis Friderici Wilhelmi Magni, electoris brandenburgici, commentariorum libri novendecim* (Berlin, 1695); German translation: [Samuel Pufendorf,] *Friederich Wilhelms des Grossen Chur-Fürstens zu Brandenburg Leben und Thaten*, trans. Erdmann Uhse (Berlin, 1710).

110. Droysen, 'Zur Kritik Pufendorfs', 314.

111. Samuel Pufendorf, *Friedrich Wilhelms des Grossen Chur-Fürsten von Brandenburg Leben und Thaten*, trans. Erdmann Uhse (Berlin, 1710), 399.

112. Ibid., 428.

113. Ibid., 401–2.

114. Elias Loccelius, *Marchia Illustrata oder Chronologische Rechnung und Bedencken über die Sachen, so sich in der Mark Brandenburg und incorporierten Ländern vom Anfange der Welt biß ad Annum Christi 1680 sollen zugetragen haben* (Crossen, 1680), 609, 611, 635, 639, 647, 702, 711, 753, 762, 808, 846–49, 861. This work was never published, but it was available to Pufendorf when he wrote his *De rebus gestis* and can be consulted in manuscript form in the Handschriftensammlung of the Staatsbibliothek Berlin, Potsdamerstrasse 33, Signatur: MS Boruss, fol. 18.

115. Erdmann Uhse, 'An den Leser', in *Friedrich Wilhelms des Grossen Chur-Fürsten von Brandenburg Leben und Thaten*, n.p.

116. [Pufendorf,] *Friederich Wilhelms des Grossen Chur-Fürstens zu Brandenburg Leben und Thaten*, 56–58.

117. Ibid., 760–62.

118. Pufendorf, *Leben und Thaten*, 194.

119. On Pufendorf as a choice theorist, see Eerik Lagerspetz, 'Pufendorf on Collective Decisions', *Public Choice* 49.2 (1986), 179–82.

120. Seidler, 'Introduction', in Pufendorf, *Present State of Germany*; as Seidler points out, Pufendorf was not the first to make this claim—Hermann Conring advanced the same argument on different grounds in his *De origine iuris Germanici* (1643).

121. Pufendorf, *Einleitung zu der Historie der vormehmsten Reiche und Staaten*, Vorrede.

122. Pufendorf, *Leben und Thaten*, 1249.

123. Max Weber, *Economy and Society: An Outline of Interpretative Sociology*, 2 vols. (Berkeley, CA, 1978), 1:227.

124. On the danger of allowing 'unknown hypotheses and patterns of interpretation' to infiltrate our understanding the Great Elector, see Ernst Opgenoorth, 'Mehrfachherrschaft im Selbstverständnis Kurfürst Friedrich Wilhelms', in Kaiser and Rohrschneider, *Membra unius capitis*, 35–52, here 37.

125. Jeremy Bentham, *An Introduction to the Principles of Morals and Legislation* (1781), http://utilitarianism.com/jeremy-bentham/index.html#one; on the orientation of security-based arguments towards the future, see Lucia Zedner, *Security* (London, 2009), 29.

126. Dietrich, *Die politischen Testamente*, 188; on 'powerlessness', see also Johann Gustav Droysen, *Der Staat des großen Kurfürsten* (Geschichte der preussischen Politik, pt. 3), 3 vols. (Leipzig, 1870–71), 2:370, Philippson, *Der Große Kurfürst*, 2:238, Albert Waddington, *Histoire de Prusse*, 2 vols. (Paris, 1922), 1:484.

127. Vera Keller, *Knowledge and Public Interest, 1575-1725* (Cambridge, 2015), 4, 8, passim.

128. Burke, 'Foreword', ix–xx.

129. J.G.A. Pocock, *Virtue, Commerce, and History. Essays on Political Thought and History, Chiefly in the Eighteenth Century* (Cambridge, 1985), 92–93.

130. Andrea Brady and Emily Butterworth, 'Introduction', in Brady and Butterworth, *Uses of the Future*, 1–18.

131. I use the term 'historical culture' in the sense proposed by D. R. Woolf: 'a convenient shorthand for the conceptual and cognitive matrix of relations among past, present and future, a matrix that gives rise to, nurtures, and is in turn influenced by the formal historical writing of that era'; see D. R. Woolf, 'Little Crosby and the Horizons of Early Modern Historical Culture', in Donald R. Kelley and David Harris Sacks (eds.), *The Historical Imagination in Early Modern Britain. History, Rhetoric and Fiction, 1500-1800* (Cambridge, 1997), 93–132, here 94.

132. Juan de Mariana, *The General History of Spain from the First Peopling of It by Tubal, till the Death of King Ferdinand, Who United the Crowns of Castile and Aragon: with a Continuation to the Death of King Philip III [. . .], to Which Are Added, Two Supplements, the First by F. Ferdinand Camargo y Salcedo, the Other by F. Basil Varen de Soto, Bringing It Down to the Present Reign*, trans. Capt. John Stevens. (London, 1699), passim, but see as an example 299–300, in which the wars of kings are depicted as a scourge brought upon the common people by the vainglory and ambition of their rulers.

133. Thus, Mariana blamed Philip II for provoking the revolt in the Low Countries by executing the counts of Egmont and Hoorn in 1568, arguing that a more conciliatory policy would have prevented the revolt.

134. On these features of Mariana's political thought, see Harald Braun, *Juan de Mariana and Early Modern Spanish Political Thought* (Aldershot, 2007).

135. Chantal Grell, *L'histoire entre erudition et Philosophie. Étude sur la connaissance historique a l'âge des Lumières* (Paris, 1993), 35, 195, 210, 212, 217; on the resistance of the early modern 'history of France' to mutations, see Philippe Ariès, *Le Temps de l'histoire*, 2nd ed. (Paris, 1986), 135–38, and Orest Ranum, *Artisans of Glory. Writers and Historical Thought in Seventeenth-Century France* (Chapel Hill, NC, 1980), 15–16; Michel Tyvaert, 'L'image du Roi: Legitimité et moralité rolales dans les histoires de France au XVIIe siècle', *Revue d'histoire modern et contemporaine* 21 (1974), 521–47.

136. Grell, *L'histoire entre erudition et Philosophie*, 35. Grell singles out Guyonnet de Vertron, *Parallèle de Louis le Grand avec les princes qui ont été surnommés Grands, dédié à Monseigneur le Dauphin* (Paris, 1685), for declaring that the magnificent attributes of Louis XIV have rendered all previous models of virtue (including Hercules) obsolete, 50–52.

137. Tony Claydon, 'Time and the Revolution of 1688/89' (paper, Workshop on History and Temporality, St Catharine's College, Cambridge, 27 May 2016); Richard S. Kay, *The Glorious Revolution and the Continuity of Law* (Washington, DC, 2014), 279.

138. There are now many studies pressing the case for the special status of early modern temporalities, some of which have been cited in this chapter; for a penetrating discussion of the issues, see Peter Burke, 'Exemplarity and Anti-exemplarity in Early Modern Europe', in A. Lianeri (ed.), *The Western Time of Ancient History: Historiographical Encounters with the Greek and Roman Pasts* (Cambridge, 2011), 48–59.

139. See Milos Vec, *Zeremonialwissenschaft im Fürstenstaat. Studien zur juristischen und politischen Theorie absolutistischer Herrshchaftspräsentation* (Frankfurt/Main, 1998); Jörg Jochen Berns, 'Der nackte Monarch und die nackte Wahrheit. Auskünfte der deutschen Zeitungs- und Zeremoniellschriften des apäten 17. und frühen 18. Jahrhunderts zum Verhältnis von Hof und Öfentlichkeit', *Daphnis* 11 (1982), 315–45; Berns, 'Die Festkultur der deutschen Höfe zwischen 1580 und 1730. Eine Problemskizze in typologischer Absicht', *Germanisch-romanische Monatsschrift* 65 (1984), 295–311.

140. Werner, Brandenburg resident in Warsaw, Report of 10 June 1700, in Max Lehmann, *Preussen und die katholische Kirche seit 1640*, 9 vols. (Leipzig, 1878–1902), 1:465.

141. Father Vota to the Elector of Brandenburg, in Lehmann, *Preussen und die katholische Kirche*, 1:468.

142. Johann von Besser, *Preussische Krönungsgeschichte oder Verlauf der Ceremonien auf welchen Der Allerdurchlauchtigste Großmächtigste Fürst und Herr Friderich der Dritte—die königliche Würde des von Ihm gestifteten Königreichs preußen angenommen und sich und seine Gemahlin ... durch die Salbung als König und Königin einweihen lassen* (Cölln/Spree, 1702), 19.

143. The discovery was said to have been made by Werner, the Prussian representative in Warsaw; see Father Vota to Elector of Brandenburg, Warsaw, 15 May 1700, in Lehmann, *Preussen und die katholische Kirche*, 1:463.

144. Besser, *Preussische Krönungsgeschichte*, 3, 6.

145. Johann Christian Lünig, *Theatrum ceremoniale historico-politicum oder historisch-politischer Schau-Platz aller Ceremonien etc.*, 2 vols. (Leipzig, 1719–20), 2:100, 96. On the importance of the king's self-unction, see Hans Liermann, 'Sakralrecht des protestantischen Herrschers', *Zeitschrift der Savigny-Stiftung für Rechtsgeschichte* 61 (1941), 311–83, esp. 333–69.

Chapter 2. The Historian King

1. On the relationship between Bach and Frederick II, see Leta E. Miller, 'C.P.E. Bach's Sonatas for Solo Flute', *Journal of Musicology* 11.2 (1993), 203–49. These reflections on the king and his music are indebted to conversations with Kate Clark, Teacher of Historical Flutes and Lecturer in the Early Music Department of the Royal Conservatorium of The Hague; on Quantz's musical dominance at court, see Tim Blanning, *Frederick the Great. King of Prussia* (London, 2015), 150–52.

2. Charles Burney, *The Present State of Music in Germany, the Netherlands and United Provinces Or: The Journal of a Tour through Those Countries, Undertaken to Collect Materials for a General History of Music*, 2 vols. (London, 1773; repr., London 2008), 2:150–51.

3. On the king's attitude to Bach, see Blanning, *Frederick the Great*, 157–59.

4. Vanessa Agnew, *Enlightenment Orpheus: The Power of Music in Other Worlds* (Oxford, 2008), esp. 59.

5. On Frederick's relationship with the Berlin court, see Thomas Biskup, 'Eines "Grossen" würdig? Hof und Zeremoniell bei Friedrich II.', in *Friederisiko— Friedrich der Große. Die Essays* (Munich, 2012), 96–113; Biskup, *Friedrichs Größe. Inszenierungen des Preußenkönigs in Fest und Zeremoniell 1740–1815* (Frankfurt/Main, 2012); Biskup, 'Höfisches Retablissement: Der Hof Friedrichs des Großen nach 1763', in Michael Kaiser and Jürgen Luh (eds.), *Friedrich der Große—eine perspektivische Bestandsaufnahme. Beiträge des ersten Colloquiums in der Reihe "Friedrich300"*, http://www.perspectivia.net/publikationen /friedrich300-colloquien/friedrich-bestandsaufnahme/biskup_retablissement.

6. The *Histoire de la guerre de Sept Ans*, which included an introit on the years of peace between the Silesian and the Seven Years' War, was written in 1763–64. In 1775, Frederick completed an overview of events from the Peace of Hubertusburg (1763) to the end of the first partition of Poland (1775); this was subsequently reworked and combined with text fragments on the years 1774–48 and the War of the Bavarian Succession (1778). A further text fragment produced in 1784 covered the history of Brandenburg-Prussia since the Peace of Teschen (1779). The key works by Frederick II discussed in this chapter include 'Histoire de mon temps' (1746 and 1775), in Johann D. E. Preuss (ed.), *Œuvres de Frédéric le Grand*, 30 vols. (Berlin, 1846–56), 2:v–160 and 3:1–240; 'Histoire de le Guerre de Sept Ans', in Preuss, *Œuvres*, 4:v–296 and 5:1–264; 'Memoires depuis da Paix de Hubertsbourg 1763, jusqu'à la fin du partage de la Pologne',

in Preuss, *Œuvres*, 6:1–123; 'De ce qui s'est passé de plus important depuis l'année 1774 jusqu'à l'année 1778', in Preuss, *Œuvres*, 6:125–49; 'Memoires de la guerre de 1778', in Preuss, *Œuvres*, 6:151–201; 'Réflexions sur les talents militaires de Charles XII, roi de Suède', in Preuss, *Œuvres*, 7:79–101; 'De le literature Allemande, des defauts qu'on peut lui reprocher, quelles en sont les causes et par quels moyens on peut les corriger', in Preuss, *Œuvres*, 7:103–40; 'Avant-propos de l'extrait du dictionnaire historique et critique de Bayle', in Preuss, *Œuvres*, 7:141–47; 'Avant-propos de l'abrégé de l'histoire écclésiastique de Fleury', in Preuss, *Œuvres*, 7:149–64; 'L'Antimachiavel, ou examen du prince de Machiavel', in Preuss, *Œuvres*, 8:65–184; 'Réfutation du prince de Machiavel' (a reworked version of the same text), in Preuss, *Œuvres*, 8:185–336; 'Ode sur la gloire', in Preuss, *Œuvres*, 11:98–101; and 'Ode sur le temps', in Preuss, *Œuvres*, 12:1–3.

7. On Frederick's research methods and ambition to create an overarching work of narrative interpetation, see the essay 'Die historischen Werke' in Gustav Berthold Volz (ed.), *Die Werke Friedrichs des Grossen in deutscher Übersetzung*, 10 vols. (Berlin, 1913), vol. 1, 'Denkwürdigkeiten zur Geschichte des Hauses Brandenburg', trans. Friedrich von Oppeln-Bronikowski, Willi Rath, and Carl Werner von Jordans, v–xii, here vii; Max Posner, 'Zur literarischen Thätigkeit Friedrichs des Grossen. Erörterungen und Actenstücke', in Königliche Preussische Archiv-Verwaltung (ed.), *Miscellaneen zur Geschichte König Friedrich des Grossen* (Berlin, 1878), 205–494, esp. 217, 227–28, 236, passim; for an important recent discussion, see Michael Knobloch, '"Handlanger der Geschichtsschreibung". Friedrich II. Als Rezipient historischer Werke zur brandenburgischen Geschichte', in Brunhilde Wehinger and Günther Lottes (eds.), *Friedrich der Große als Leser* (Berlin, 2012), 43–70.

8. 'Die staatliche Existenz Preußens und den eigenen Standort näher zu bestimmen'; see Wilfried Herderhorst, *Zur Geschichtsschreibung Friedrichs des Großen*, Historisch-Politische Hefte der Ranke-Gesellschaft, 10 (Göttingen, 1962), 5.

9. Frederick II, Avant-Propos (1748) to the 'Mémoires pour servir à l'histoire de la maison de Brandebourg', in Preuss, *Œuvres*, 1:xliii–xliv, here xliii; on the relationship between the mid-eighteenth-century natural sciences and history, see Peter Hanns Reill, 'Die Historisierung von Natur und Mensch. Der Zusammenhang von Naturwissenschaften und historischem Denken im Entstehungsprozess der modernen Naturwissenschaften', in Küttler, Rüsen, and Schulin, *Geschichtsdiskurs*, 2:48–61, esp. 49–51, 58–59.

10. Frederick II, 'Discours Préliminaire' (1751), in Preuss, *Œuvres*, 1:xlv–lii, here xlv.

11. Ibid., 1:xlvii.

12. On the danger of reading Frederick's literary and political texts as 'Bekenntnisschriften' that express an inner state of mind in a straightforward way, see Andreas Pečar, 'Friedrich der Große als Autor. Plädoyer für eine adressatenorientierte Lektüre seiner Schriften', in Stiftung Preussische Schlösser

und Gärten (ed.), *Friedrich300*, www.perspectivia.net/content/publikationen /friedrich300-colloquien/friedrich-bestandsaufnahme/pecar_autor/.

13. Frederick II, 'Histoire de mon temps', 'Avant-Propos' (1746), in Preuss, *Œuvres*, 2:v–xii, here vii.

14. Frederick II, 'Histoire de mon temps', 'Avant-Propos' (1775), in Preuss, *Œuvres*, 3:xiii–xxiv, here xvii.

15. See, for example, Frederick II, 'Histoire de mon temps', 'Avant-Propos' (1746), in Preuss, *Œuvres*, 2:vii.

16. See Michael Rohrschneider, 'Friedrich der Grosse als Historiograph des Hauses Brandenburg. Herrscherideal, Selbststilisierung und Rechtfertigungstendenzen in den Mémoiren pour servir à l'histoire de la maison de Brandebourg', *Forschungen zur Brandenburgischen und Preußischen Geschichte* 17 (2007), 103–21; for discussions emphasising the reflective function of the historical texts, see also Herderhorst, *Zur Geschichtsschreibung*, 12–13 and 31; Horst Möller, 'Friedrich der Große und der Geist seiner Zeit', in Johannes Kunisch (ed.), *Analecta Fridericiana* (= Zeitschrift für historische Forschung Beih. 4) (Berlin, 1987), 55–74, esp. 61.

17. Jürgen Luh, *Der Große. Friedrich II. von Preußen* (Munich, 2011); on Churchill's determination to do the same, see David Reynolds, *In Command of History. Churchill Fighting and Writing the Second World War* (London, 2005).

18. Frederick II, 'Histoire de mon temps', 'Avant-Propos' (1746), in Preuss, *Œuvres*, 2:vii.

19. Ibid., 2:vii.

20. Frederick II, 'Avant-Propos' (1748) to the 'Mémoires pour servir à l'histoire de la maison de Brandebourg', in Preuss, *Œuvres*, 1:xliii–xliv, here xliv.

21. Frederick II, 'Réflexions sur les talents militaries et sur le caractère de Charles XII, Roi de Suède', Preuss, *Œuvres*, 7:79–105, here 81; 'Histoire de mon temps', 'Avant-Propos' (1775), in Preuss, *Œuvres*, 2:xiv.

22. Frederick II, 'Avant-Propos' (1775), 'Histoire de mon temps', in Preuss, *Œuvres*, 2:xiv.

23. On this essay as an act of politico-military instruction, see Sven Externbrink, 'Der Feldherr als Historiker. Friedrich der Große und die Histoire de la guerre de Sept Ans', in Wehinger and Lottes, *Friedrich der Große als Leser*, 99–120.

24. See Ulrich Muhlack, 'Geschichte und Geschichtsschreibung bei Voltaire and Friedrich dem Grossen', in Johannes Kunisch (ed.), *Persönlichkeiten im Umkreis Friedrichs des Großen* (Cologne, 1988), S29–57.

25. Frederick II, 'Avant-Propos' (1775), 'Histoire de mon temps', in Preuss, *Œuvres*, 2:xv.

26. Frederick II, 'Avant-Propos', 'Histoire de le guerre de sept ans', Preuss, *Œuvres*, 4:v–xii, here xi.

27. Johannes Kunisch, *Friedrich der Grosse. Der König und Seine Zeit* (Munich, 2004), 65–68; see also Rohrschneider, 'Friedrich der Grosse', 105; on the impact of the dysfunctional relationship with his father on the king's psyche, see Blanning, *Frederick the Great*, xxi–xxiv, 25–45.

28. Pečar, 'Friedrich der Große als Autor', 20–21; for other readings of Frederick's writings as acts of propagandistic manipulation or tools of foreign policy, see Friedrich Meinecke, 'Des Kronprinzen Friedrich Considérations sur l'état présent du corps politique de l'Europe', in Meinecke, *Brandenburg—Preußen—Deutschland. Kleine Schriften zur Geschichte und Politik*, ed. Eberhard Kessel (= Werke 9; Stuttgart 1979), 174–200; Reinhold Koser, *Geschichte Friedrichs des Großen*, 4 vols. (repr., Darmstadt, 1963), 1:145–50.

29. On the quest for 'useful truth' (*vérités utiles*) as the defining characteristic of a 'philosophical' as opposed to a merely 'historical' history, see Voltaire, *Essai sur les mœurs et sur l'esprit des nations*, vol. 1, Introduction, https://fr.wikisource.org/wiki/Essai_sur_les_mœurs/Introduction; on Frederick's interest in Montesquieu, see Georg Küntzel, 'Der junge Friedrich und die Anfänge seiner Geschichtsschreibung', in Unnamed students and colleagues (eds.), *Festgabe Friedrich von Bezold dargebracht zum 70. Geburtstag* (Bonn, 1921), 234–49, here 241–44.

30. For a fuller discussion of the relationship between the Mémoires and the Siècle, see Muhlack, 'Geschichte und Geschichtsschreibung', passim; Muhlack, *Geschichtswissenschaft im Humanismus und in der Aufklärung. Die Vorgeschichte des Historismus* (Munich, 1991), 258–68.

31. Möller, 'Friedrich der Große', 58; on the historical sensibility of the Prussian Enlightenment, see also Matt Erlin, *Berlin's Forgotten Future. City, History, and Enlightenment in Eighteenth-Century Germany* (Chapel Hill, NC, 2004).

32. Johann Martin Chladenius, *Einleitung zur richtigen Auslegung vernünftiger Schriften und Reden*, ed. Lutz Goldsetzer ([1742] Düsseldorf, 1969), 195; see also Frederick Beiser, *The German Historicist Tradition* (Oxford, 2011), 29, 40, 47–54; on enlightened perspective awareness in general, see Reinhard Koselleck, 'Standortbindung und Zeitlichkeit: Ein Beitrag zur historischen Eschließung der geschichtlichen Welt', in Koselleck, *Vergangene Zukunft*, 178–88.

33. Frederick II, 'Mémoires pour servir', Preuss, *Œuvres*, 1:241.

34. Frederick II, 'Avant-Propos de l'abrégé de l'Histoire écclésiastique de Fleury', Preuss, *Œuvres*, 7:149–64, here 151–53; for Preuss's comments on the publication and impact of this work, see his 'Avertissment', xiv–xv. David Friedrich Strauss would later incorporate the same line of argument into his critique of 'myth' in *Das Leben Jesu kritisch bearbeitet*, 2 vols. (Tübingen, 1835), 1:173–77.

35. Frederick II, 'Mémoires pour servir', Preuss, *Œuvres*, 1:14.

36. Ibid., 1:244.

37. Frederick II, 'Discours Preliminaire' (1751), Mémoires, Preuss, *Œuvres*, 1:xlv–lii, here xlvii–xlviii. On Christoph Hartknoch (1644–87), author of celebrated histories of Prussia (meaning Ducal and Royal Prussia), see below.

38. Frederick II, 'Des moeurs, des coutumes, de l'industrie, des progrès de l'esprit humain dans les arts et dans les sciences' (supplementary chapter of Mémoires), in Preuss, *Œuvres*, 1:264.

39. On the disregard for Pufendorf, see Notker Hammerstein, 'Reichshistorie', in Hans Erich Bödeker, Georg G. Iggers, Jonathan B. Knudsen, and

Peter H. Reill (eds.), *Aufklärung und Geschichte. Studien zur deutschen Geschichtswissenschaft im 18. Jahrhundert* (Göttingen, 1986), 82–104; on the valorisation of philosophical history and the denigration of 'erudition', see Henning Wrede, 'Die Entstehung der Archäologie und des Einsetzen der neuzeitlichen Geschichtsbetrachtung', in Küttler, Rüsen, and Schulin, *Geschichtsdiskurs*, 2:95–119, 99; Ursula Goldenmann, 'Die philosophische Methodendiskussion des 17. Jahrhunderts in ihrer Bedeutung für den Mondernisierungsschub in der Historiographie', in Küttler, Rüsen, and Schulin, *Geschichtsdiskurs*, 2:148–61, here 148–49.

40. Posner, 'Zur literarischen Thätigkeit Friedrichs des Grossen', 238–39; among the works by Hartknoch available in German when Frederick was composing the memoires are *Preussische Kirchen-historia: darinnen von Einführung der christlichen Religion in diese Lande / wie auch von der Conservation, Fortpflantzung / Reformation und dem heutigen Zustande derselben Ausführlich gehandelt wird. Nebst vielen denckwürdigen Begebenheiten . . . aus vielen gedruckten und geschriebenen Documenten* (Frankfurt/Main and Leipzig, 1686) and *Alt- und Neues Preussen Oder Preussischer Historien Zwey Theile* (Frankfurt/Main and Leipzig, 1684).

41. Loccelius, *Marchia Illustrata*, 609, 611, 635, 639, 647, 702, 711, 753, 762, 808, 846–49, 861.

42. Jaroslav Miller, *Urban Societies in East Central Europe, 1500–1700*, 2nd ed. (Abingdon, 2016), 167; on Hartknoch as a historian and propagandist of Prussian liberty, see Karin Friedrich, *The Other Prussia. Royal Prussia, Poland and Liberty, 1569–1772* (Cambridge, 2000), esp. 103–5.

43. Hartknoch, *Alt- und Neues Preussen*, pt. 1, 232.

44. Ibid., pt. 1, 238.

45. Ibid., pt. 2, 309–12, 314–15, passim.

46. See Friedrich, *Other Prussia*, 51, 70, 79.

47. Frederick II, 'Du Gouvernement ancien et moderne de Brandebourg', supplementary chapter to Mémoires, in Preuss, *Œuvres*, 1:275–76.

48. Even Voltaire was struck by the hostility of the king's account of Schwarzenberg, which he felt was not justified by the evidence provided in the text; see the transcription of Voltaire's notes on Frederick's *Mémoires* in Posner, 'Zur literarischen Thätigkeit Friedrich des Grossen', 273.

49. See, for example, Hartknoch, *Alt- und Neues Preussen*, esp. the chapter titled 'Von der Republic und Regierungs-Art der Lande Preussen', 601–65, which traces the history of the lands of Ducal and Royal Prussia as a history of political argument and competing corporate interests.

50. Voltaire, *Henriade. An Epick Poem in Ten Cantos*, trans. anon. (London, 1732), canto 6, 120; see also canto 3, 61; on Frederick's admiration for this and other works by Voltaire, see Blanning, *Frederick the Great*, 119–20, 329–30.

51. Voltaire, *Le Siècle de Louis XIV* (London, 1752), vol. 1, introduction, 4, and see also 319: 'plus le service en tout genre prévaut sur les titres, plus un état est florissant'.

52. On 'corporate latency', see Wolfgang Neugebauer, *Politischer Wandel im Osten. Ost- und Westpreussen von den alten Ständen zum Konstitutionalismus* (Stuttgart, 1992), 65–86.

53. Hanna Schissler, *Preussische Agrargesellschaft im Wandel. Wirtshcaftliche, gesellschaftliche und politische Transformationsprozesse von 1763 bis 1847* (Göttingen, 1978), 217; Johannes Ziekursch, *Hundert Jahre Schlesischer Agrargeschichte* (Breslau, 1915), 23–26; Robert Berdahl, *The Politics of the Prussian Nobility. The Development of a Conservative Ideology 1770-1848* (Princeton, NJ, 1988), 80–85; on the presence of non-noble landowners in the district assemblies (Kreistage) of the Mark Brandenburg, see Klaus Vetter, 'Zusammensetzung, Function und politische Bedeutung der kurmärkischen Kreistage im 18. Jh', *Jahrbuch für die Geschichte des Feudalismus* 3 (1979), 393–416; Peter Baumgart, 'Zur Geschichte der kurmärkischen Stände im 17. und 18. Jh', in Dieter Gerhard (ed.), *Ständische Vertretungen in Europe im 17. u. 18. Jahrhundert* (Göttingen, 1969), 131–61.

54. T.C.W. Blanning, 'Frederick the Great', in H. M. Scott, ed., *Enlightened Absolutism* (Basingstoke, 1990), 265–88.

55. On the king's awareness of his aristocratic corporate status, see Luh, *Der Große*, 170–74.

56. Gustavo Corni, *Stato assoluto e società agraria in Prussia nell'età di Federico II* (=Annali dell'Istituto storico italo-germanico, 4; Bologna, 1982), 283–84, 288, 292, 299–300.

57. Edgar Melton, 'The Prussian Junkers, 1600–1786', in H. M. Scott (ed.), *The European Nobilities in the Seventeenth and Eighteenth Centuries*, 2 vols. (London 1995), vol. 2, Northern, Central and Eastern Europe, 71–109, here 72; Hanna Schissler, 'The Junkers: Notes on the Social and Historical Significance of the Agrarian Elite in Prussia', in Robert G. Moeller (ed.), *Peasants and Lords in Modern Germany. Recent Studies in Agricultural History* (Boston, 1986), 24–51; Berdahl, *Politics*, 79; Schissler, *Preussische Agrargesellschaft*, esp. 217.

58. Frederick II, 'Mémoires depuis la paix de Hubertusbourg 1763, jusqu'à la fin du partage de la Pologne, 1775', in Preuss, *Œuvres*, 6:90.

59. On the 'second reign', see H. M. Scott, '1763–1786: The Second Reign of Frederick the Great', in Philip Dwyer (ed.), *The Rise of Prussia 1700-1830* (London, 2000), 177–200.

60. Frederick II, 'Lettres sur l'amour de la patrie, ou correspondence d'Anapistémon et de Philopatros', in Preuss, *Œuvres*, 9:241–78, here 246–47.

61. This passage is discussed in Adolf Dock, *Der Souveränetätsbegriff von Bodin bis zu Friedrich dem Grossen* (Strasbourg, 1897), 148.

62. 'Dans tous le recueils immenses qu'on ne peut embrasser, il faut se borner et choisir. C'est un vaste magasin où vous prendrez ce qui est à votre usage'. Voltaire, *Essai sur les mœurs et l'esprit des nations et sur les principaux faits de l'histoire depuis Charlemagne jusqu'à Louis XIII*, ed. René Pomeau, 2 vols. (Paris, 1963), 1:196.

63. Frederick II, Mémoires, in Preuss, *Œuvres*, 1:244.

64. Muhlack, *Geschichtswissenschaft im Humanismus und in der Aufklärung*, 266–67.

65. Schindele, 'Friedrich der Große über den Staat', in *Abhandlungen aus dem Gebiete der Philosophie und ihrer Geschichte. Eine Festgabe zum 70. Geburtstag Georg Freiherrn von Hertling* (Freiburg i. Breisgau, 1913), 289–308, here 291–92.

66. Frederick II, 'Mémoires pour servir', Preuss, *Œuvres*, 1:272.

67. Frederick II, 'Histoire de mon temps', in Preuss, *Œuvres*, 2:38.

68. Frederick II, 'Mémoires pour servir', in Preuss, *Œuvres*, 1:272–73.

69. Frederick II, *The Refutation of Machiavelli's Prince, or: Anti-Machiavel*, ed. and trans. Paul Sonnino (Athens, OH, 1981), 40.

70. Ibid., 41.

71. Ibid., 43.

72. Ibid., 4–5.

73. Frederick II, 'Instruction for Major Count Borcke (24 September 1751)', in Preuss, *Œuvres*, 9:35–40, here 37.

74. Frederick II, *Der Antimachiavell*, 47.

75. Ibid., 38.

76. Frederick II, 'The Political Testament of 1752', in Adolph von Menze (ed.), *Die Werke Friedrichs des Großen in deutscher Übersetzung*, 10 vols. (1913), in Gustav Berthold Volz (ed.), vol. 7, *Antimachiavell und Testamente*, trans. Eberhard König, Friedrich v. Oppeln Bronikowski, and Willy Rath (Berlin, 1913), 136, 137, 138, 140.

77. Ibid., 153.

78. Ibid., 160.

79. Ibid., 161.

80. Ibid., 165.

81. Norman Bryson, 'Watteau and "Reverie": A Case Test in "Combined Analysis"', *Eighteenth Century* 22 (1981), 97–126, here 109.

82. On Frederick's acquisition of this painting and its place in his collections, see Stiftung Preussischer Schlösser und Gärten (ed.), *Bestandskataloge der Kunstsammlungen. Französische Gemälde I. Watteau, Pater, Lancret, Lajoue* (Berlin, 2011), 702–8 and 754.

83. René Huyghe, 'L'Univers de Watteau', in Hélène Adhémar, *Watteau: sa vie, son œuvre. Catalogue des peintures et illustration* (Paris, 1950), 1–46, here 1.

84. Anne Claude Caylus, *La Vie de Antoine Watteau par le Comte de Caylus, publiée pour la première fois d'après l'autographe*, ed. Charles Henry (Paris, 1887), 41–42.

85. Thomas M. Kavanagh, *Esthetics of the Moment. Literature and Art in the French Enlightenment* (Philadelphia, 1996) 169.

86. Frederick to Jordan, 2 February 1742, in Johann D. E. Preuss (ed.), *Oeuvres de Frédéric le Grand*, 31 vols. (1846–56), 17:163, http://friedrich.uni-trier.de /oeuvres/17/163/text/.

87. Frederick, poem sent to Jordan, July 1742 in Preuss, *Oeuvres*, vol. 18, Correspondance de Frédéric avec le comte Algarott, 58, http://friedrich.uni -trier.de/de/oeuvres/18/58/text/:

Ton esprit me transporte en une galerie
Où des plus précieux tableaux
Le spectacle enchanteur sans cesse se varie,
Où les derniers sont les plus beaux,
Où Corrége et Poussin étalent leur génie
Avec les Lancrets, les Watteaux.

On Frederick's ode to the orgasm, see Vanessa de Senarclens, 'Friedrichs Schossgebet', *Die Zeit*, 15 September 2011, 21; also Blanning, *Frederick the Great*, 68–69.

88. Frederick to Amélie of Prussia, Meissen, 15 April 1761, in Frederick the Great et al., *Politische Korrespondenz Friedrich's des Großen*, ed. Johann Gustav Droysen et al., 40 vols. (Berlin, 1879–1939), 20:336–37, http://friedrich.uni-trier .de/de/politKorr/20/336/text/.

89. Astrid Dostert, 'Friedrich der Große als Sammler antiker Skulptur', in Stiftung Preussische Schlösser und Gärten (ed.), *Friedrich300*, http://www .perspectivia.net/content/publikationen/friedrich300-colloquien/friedrich -bestandsaufnahme/pecar_autor/; on the evolution of Frederick's collection, and his insistence that it be made known to the public, see Blanning, *Frederick the Great*, 170–73.

90. On the king's continuing interest in paintings in the *fêtes galantes* tradition, even after the Seven Years' War and their prominence in his private rooms, see Christoph Martin Vogtherr, 'Friedrich II als Sammler von Fêtes galantes. Zur Geschichte der Sammlung im 18. Jahrhundert', in Stiftung Preussischer Schlösser und Gärten, *Bestandskataloge der Kunstsammlungen*, 3–20, here 8, 12–15.

91. Vogtherr, 'Friedrich II als Sammler', 15.

92. Frederick II, 'Ode sur le Temps', in Preuss, *Œuvres*, 12:1–3.

93. Record of a conversation in May 1758, in Henri de Catt, *Unterhaltungen mit Friedrich dem Großen*, ed. Reinhold Koser (Leipzig, 1884), 60–61.

94. Conversation of April–June 1760, in Catt, *Unterhaltungen*, 314.

95. Gregor Vogt-Spira, 'Das antike Rom im geistigen Haushalt eines Königs', in Bernd Sösemann and Gregor Vogt-Spira (eds.), *Friedrich der Grosse in Europa. Geschichte einer wechselvollen Beziehung*, 2 vols. (Frankfurt, 2012), 1:128–29.

96. Friedrich to Voltaire, 7 April 1737; Voltaire to Frederick, 27 May 1737; Friedrich to Voltaire, 6 July 1737, in Reinhold Koser and Hans Droysen (eds.), *Briefwechsel Friedrichs des Großen mit Voltaire*, 3 vols. (Leipzig, 1908–11), 1:49, 61–64, 67–68.

97. Frederick to Grumbkow, 26 January 1732, cited in Ulrich Sachse, 'Groß im Tod sein. Friedrichs des Großen erste Verfügung zur Inszenierung seines Nachlebens', in Stiftung Preussische Schlösser und Gärten (ed.), *Friedrich300*,

http://www.perspectivia.net/content/publikationen/friedrich300-colloquien
/friedrich-bestandsaufnahme/pecar_autor; see also Ullrich Sachse, *Cäsar in
Sanssouci. Die Politik Friedrichs des Großen und die Antike* (Munich, 2008),
esp. 191–221.

98. Blanning, *Frederick the Great*, 444.

99. Frederick II to Cabinet Minister von Podewils, March 1741, in Volz,
Antimachiavell und Testamente [= vol. 7 of Menze, *Die Werke Friedrichs des
Großen*], 237.

100. Andreas Pečar, 'Regelbruch als Markenzeichen', in Stiftung Preussische Schlösser und Gärten (ed.), *Friedrich300*, http://www.perspectivia
.net/publikationen/friedrich300-colloquien/friedrich_repraesentation/pecar
_regelbruch/#sdfootnote1anc.

101. Horace, *Carmina*, 2.6 (my translation): ver ubi longum tepidasque
praebet / Iuppiter brumas et amicus Aulon / fertili Baccho minimum Falernis /
invidet uvis Ille te mecum locus et beatae / postulant arces: ibi tu calentem /
debita sparges lacrima favillam / vatis amici. On the relevance of this passage
to Frederick's burial plans, see Sachse, 'Groß im Tod sein'. On Horace as one of
Frederick's favourite authors, see Blanning, *Frederick the Great*, 50.

102. Luh, *Der Große*, passim.

103. Frederick II, Ode sur la Gloire (1734), in Preuss, *Œuvres*, 11:98–101,
here 98 and 100.

104. Ibid., 100.

105. Pečar, 'Regelbruch als Markenzeichen'.

106. Friedrich Nicolai, *Anekdoten von König Friedrich dem Zweiten von
Preußen* (Berlin and Stettin, 1788–92; repr., Hildesheim, 1985) (= Friedrich
Nicolai, *Gesammelte Werke*, ed. Bernhard Fabian and Marie-Luise Spiecker-
mann, vol. 7 [Hildesheim, 1985]), i–xvii.

107. On these aspects of anecdote more generally, see Volker Weber, *Anekdote. Die andere Geschichte. Erscheinungsformen der Anekdote in der deutschen
Literatur, Geschichtsschreibung und Philosophie* (Tübingen, 1993), 25, 48, 59,
60, 62–65, 66.

108. Judith Butler, *The Psychic Life of Power* (Stanford, CA, 1997), 2.

109. For analogical reflections on the oedipal dimension of power in the
writings of Kafka, see Gilles Deleuze and Félix Guattari, *Kafka: Pour une littéra-
ture mineure* (Paris, 1975).

110. The Temple of Friendship at the western end of the park at Sanssouci
was decorated with statues of lovers from classical antiquity: Orestes and
Pylades, Nisus and Euryalus, Heracles and Philoctetes, and Theseus and Pir-
ithous; on homoerotic themes in the art and statuary around the king, see Blanning, *Frederick the Great*, 175–80.

111. David Shuttleton, 'The Queer Politics of Gay Pastoral', in Richard Phillips, Diane Watt, and David Shuttleton (eds.), *De-centring Sexualities: Politics
and Representations beyond the Metropolis* (London, 2000), 125–46, here 128;
Byrne Fone, 'This Other Eden: Arcadia and the Homosexual Imagination', *Jour-*

nal of Homsexuality 8 (1983), 13–34; for an overview of texts in this tradition, see Rictor Norton, 'The Homosexual Pastoral Tradition', http://rictornorton. co.uk/pastor01.htm.

112. On 'queer temporality' more generally, see Jodie Taylor, 'Queer Temporalities and the Significance of "Music Scene" Participation in the Social Identity of Middle-Aged Queers', *Sociology* 44 (2010), 893–907, here 894; Judith Halberstam, *In a Queer Time and Place. Transgender Bodies, Subcultural Lives* (New York, 2005), esp. chap. 1, 1–21; Carolyn Dinshaw, Lee Edelman, Roderick A. Ferguson, Carla Freccero, Elizabeth Freeman, Judith Halberstam, Annamarie Jagose, Christopher Nealon, and Nguyen Tan Hoang, 'Theorizing Queer Temporalities: A Roundtable Discussion', https://blogs.commons.georgetown.edu /modernities-working-group/files/2015/08/TheorizingQueerTemporalities GLQ.pdf.

113. On the contrast between the developmental character of domestic political narratives and the 'sameness and repetition' characteristic of realist understandings of international relations, see Kimberly Hutchings, *Time and World Politics. Thinking the Present* (Manchester, 2008), 13.

114. Muhlack, *Geschichtswissenschaft im Humanismus und in der Aufklärung*, 268.

115. Frederick II, 'Histoire de mon temps', Preuss, *Œuvres*, 2:20.

116. Ibid., 2:29, where the monarch in question is wrongly identified as August II; German trans. in Volz, *Werke Friedrichs*, 2:37.

Chapter 3. Boatman on the River of Time

1. Bismarck to Luitgard von Puttkamer, 5 February 1852, cited in Hans Rothfels (ed.), *Bismarck-Briefe* (Göttingen, 1955), 163–165, here 165.

2. For a lyrical discussion of this theme, see Pflanze's reflection on 'The Stream of Time' in Otto Pflanze, *Bismarck and the Development of Germany. The Period of Unification, 1815–1871* (Princeton, NJ, 1963), 17–48; for a list of passages in which Bismarck employs the stream of time metaphor, see Hellmut Seier, 'Bismarck und der "Strom der Zeit". Drei neue Biographien und ein Tagungsband', *Historische Zeitschrift* 256.3 (1993), 689–709. For the contemporary resonance of the metaphor, see, for example, the best-selling digest by Fedor von Köppen, *Fürst Bismarck, der Deutsche Reichskanzler* (Berlin and Heidelberg, 1889), the eighth chapter of which, dedicated to the year revolution, bears the title 'Im Strom der Zeit'.

3. 'Die Geschichte ist dann nicht mehr bloß eine Beispielsammlung, sondern der einzige Weg zur wahren Erkenntnis unseres eigenen Zustandes'. Friedrich Carl von Savigny, 'Über den Zweck dieser Zeitschrift', *Zeitschrift für geschichtliche Rechtswissenschaft* 1 (1815), 4, http://www.gleichsatz.de/b-u-t/can /rec/savigny.html.

4. Leopold von Ranke, *Geschichte und Politik. Friedrich der Große, Politisches Gespräch und andere Meisterschriften*, ed. Hans Hofmann (Leipzig, 1868), 136–37.

5. On Ranke's belief, despite his insistence on the centrality of individuals and particularities, that the historians must always grasp 'the universality inherent in the particular', see Beiser, *German Historicist Tradition*, 260.

6. Beiser, *German Historicist Tradition*, 2.

7. Ernst Troeltsch, *Der Historismus und seine Probleme. Erstes Buch: Das logische Problem der Geschichtsphilosophie (1922)*, ed. Friedrich Wilhelm Graf (Berlin, 2008), 228.

8. *Zwischen Berlin und Rom*, satirical engraving by Wilhelm Scholz in *Kladderadatsch*, 16 May 1875, 92. Note that the artist has—presumably in error—reversed the order of the black-and-white squares on the board (the left-most squares for both players should be black).

9. Margaret Connolly, 'Chaucer and Chess', *Chaucer Review* 29.1 (1994), 40–44, here 43; Mark N. Taylor, 'Chaucer's Knowledge of Chess', *Chaucer Review* 38.4 (2004), 299–313, esp. 299–301 and 304–5; Guillemette Bolens and Paul Beckman Taylor, 'The Game of Chess in Chaucer's "Book of the Duchess"', *Chaucer Review* 32.4 (1988), 325–34.

10. William Poole, 'False Play: Shakespeare and Chess', *Shakespeare Quarterly* 55.1 (2004), 50–70, here 50–51, 53; on chess as an accoutrement of courtly culture, see also Olivia Remie Constable, 'Chess and Courtly Culture in Medieval Castile: The "Libro de ajedrez" of Alfonso X, el Sabio', *Speculum* 82.2 (2007), 301–47. For an overview, see Jenny Adams, *Power Play. The Literature and Politics of Chess in the Late Middle Ages* (Philadelphia, 2006).

11. On the sixteenth- and seventeenth-century meanings of chess, see Robin O'Bryan, 'A Duke, a Dwarf and a Game of Chess', *Source: Notes in the History of Art* 34.2 (2015), 27–33; Richard A. Davies and Alan R. Young, '"Strange Cunning" in Thomas Middleton's *A Game at Chess*', *University of Toronto Quarterly* 45.3 (1976), 236–45; Paul Yachnin, '*A Game at Chess* and Chess Allegory', *Studies in English Literature, 1500–1900* 22.2 (1982), 317–30; Neil Taylor and Brian Loughrey, 'Middleton's Chess Strategies in *Women Beware Women*', *Studies in English Literature, 1500–1900* 24.2 (1984), 341–54; Margot Heinemann, 'Middleton's "A Game at Chess": Parliamentary-Puritans and Opposition Drama', *English Literary Renaissance* 5.2 (1975), 232–50; on nineteenth-century resonances of the game, William Hauptman, 'Thomas Eakins's *The Chess Players* Replayed', *Metropolitan Museum Journal* 47.1 (2012), 149–68, esp. 158–59; Michael Clapper, 'Thomas Eakins and *The Chess Players*', *American Art* 24.3 (2010), 78–99.

12. Edwyn Anthony, 'The Inexhaustibility of Chess', *Chess Player's Chronicle*, New Series 2 (1878), 193–96. Anthony's estimate has since been extensively discussed and critiqued by mathematicians of chess; see, for example, Karl Fabel, 'X = 169518829100544000000000000000000?', *Die Schwalbe* 5 (1968), 55–56, which proposed a downward revision of Antony's total to 10^{29}.

13. Lewis Carroll, *Through the Looking Glass and What Alice Found There* (London, 1872), 39.

14. William Steinitz, *The Modern Chess Instructor* (New York, 1889), xxvii.

15. Carroll, *Through the Looking Glass*, 95.

16. Steinitz, *Modern Chess Instructor*, xxx.

17. William Steinitz, *The Steinitz Papers. Letters and Documents of the First World Chess Champion*, ed. Kurt Landsberger (Jefferson, NC, 2002), 152, 190; on Steinitz's openings, see Richard Réti, *Modern Ideas in Chess* (Milford, CT, 2009), 28.

18. On Steinitz as 'the greatest representative of the scientific tendency in chess', see Réti, *Modern Ideas*, 27.

19. Emanuel Lasker, *Lasker's Manual of Chess* (London, 1932), 255. The original German edition appeared in 1925.

20. Edmund Bruns, *Das Schachspiel als Phänomen der Kulturgeschichte des 19. Und 20. Jahrhunderts* (Münster, 2003), 42–43.

21. Oliver Kohns, 'Fiktionen politischer Existenz: Skizze zum Politiker als Schriftsteller: Bismarck, Disraeli, Goebbels', in Patrick Ramponi and Saski Viedler (eds.), *Dichter und Lenker. Die Literatur der Staatsmänner, Päpste und Despoten von der frühen Neuzeit bis in die Gegenwart* (Tübingen, 2014), 49–72, here 61–62; chess was frequently employed as a metaphor for politics in the German press of the Bismarck era: for examples in Kladderadatsch, see 'Der Baron von Strudelwitz an den Baron von Prudelwitz', *Kladderadatsch* 16 (15 November 1863), 210; 'Ein gewagter Zug', *Kladderadatsch* 20 (3 November 1867) and 'Vom Schach-Congress', *Kladderadatsch* 34 (11 September 1881), 168; 'Schreiben des Barons von Prudelwitz an den Baron von Strudelnitz', *Kladderadatsch* 37 (17 August 1884), 147. A search of the Austrian National Library's online historical press archive, ANNO Historische österreichische Zeitungen und Zeitschriften, reveals a sharp rise during the later 1850s and 1860s in the use of the term *Schachzug* (denoting a move in chess); an analysis of the individual occurrences reveals that the term is almost always used as a political metaphor, denoting a strategic or tactical initiative. There is only one occurrence in the years 1837 and 1848 and none at all in any of the other years between 1800 and 1850. http://anno.onb.ac.at/anno-suche/#searchMode=simple&resultMode=list&from=1. Sadly, a comparable digital library of nineteenth-century German periodicals does not exist.

22. Morier to Russell, 2 September 1870, cited in Thomas Otte, *The Foreign Office Mind. The Making of British Foreign Policy, 1865–1914* (Cambridge, 2011) 72; for a discussion of this passage, see Jonathan Steinberg, *Bismarck. A Life* (Oxford, 2011), 128.

23. [Horst Kohl], 'Die gewonnene Partie. Ein orientalisches Märchen', *Kladderadatsch*, 4 March 1866, 1; for Kohl's later explanation, see Horst Kohl, *Bismarck-Gedichte des Kladderadatsch mit Erläuterungen herausgegeben* (Berlin, 1894), 63–64.

24. Cited in Steinberg, *Bismarck*, 445. On Bismarck's flirtations with a coup d'état, see Michael Stürmer, 'Staatsstreichgedanken im Bismarckreich', *Historische Zeitschrift* 209 (1969), 566–615; specifically on the terminal crisis of his career: John C. G. Röhl, 'Staatsstreichplan oder Staatsstreichbereitschaft?

Bismarcks Politik in der Entlasssungskrise', *Historische Zeitschrift* 203 (1966), 610–24.

25. Otto von Bismarck, *Gedanken und Erinnerungen*, 3 vols. (Stuttgart, 1898), 1:228.

26. Ibid., 1:314.

27. Ibid., 1:331 (in reference to Bismarck's conflict with the Austrian minister Rechberg at Frankfurt); ibid., 1:340 (in reference to the King of Saxony's unexpected support for the Congress of Princes in Frankfurt); ibid., 2:56 (in reference to the need to measure the utility of 'chess moves' in domestic politics by their impact on Prussia's external reputation); ibid., 2:165 (in reference to the foundation of the Old Catholic Church in Prussia as a means of weakening the influence of the Roman curia); ibid., 2:197 (in reference to the manoeuvres of his political enemies in 1878–79). For examples from the correspondence, see, for example, Bismarck to Count Reuß, Berlin, 28 February 1874, in Rainer Bendick (ed.), *Schriften, 1874–1876* (=Konrad Canis, Lothar Gall, Klaus Hildebrand, and Eberhard Kolb [eds.], *Otto von Bismarck, Gesammelte Werke. Neue Friedrichsruher Ausgabe*, Abteilung III, vol. 2) (Paderborn, 2005), nr. 76, 119 (expressing concern that the Austrians will use France as a 'piece to be turned against us on the chessboard'); Bismarck to Stroßenreuter, Berlin, 10 December 1874, in ibid., nr. 157, 229 (in reference to the manoeuvres of the Centre Party); Bismarck to Bülow, Varzin, 17 October 1876 (in reference to Anglo-Turkish policy vis-à-vis Russia) in ibid., nr. 420, 615–16; Bismarck to Bülow, Friedrichsruh, 23 April 1877, in Michael Epkenhans and Erik Lommatzsch (eds.), *Schriften, 1877–1878* (=Konrad Canis, Lothar Gall, Klaus Hildebrand, and Eberhard Kolb [eds.], *Otto von Bismarck, Gesammelte Werke. Neue Friedrichsruher Ausgabe*, Abteilung III, vol. 3) (Paderborn, 2008), nr. 58, 88 (in reference to English policy vis-à-vis Russia); Bismarck to Bülow, ibid., nr. 311, 375 (in reference to Austrian foreign policy); Bismarck to Stolberg, Gastein, 28 August 1878 (in reference to actions by the Ministry of Justice); see also Bismarck to Reuß, Varzin, 22 January 1880 in ibid., nr. 184, 294; Bismarck to Reuß, Berlin, 11 February 1880, in ibid., nr. 205, 331; Bismarck to Crown Prince Frederick William, Varzin, 7 September 1882, nr. 187, 236 in Ulrich Lappenküper (ed.), *Schriften, 1882–1883* (=Konrad Canis, Lothar Gall, Klaus Hildebrand, and Eberhard Kolb [eds.], *Otto von Bismarck, Gesammelte Werke. Neue Friedrichsruher Ausgabe*, Abteilung III, vol. 5) (Paderborn, 2010); Bismarck to Schlözer, Berlin, 22 December 1882, in ibid., nr. 253, 314, passim.

28. Bismarck to Gerlach, 2 May 1860, cited in Pflanze, *Bismarck and the Development of Germany*, 134; for a discussion of this letter see also Steinberg, *Bismarck*, 133.

29. Bismarck, *Gedanken und Erinnerungen*, 2:44.

30. Bismarck to Gerlach, 21 May 1857, transcribed in Bismarck, *Gedanken und Erinnerungen*, 1:171.

31. Bismarck, *Gedanken und Erinnerungen*, 1:19–20.

32. Ibid., 1:25.

33. Bismarck discusses this speech in his memoirs; see ibid., 1:32. The text is in Horst Kohl (ed.), *Die politischen Reden des Fürsten Bismarck 1847–1897*, 14 vols. (Stuttgart, 1892–1895: vol. 1, Stuttgart 1895), 45–46. For a discussion, see Lothar Gall, *Bismarck: Der weisse Revolutionär* (Frankfurt/Main, 1908), 74–75; Ernst Engelberg, *Bismarck: Urpreuße und Reichsgründer* (Berlin, 1985), 280.

34. Heinz Wolter, 'Bismarck und das Problem der Revolution im 19. Jahrhundert', in Johannes Kunisch (ed.), *Bismarck und seine Zeit. Forschungen zur Brandenburgischen und Preussischen Geschichte, Beiheft 1* (Berlin, 1992), 191–204, here 194.

35. Bismarck claimed to have posted the article to a newspaper between the Second United Diet and the elections to the National Assembly, but was unable to remember to which newspaper he had sent it. Bismarck, *Gedanken und Erinnerungen*, 1:36; the version Bismarck used to write this passage of his memoirs was still in draft, so the article may never actually have been published; on this, see Engelberg, *Bismarck*, 283.

36. Carl Schmitt, *Verfassungslehre* (Munich, 1928), 53–54; for an insightful discussion, see Hans-Christof Kraus, 'Ursprung und Genese der "Lückentheorie" im preußischen Verfassungskonflikt', *Der Staat* 29.2 (1990), 209–34.

37. Günther Grünthal, *Parlamentarismus in Preussen 1848/49–1857/58. Preussischer Konstitutionalismus, Parlament und Regierung in der Reaktionsära* (Düsseldorf, 1982), 44, 114–15, 118–25.

38. Art. 98: [1] Alle Einnahmen und Ausgaben des Staats müssen für jedes Jahr im Voraus veranschlagt und auf den Staatshaushalts-Etat gebracht werden. [2] Letzterer wird jährlich durch ein Gesetz festgestellt. Art. 60: [1] Die gesetzgebende Gewalt wird gemeinschaftlich durch den König und durch zwei Kammern ausgeübt. [2] Die Übereinstimmung des Königs und beider Kammern ist zu jedem Gesetze erforderlich, *Verfassungsurkunde für den preußischen Staat vom 5. Dezember 1848*, http://www.documentarchiv.de/nzjh /verfpr1848.html.

39. Art. 108: Die bestehenden Steuern und Abgaben werden forterhoben, und alle Bestimmungen der bestehenden Gesetzbücher, einzelnen Gesetze und Verordnungen, welche der gegenwärtigen Verfassung nicht zuwiderlaufen, bleiben in Kraft, bis sie durch ein Gesetz abgeändert werden. The classical discussion of this problem is Grünthal, *Parlamentarismus in Preussen*, 126–28.

40. Otto von Bismarck, *Die Gesammelten Werke*, 15 vols. (Berlin, 1924–32), 10:44, cited in Kraus, 'Ursprung und Genese', 216.

41. Hans Rothfels, *Bismarck und der Staat. Ausgewählte Dokumente* (Stuttgart, 1925), xxiii.

42. The Nachmärz, or post-March, refers to the aftermath of the revolutions, which broke out in the 'March Days' of 1848; on the significance of this term as an epochal rubric, see Thomas Koebner and Sigrid Weigel (eds.), *Nachmärz. Der Ursprung der ästhetischen Moderne in einer nachrevolutionären Konstellation* (Opladen, 1996); Norbert Otto Eke and Renate Werner (eds.), *Vormärz—Nachmärz. Bruch oder Kontinuität?* (Bielefeld, 2000).

43. Grünthal, *Parlamentarismus in Preussen*, 476.

44. Anna Ross, 'Post-revolutionary Politics in Prussia, 1848–1858' (PhD thesis, Cambridge, 2014), passim, and now *Beyond the Barricades: Government and State-Building in Post-Revolutionary Prussia, 1848–58* (Oxford, 2018).

45. On the instabilities of Prussian high politics after 1848, see David Barclay, *Frederick William IV and the Prussian Monarchy, 1840–1861* (Oxford, 1995), 252–55.

46. Gerlach to Bismarck, 20 June 1853, reported by Bismarck in *Gedanken und Erinnerungen*, 1:143.

47. Barclay, *Frederick William IV*, 262, Kurt Wappler, *Regierung und Presse. Geschichte der amtlichen preussischen Pressestellen, 1848–1862* (Leipzig, 1935), 3–4, 16–17.

48. On the mid-nineteenth-century transition from censorship to news management in the German states, see Abigail Green, *Fatherlands. Statebuilding and Nationhood in Nineteenth-Century Germany* (Cambridge, 2001), 148–88.

49. Manteuffel to Rochow, 3 July 1851, cited in Wappler, *Regierung und Presse*, 91.

50. Heinrich von Poschinger, *Unter Friedrich Wilhelm IV: Denkwürdigkeiten des Ministers Otto Freiherrn von Manteuffel*, 3 vols. (Berlin, 1901), 1:133–34.

51. On Bismarck's handling of the press, see Irene Fischer-Frauendienst, *Bismarcks Pressepolitik* (= Studien zur Publizistik. Bremer Reihe, Deutsche Presseforschung, vol. 4) (Münster, 1963); Robert H. Keyserlingk, *Media Manipulation. The Press and Bismarck in Imperial Germany* (Montreal, 1977); Andreas Biefang, *Die andere Seite der Macht. Reichstag und Öffentlichkeit im 'System Bismarck' 1871–1890* (= Beiträge zur Geschichte des Parlamentarismus und der politischen Parteien 156) (Düsseldorf, 2009); Rudolf Stöber, 'Bismarcks Geheime Presseorganisation von 1882', *Historische Zeitschrift* 262.2 (1996), 423–51.

52. Bismarck, *Gedanken und Erinnerungen*, 1:2.

53. Reinhart Koselleck, 'Revolution. Rebellion, Aufruhr, Bürgerkrieg', in Brunner, Conze, and Koselleck, *Geschichtliche Grundbegriffe*, 5:653–788, here 653, 734, 736, 739, 749, 764–65.

54. Friedrich Julius Stahl, *Was ist die Revolution? Ein Vortrag auf Veranstaltung des Evangelischen Vereins für Kirchliche Zwecke am 8 Märze 1852* (Berlin, 1852), 3; on the semantic inflation of 'revolution' in this period more generally, see Koselleck, 'Revolution', 5:653–788. On Bismarck's relationship with Stahl, see Pflanze, *Bismarck and the Development of Germany*, 56–57, 67–68.

55. Bismarck, *Gedanken und Erinnerungen*, 3:95–100.

56. Helmuth Wolff, *Geschichtsauffassung und Politik in Bismarcks Bewusstsein* (Munich, 1926), 158.

57. Ibid., 159–72.

58. See, for example, Bismarck, *Gedanken und Erinnerungen*, 1:142.

59. For an articulation of this distinction between a politics of affiliation and one of detachment, see the discussion with Leopold von Gerlach cited in Pflanze, *Bismarck and the Development of Germany*, 105.

60. Cited in Andrea Hopp, 'Vorwort', in Hopp (ed.), *Schriften, 1871–1873* (Paderborn, 2004), xiii.

61. Cited in Erich Eyck, *Bismarck and the German Empire*, 3rd ed. (London, 1968), 116.

62. Wolfgang Schwentker, *Konservative Vereine und Revolution in Preussen, 1848–49: Die Konstituierung des Konservativismus als Partei* (Düsseldorf, 1988).

63. Bismarck, *Gedanken und Erinnerungen*, 2:58–61.

64. On the locomotive as the unequivocal metaphor for linear time, see Michel Serres and Bruno Latour, *Conversations on Science, Culture and Time*, trans. Roxanne Lapidus (Ann Arbor, MI, 1995), 79.

65. Oliver Haardt, 'The Kaiser in the Federal State, 1871–1918', *German History* 34 (2016), 529–54.

66. Ludwig Rochau, *Grundsätze der Realpolitik, angewendet auf die staatlichen Zustände*, 2 vols. (Stuttgart, 1853, 1869), vol. 1 (2nd ed., Stuttgart 1869), 11.

67. Duncan Kelly, '"The Goal of That Pure and Noble Yearning". Friedrich Meinecke's Visions of 1848', in Douglas Moggach and Gareth Stedman Jones (eds.), *The 1848 Revolutions and European Political Thought* (Cambridge, 2018), 293–321, here 294–96.

68. Rochau, *Grundsätze der Realpolitik*, 1:4. On the relationship between Rochau's thought and the 1848 revolutions, see Duncan Kelly, 'August Ludwig von Rochau and Realpolitik as historical political theory', *Global Intellectual History* (2017), doi:10.1080/23801883.2017.1387331.

69. Nina Lübbren, 'Eloquent Objects: Gérôme, Laurens and the Art of Inanimate Narration', in Peter Cooke and Nina Lübbren (eds.), *Painting and Narrative in France, from Poussin to Gauguin* (Abingdon, 2016), 129–44.

70. Referring to a conversation with Count Brandenburg: Bismarck, *Gedanken und Erinnerungen*, 1:61.

71. Bismarck to William I, Berlin, 16 May 1873, in Hopp, *Schriften, 1871–1873*, nr. 438, 523.

72. Bismarck to Ludwig II, 12 August 1878, in Bismarck, *Gedanken und Erinnerungen*, 1:342–45, here 345.

73. Bismarck, *Gedanken und Erinnerungen*, 1:277.

74. Ibid., 2:117–18.

75. Droysen to Theodor von Schön, 29 December 1851, in Johann Gustav Droysen, *Briefwechsel*, ed. R. Hübner, 2 vols. (Stuttgart, 1929), 2:34–36, here 35; this passage is discussed in Wolfgang Hardtwig, 'Von Preußens Aufgabe in Deutschland zu Deutschlands Aufgabe in der Welt. Liberalismus und Borussianisches Geschichtsbild zwischen Revolution und Imperialismus', *Historische Zeitschrift* 231.2 (1980), 265–324, here 309.

76. Wenzlhuemer, '"Less Than No Time"'.

77. Sue Zemka, *Time and the Moment in Victorian Literature and Society* (Cambridge, 2012), 2, 8.

78. Ulrich Raulff, *Der unsichtbare Augenblick. Zeitkonzepte in der Geschichte* (Göttingen, 1999), esp. 50–84.

79. John Lothrop Motley, *History of the United Netherlands. From the Death of William the Silent to the Twelve Years' Truce—1609*, 4 vols. (New York, [1874]; vols. 1 and 2 orig. pub. London, 1860). Examples include the following: 1:7: 'The contest between those . . . Provinces . . . and the great Spanish Empire, seemed at the moment with which we are now occupied a sufficiently desperate one'; 1:60: 'at that moment, the reformers were full of confidence, not foreseeing the long procession of battles and sieges which were soon to sweep through the land'; 1:136: 'If there had ever been a time when every nerve in Protestant Christendom should be strained to wield all those provinces together into one great commonwealth, as a bulwark for European liberty . . . , that moment had arrived'; 1:155: 'The Prince was not aware that his brave but venal ally had, at the very same moment, been secretly treating with William of Orange. . .'; 1:500: 'at almost the very moment when Elizabeth had so suddenly overturned her last vial of wrath upon the discomfited Heneage . . . ; at that very instant, Parma was writing secretly, and in cipher, to Philip'; 2:168: 'Never was a more dangerous moment than this for a country to be left to its fate'; 2:402–3: 'The most important point for the reader to remark is the date of this letter. It was received in the very *last days of the month of July*. Let him observe—as he will soon have occasion to do—the events which were occurring on land and sea, exactly at the moment when this classic despatch reached its destination'. Moments of this kind occur too frequently in the text to permit a fuller analysis.

80. Bismarck, *Gedanken und Erinnerungen*, 1:72.

81. Ibid., 2:96–97.

82. Ibid., 1:40–43.

83. An example of a πρῶτον ψεῦδος:

Pips is a penguin.
Penguins are birds.
All birds can fly.
Therefore: Pips can fly.

The πρῶτον ψεῦδος is the third premiss. As penguins demonstrate, not all birds can fly.

84. On the place of (daring and high-risk) decision making by eighteenth-century commanders in battle, see Marian Füssel, 'Vom Dämon des Zufalls: Die Schlacht als kalkuliertes Wagnis im langen 18. Jahrhundert', in Stefan Brakensiek, Christof Marx, and Benjamin Scheller (eds.), *Wagnisse. Risiken eingehen, Risiken analysieren, von Risiken erzählen* (Frankfurt/Main, 2017), 91–110, on Frederick, 98–104.

85. Bismarck, *Gedanken und Erinnerungen*, 1:277–78.

86. William I to Bismarck, Berlin, 23 December 1887, cited in ibid., 2:299–230.

87. Helmuth Wolff comes close to capturing this tension in his discussion of the 'genetic' and 'comparative'

88. See, for example, Bismarck, *Gedanken und Erinnerungen*, 2:8 ('Die Abstufungen, welche in der dänischen Frage erreichbar erschienen') and 2:9 ('Ich habe von Anfang an die Annexion unverrückt im Auge behalten, ohne die andern Abstufungen aus dem Gesichtsfelde zu verlieren').

89. On Bismarck's planning, see Jochen Dittrich, *Bismarck, Frankreich und die spanische Thronkandidatur der Hohenzollern* (Munich, 1962); Eberhard Kolb, *Der Kriegsausbruch 1870* (Göttingen, 1970); Josef Becker, 'Zum Problem der Bismarckschen Politik in der spanischen Thronfrage', *Historische Zeitschrift* 212 (1971), 529–605 and Becker, 'Von Bismarcks "spanischer Diversion" zur "Emser Legende" des Reichsgründers', in Johannes Burkhardt (ed.), *Lange und Kurze Wege in den Krieg* (Augsburg, 1996), 87–113. Becker makes the case for a planned preventive war; the contrary position is set out in Eberhard Kolb, 'Mächtepolitik und Kriegsrisiko am Vorabend des Krieges von 1870', in Kolb (ed.), *Europa vor dem Krieg von 1870* (Munich, 1987), 203–9. For Becker's defence of his view against the objections of an American critic, David Wetzel, see Josef Becker, 'The Franco-Prussian Conflict of 1870 and Bismarck's Concept of a "Provoked Defensive War": A Response to David Wetzel', *Central European History* 41.1 (2008), 93–109.

90. Bismarck, *Gedanken und Erinnerungen*, 1:1.

91. Steinberg, *Bismarck*, 197, 480.

92. Bismarck to State Secretary of the Interior v. Boetticher, Friedrichsruh, 27 March 1882, transcribed in Rothfels, *Bismarck und der Staat*, 369.

93. William I to Otto von Manteuffel, Director in the Interior Ministry under Camphausen, 7 April 1848, cited in Karl-Heinz Börner, *Wilhelm I Deutscher Kaiser und König von Preußen. Eine Biographie* (Berlin, 1984), 81.

94. Bismarck, *Gedanken und Erinnerungen*, 1:197 (my emphases).

95. On the origins of the gap theory in the constitutional debates of 1849–51, see Kraus, 'Ursprung und Genese'.

96. Pflanze, *Bismarck and the Development of Germany*, 213–14.

97. Egmont Zechlin, *Staatsstreichpläne Bismarcks und Wilhelms II. 1890–1894* (Stuttgart, 1929); on Bismarck's readiness to embark on a *Staatsstreich*, see also Hans Delbrück, 'Die Hohenlohe-Memoiren und Bismarcks Entlassung', *Preussische Jahrbücher* 126 (1906), 501–17 and Delbrück, 'Bismarcks letzte politische Idee', *Preussische Jahrbücher* 147 (1912), 1–12; Röhl, 'Staatsstreichplan oder Staatsstreichbereitschaft?'; for a subtle discussion of the issues at stake in the 1890 crisis, see also J.C.G. Röhl, 'The Disintegration of the Kartell and the Politics of Bismarck's Fall from Power, 1887–1890', *Historical Journal* 9.1 (1966), 60–89.

98. Bismarck to Ludwig of Bavaria, Kissingen, 12 August 1878, transcribed in Bismarck, *Gedanken und Erinnerungen*, 1:364.

99. Matthew P. Fitzpatrick, *Purging the Empire. Mass Expulsions in Germany, 1871–1914* (Oxford, 2015), 86–87.

100. Bismarck, *Gedanken und Erinnerungen*, 3:42–43.

101. Troeltsch, *Der Historismus*, 230–31.

102. Otto von Bismarck, *Briefe an seine Braut und Gattin*, ed. Herbert von Bismarck (Stuttgart, 1900), 268–69.

103. On Bismarck's 'weak' providentialism, see Helmuth Wolff, *Geschichtsauffassung und Politik in Bismarcks Bewusstsein* (Oldenburg, 1926), 134–50.

104. Otto Hintze, review of Otto von Bismarck, *Deutscher Staat. (Der deutsche Staatsgedanke. Eine Sammlung, Erste Reihe: Führer und Denker XXI)*, ed. Hans Rothfels, *Zeitschrift für Politik* 15 (1926), 380–84, here 383.

105. On Clausewitz as a theorist of complexity and immersive reasoning who situated war in an environment saturated with contingency, see Anders Engberg-Petersen, *Empire of Chance. The Napoleonic Wars and the Disorder of Things* (Cambridge, MA, 2015), passim, esp. 92.

106. On this dimension of Clausewitz's thought, see Emile Simpson, *War from the Ground Up. Twenty-First Century Combat as Politics* (New York, 2012), esp. 41–66.

107. George G. Iggers, *The German Conception of History. The National Tradition of Historical Thought from Herder to the Present* (Middletown, CT, 1968), 82, 88–89; on the centrality and 'intellectual-cultural significance' of the state for Ranke, see also Troeltsch, *Der Historismus*, 476.

108. On Rodbertus, see Wilhelm Andreae, 'Der staatssozialistische Ideenkreis', *Archiv für Rechts- und Wirtschaftsphilosophie* 24 (1930), 169–91, esp. 180–88; Hermann Beck, *The Origins of the Authoritarian Welfare State in Prussia. Conservatives, Bureaucracy and the Social Question, 1815–1870* (Providence, RI, 1993), 93–100.

109. Gerd Heinrich, *Geschichte Preußens. Staat und Dynastie* (Frankfurt, 1981), 283–84; on Wagener and Gerlach, see Hans-Julius Schoeps, *Das andere Preußen. Konservative Gestalten und Probleme im Zeitalter Friedrich Wilhelms IV*, 3rd ed. (Berlin, 1966), 203–28.

110. On the links between Stein and Schmoller, see Giles Pope, 'The Political Ideas of Lorenz Stein and Their Influence on Rudolf Gneist and Gustav Schmoller' (DPhil thesis, Oxford University, 1985); Karl Heinz Metz, 'Preussen als Modell einer Idee der Sozialpolitik. Das soziale Königtum', in Patrick Bahners and Gerd Roellecke (eds.), *Preussische Stile. Ein Staat als Kunststück* (Stuttgart, 2001), 355–63, here 358.

111. On these debates, see Damian Valdez, 'Prussian Faust or Universalist Puritan?', *Modern Intellectual History* 14.2 (August 2017), 585–96.

112. Jörn Leonhard, *Die Büchse der Pandora. Geschichte des Ersten Weltkriegs* (Munich, 2014), passim.

113. Lothar Machtan, *Die Abdankung: Wie Deutschlands gekrönte Häupter aus der Geschichte fielen* (Munich, 2008).

114. Carl Schmitt, *State, Movement, People. The Triadic Structure of the Political Unity (1933). The Question of Legality (1950)*, trans. Simona Draghici (Cornwallis, OR, 2001), 34.

115. Troeltsch, *Der Historismus*, 173.

116. Ibid., 169; for an account of the crisis of historicism that is sceptical about whether such a crisis ever really took place, see Beiser, *German Historicist Tradition*, 23–26.

117. Kurt Flasch, *Die geistige Mobilmachung. Die deutschen Intellektuellen und der Erste Weltkrieg: ein Versuch* (Berlin, 2000).

118. Lucian Hölscher, 'Mysteries of Historical Order: Ruptures, Simultaneity and the Relationship of the Past, Present and Future', in Chris Lorenz and Berber Bevernage (eds.), *Breaking Up Time. Negotiating the Borders between Present, Past and Future* (Goettingen, 2013), 134–51.

119. Friedrich Meinecke, *Machiavellism. The Doctrine of Raison d'Etat and Its Place in Modern History*, trans. Douglas Scott (Epping, 1984), 19.

120. Ibid., 432.

121. J. Kaerst, 'Die Geschichtsauffassung Rankes und Droysens in ihrer nationalen Bedeutung', *Vierteljahrschrift für Sozial- und Wirtschaftsgeschichte* 20. Bd., H. 1/2 (1928), 219–33, here 229.

122. Röhl, 'Disintegration of the Kartell'.

123. Rothfels, 'Deutschlands Krise', in Alfred Bozi and Alfred Niemann (eds.), *Die Einheit der nationalen Politik* (Stuttgart, 1925), 1–15, here 10. For a discussion of this passage, see Jan Eckel, *Hans Rothfels: Eine intellektuelle Biographie im 20. Jahrhundert* (Göttingen 2005), 55.

124. Otto Hintze, review of Otto von Bismarck, *Deutscher Staat*, ed. Hans Rothfels, *Zeitschrift für Politik* 15 (1926), 380–84, here 382.

125. On the theological dignity of nineteenth- and early twentieth-century history as a form of bourgeois religion, see Wolfgang Hardtwig, 'Geschichtsreligion—Wissenschaft als Arbeit—Objektivität. Der Historismus in neuer Sicht', *Historische Zeitschrift* 252.1 (1991), 1–32, here 9; on the crisis as 'a problem for life and culture', see Franz Schnabel, 'Vom Sinn des geschichtlichen Studiums in der Gegenwart' (1923), in Schnabel, *Abhandlungen und Vorträge 1914–1965*, ed. Heinrich von Lutz et al. (Freiburg, 1970), 147.

126. Troeltsch discusses his proposal for a new history in *Christian Thought, Its History and Application; Lectures Written for Delivery in England during March 1923*, trans. Baron F. von Hügel (London, 1923); my understanding of Troeltsch's role in these debates was informed by Stefan Eich and Adam Tooze, 'Max Weber, Politics and the Crisis of Historicism' (paper, Yale University, January 2012). I am grateful to Stefan Eich and Adam Tooze for letting me see this paper.

127. 'Le prophète est dans le même sac que l'historien', Paul Valéry, 'La Crise de l'Esprit', in Valéry, *Oeuvres*, ed. Jean Hytier, 2 vols. (Paris, 1957), 1:988–1014, here 991; on the date of the original publication (1919), see the notes on 1768–69.

128. Paul Valéry, 'De l'Histoire', in Valéry, *Oeuvres*, 2:935–37. This essay was probably written in 1928; see the note on 1540–41.

129. Theodor Lessing, *Geschichte als Sinngebung des Sinnlosen* (Munich, 1919), 11, 12, 13, 153. On these themes, see Matthias Lentz, 'Eine Philosophie

der Tat, eine Tat der Philosophie. Theodor Lessings Kampf gegen den Lärm', *Zeitschrift für Religions- und Geistesgeschichte* 50.3 (1998), 242–64.

130. Lessing, *Geschichte als Sinngebung*, 152.

131. Mircea Eliade, *Myth of the Eternal Return, or: Cosmos and History* (London, 1989), 38. See also Raul Carstocea, 'Breaking the Teeth of Time: Mythical Time and the "Terror of History" in the Rhetoric of the Legionary Movement in Interwar Romania', *Journal of Modern European History* 13.2 (2015), 79–97, esp. 80–83.

Chapter 4. Time of the Nazis

1. Max Frisch, 'Kleines Tagebuch einer deutschen Reise', *Neue Zürcher Zeitung*, 30 April 1935, excerpted and anthologised in Oliver Lubrich (ed.), *Travels in the Reich, 1933–1945. Foreign Authors Report from Germany*, trans. Kenneth Northcott, Sonia Wichmann, and Dean Krouk (Chicago, 2010), 65–72, here 67–68; for a more detailed description of the bell of life and the hourglass beneath it, see the article 'Wunder des Lebens' by the anonymous German correspondent 'F.G.' in the *Spectator*, 5 April 1935, 15. Frisch took no notes in the exhibition for fear of having them confiscated and read, and subsequently misremembered the purpose of the bell. He thought it chimed to signify that too many Germans had died and too few had been born and that its clanging was intended as a warning to the visitors to procreate as a matter of urgency (an understandable error, since other exhibits made exactly this appeal, warning that if persons of 'superior' racial quality failed to spawn enough children, the result would be a steep 'qualitative decline'). A correction was published after the designers of the exhibition wrote to the *NZZ* to complain.

2. For landmark contributions and useful discussions, see Philippe Burrin, 'Political Religion: The Relevance of a Concept', *History and Memory* 9 (1997), 321–49; Elilio Gentile, 'Fascism as Political Religion', *Journal of Contemporary History* 25 (1990), 229–51; Stanley Stowers, 'The Concepts of "Religion", "Political Religion" and the Study of Nazism', *Journal of Contemporary History* 42.1 (2007), 9–24; David D. Roberts, '"Political Religion" and the Totalitarian Departures of Inter-war Europe: On the Uses and Disadvantages of an Analytical Category', *Contemporary European History* 18 (2009); Hans Maier, 'Political Religion. The Potentialities and Limitations of a Concept', in Hans Maier (ed.), *Totalitarianism and Political Religion*, trans. Jodi Bruhn (London, 2007), 272–82. Sabine Behrenbeck, *Der Kult um die toten Helden. Nationalsozialistische Mythen, Riten und Symbole 1923 bis 1945* (Vierow, 1996), is an excellent example of an empirical study driven by the political religion paradigm. For a powerful recent exposition of the generic fascism approach (which tends now to overlap considerably with the political religion school), see Ferdando Esposito and Sven Reichardt, 'Revolution and Eternity. Introductory Remarks on Fascist Temporalities', *Journal of Modern European History* 13 (2015), 24–43.

3. Richard Steigmann-Gall, *The Holy Reich. Nazi Conceptions of Christianity, 1919–1945* (Cambridge, 2003), esp. 86–113.

4. See Confino, 'Why Did the Nazis Burn the Hebrew Bible?', 381.

5. Crawford Photographs Collection, Institute of Archaeology, Oxford.

6. There is some uncertainty about the location of the Berlin Revolutionsmuseum: in a review of the exhibition dated 25 November 1933, the party organ *Der S.A.-Mann* described the museum as occupying a house on the corner of Jüden- and Parochialstraße (Horst and Werner Wessel had grown up in Jüdenstraße 51/52). The photographs taken of the museum by O.G.S. Crawford in September 1934, however, show an entrance on Neue Friedrichstraße 83, near the corner with Königstraße. An article by Joseph Goebbels ('Der Spiegel des Grauens. In der Schreckenskammer der Hochtage des Kommunistenterrors', in *Völkischer Beobachter*, North German edition, 12 December 1933, feature page: 'Aus der Bewegung') confirms this location and reports that the museum had been founded on 15 September. It may well be that the museum was in fact refounded on a larger and more ambitious footing at that time; this would explain an early reference by the Social Democrat exile journalist in Paris, Hermann Wendel, who reported on 30 July 1933 that a 'Museum der nationalen Revolution' had just been opened in Berlin. See Hermann Wendel, 'Revolutionsmuseum', in Lutz Winckler (ed.), *Unter der 'Coupole'. Die Paris-Feuilletons Hermann Wendels 1933–36* (Tübingen, 1995), 116–19. A lengthy commentary in the *Märkische SA* of 10 April 1937, 1–2, reports on the recent reopening of the museum ('Erstes NS.-Revolutionsmuseum der Standarte 6 neu eröffnet') and situates it in Taubenstraße 6. It may be that the museum was moved, possibly after a travelling show of the exhibits, because its earlier premises had been turned over to another use. There is some confusion on these matters in the secondary literature. Eva Zwach, *Deutsche und englische Militärmuseen im 20. Jahrhundert. Eine kulturgeschichtliche Analyse des gesellschaftlichen Umgangs mit Krieg* (Münster, 1999), 116, suggests that the Revolutionsmuseum was installed in the premises of what had previously been Ernst Friedrich's pacifist *Anti-Kriegs-Museum* at Parochialstraße 29; but this claim appears to be based on an article in the NSDAP party organ *Der Angriff* (see 'sul.', Vom Antikriegsmuseum zur S.-A. Heim, in *Der Angriff*, Nr. 72, 25.3.1933, 4), which describes the sacking of the *Anti-Kriegs-Museum* and its conversion into a locale for the SA, but does not place the Revolutionsmuseum at that location. Martin Roth, *Heimatmuseum. Zur Geschichte einer deutschen Institution* (Berlin, 1990), 159, also states that the *Anti-Kriegs-Museum* was attacked and renamed 'Erstes Revolutions-Museum der SA-Standarte 6 Berlin' in 1932, a claim for which I can find no other supporting evidence. For references to the museum as a NS tourist destination, see *Berlin und Umgebung. Kleine Ausgabe mit Angaben für Automobilisten* (Berlin, 1936), 60; and Julek Karl von Engelbrechten and Hans Volz, *Wir wandern durch das nationalsozialistische Berlin. Ein Führer durch die Gedenkstätten des Kampfes um die Reichshauptstadt* (Munich, 1937), 59. A good recent discussion of the museum is Hans-Georg Hiller von Gaertringen and Katrin

Hiller von Gaetringen, 'NS-Revolutionsmuseum statt Anti-Kriegsmuseum? Zur Entwicklung der Berliner Museumslandschaft in der NS-Zeit', in Tanja Baensch, Kristina Kratz-Kessemeier, and Dorothee Wimmer (eds.), *Museen im National-sozialismus. Akteure—Orte—Politik* (Vienna, 2016), 99–112.

7. The 'Ehrenhalle' at Buchholz in der Nordheide, for example, was the work of Gauleiter for Osthannover Otto Telschow, in collaboration with the local SA; see Thomas Clausen, 'Otto Telschow—Hitlers Gauleiter in Osthannover' (unpublished manuscript); I am grateful to Thomas Clausen for letting me see this document.

8. On Ernst Friedrich as a 'renewer of the museum' and a critic of conventional museum practice, see Zwach, *Deutsche und englische Militärmuseen*, 113; on the SA seizure of power, see Martin Schuster, 'Die SA in der nationalsozialistischen "Machtergreifung" in Berlin und Brandenburg 1926-1934' (PhD thesis, Technische Universität Berlin, 2004), 237 (http://edocs.tu-berlin.de/diss/2004/schuster_martin.pdf); on the destruction of the museum by the very SA-men who subsequently set up the Revolutionsmuseum, see Hiller von Gaertringen and Hiller von Gaetringen, 'NS-Revolutionsmuseum statt Anti-Kriegsmuseum?', 102.

9. Dietz Bering, *Der Name als Stigma. Antisemitismus im deutschen Alltag, 1812-1933* (Stuttgart, 1988); photo of the exhibit: Crawford Photographs Collection, Institute of Archaeology, Oxford.

10. Goebbels, 'Spiegel des Grauens'; on 'sarcasm' as a feature of the exhibits, see Hiller von Gaertringen and Hiller von Gaetringen, 'NS-Revolutionsmuseum statt Anti-Kriegsmuseum?', 104.

11. See, for example, 'Revolutionsaustellung in Karlsruhe', in *Völkischer Beobachter*, North German edition, 14 September 1933, Zweites Beiblatt, which speaks of 'a piled up magazine of revolvers, pistols, carbines, daggers, knuckledusters, machine-guns, explosive cartridges, hand grenades etc.'

12. See, for example, 'Hochverratsprozeß against 111 Kommunisten in Breslau', in *Völkischer Beobachter*, 31 May 1934, 1; 'Geständnisse und Lügen der Mörder vom Bülowplatz', in *Völkischer Beobachter*, 6 June 1934, 2; 'Kommunistische Bombenanfertiger vor dem Volksgericht', in *Völkischer Beobachter*, 4 September 1934, 4; 'Gift als politisches Kampfmittel in den Händen der Kommunisten' (reports that cyanide had been found in the hands of a communist group in quantities sufficient to kill 100–150 people), in *Völkischer Beobachter*, 14 September 1934, 2; 'Kommunistische Enthüllungen vor dem Dortmunder Gericht. Zechen, Eisenbahn und Brücken sollten gesprengt werden', in *Völkischer Beobachter*, 22 September 1934, 8.

13. Stein, 'Im Revolutionsmuseum', in *Rumpelstilzchen: Nee aber sowas!* (= *Rumpelstilzchen* 15 [1934/35], Berlin 1935), entry dated 11 July 1935, 273.

14. On this feature of modern museums, see Jennifer Anne Walklate, 'Timescapes. The Production of Temporality in Literature and Museums' (PhD thesis, School of Museum Studies, University of Leeds, 2012), esp. 6–9, 135–61.

15. Roth, *Heimatmuseum*, 35, 64, 157, 162.

16. 'Das Revolutionsmuseum zeigt die Symbole einer überwundenen Zeit'.

17. Goebbels, 'Spiegel des Grauens'.

18. 'ffh', 'Erstes NS-Revolutionsmuseum der Standarte 6 neu eröffnet', in *Märkische SA*, 10 April 1937, 1 (supplement to the *SA-Mann* of the same date).

19. Karsten Fischer, '"Systemzeit" und Weltgeschichte. Zum Motiv der Epochenwende in der NS-Ideologie', in Fischer (ed.), *Neustart des Weltlaufs? Fiktion und Faszination der Zeitwende* (Frankfurt/Main, 1999), 184–202.

20. Hitler speech of 13 July 1934, cited in *Völkischer Beobachter*, North German edition, 15–16 July 1934, 1.

21. On the 'anti-religious museum' as a Soviet institution, see the excellent article by Crispin Paine, 'Militant Atheist Objects: Anti-religion Museums in the Soviet Union', *Present Pasts* 1(1), http://doi.org/10.5334/pp.13; Mark Elliott, 'The Leningrad Museum of the History of Religion and Atheism', *Religion in Communist Lands* 11 (1983), 124–29; Catriona Kelly, 'Socialist Churches, Heritage Preservation and "Cultic Buildings" in Leningrad, 1924–1940', *Slavic Review* 71 (2012), 792–823, esp. 816, 821.

22. 'Das erste nationalsozialistische Museum in Halle eröffnet', *Völkischer Beobachter*, North German edition, 15 June 1934, 7.

23. *Führer durch das NS-Museum des Gaues Halle-Merseburg der NSDAP. Ehrenhalle der nationalsozialistischen Erhebung. Revolutionsmuseum. NS-Archiv* (Halle, 1934), 33.

24. 'Aufruf des Gauleiters Staatsrats Jordan', in ibid., 4.

25. Vorspruch vom Leiter des Museums Universitäts-Professor Dr. Hahne, in *Führer durch das NS-Museum*, 9–11.

26. Schnapp, 'Fascism's Museum in Motion', 87–97, esp. 88, 93; on the Mostra, see also Susanne von Falkenhausen, *Der zweite Futurismus und die Kunstpolitik des Faschismus in Italien von 1922–1943* (Frankfurt/Main, 1979); and Stone, 'Staging Fascism', 215–43.

27. Stone, 'Staging Fascism', 223.

28. On Room O as the dramatization of a 'moment of transformation', see Falkenhausen, *Der zweite Futurismus*, 206.

29. Schnapp, 'Fascism's Museum in Motion', 94; Gigliola Fioravanti, *La Mostra della Rivoluzione Fascista* (Rome, 1992), 32; Claudio Fogu, 'The Fascist Stylisation of Time', *Journal of Modern European History* 13.2 (2015), 98–114, here 109.

30. Ottavio Dinale, 'La Mostra della Rivoluzione—Visioni d'Arte', in *Rivista Illustrata del Popolo d'Italia*, 11 June 1933, cited in Stone, 'Staging Fascism', 220.

31. Louis Gillet, 'Rome Nouvelle', in *Revue des deux Mondes*, 15 December 1932, 792–826, here 810.

32. Hanson, *Time and Revolution*, viii–ix, 180–99.

33. Francine Hirsch, *Empire of Nations. Ethnographic Knowledge and the Making of the Soviet Union* (Ithaca, NY, 2005), 264–72. It is true that early Bolshevik official temporality retained a millenarian dimension, in the sense that it nurtured the apocalyptic belief in a future society marked by the 'complete

abolition of all power' and the permanent suspension of historical time. But as the regime consolidated itself, this vision receded into an ever more remote future. The invocation of sacred time through the language of apocalypse served above all to motivate historical action in the present. The association of the revolution itself and of Stalinism with apocalypse or with millennial cycles of violence and renewal was a feature above all of anti-Bolshevik, utopian, and émigré discourses; see Williams, 'Russian Revolution and the End of Time', esp. 369–87, 393–95.

34. Auguste Sartory and E. Bailly, *Visions Rouges. Souvenirs de Voyages en U.R.S.S., Allemagne, Provinces Baltiques et Pologne* (Paris, 1935), 187.

35. Stefan Plaggenborg's interesting reflections on the 'historylessness' (Geschichtslosigkeit) of the Soviet regime (*Experiment Moderne*, 105–19) do not contradict this observation, since Plaggenborg uses this term to denote a temporal order in which the forwards momentum of history has become inseparable from the regime itself. The 'disappearance' of history thus amounts to an absorption of history into the present, rather than signifying the rejection of linear history as a temporal logic.

36. Carl Maria Holzapfel, 'Vom Rhythmus der Zeit', in *Völkischer Beobachter* (North German edition), 10–11 May 1934; Beiblatt, *Volkstum, Kunst, Wissenschaft, Unterhaltung*; 'Deutsche Vorgeschichte ist Ehrensache des ganzen deutschen Volkes', in *Völkischer Beobachter* (North German Edition), 16 October 1934, 1.

37. Eliade, *Myth of the Eternal Return*, 95.

38. Adolf Hitler, *Mein Kampf: eine kritische Edition*, ed. Christian Hartmann, Thomas Vordermayer, Othmar Plöckinger, and Roman Töppel, 2 vols. (Munich, 2016), 1:1003. The reference to the state as a 'monster of human mechanism' comes from 2:991.

39. Ibid., 2:1001.

40. Ibid., 1:821.

41. Ibid., 2:1071.

42. Ibid., 1:115.

43. Ibid., 1:855.

44. Kristina Kratz-Kessemeier, 'Für die "Erkämpfung einer neuen Museumskultur". Zur Rolle des deutschen Museumsbundes im Nationalsozialismus', in Baensch, Kratz-Kessemeier, and Wimmer, *Museen im Nationalsozialismus*, 23–43, here 35; Petra Winter, '"Das hören wir uns nicht weiter an!" Die vom Reichserziehungsministerium veranstaltete "Erste Tagung deutscher Museumsdirektoren" im November 1937 in Berlin', in Baensch, Kratz-Kessemeier, and Wimmer, *Museen im Nationalsozialismus*, 45–59, here 57.

45. Ulfert Tschirner, 'Museumsgestalter mit eigener Position. Handlungsspielräume von Wissenschaftlern am Museum Lüneburg im Nationalsozialismus', in Baensch, Kratz-Kessemeier, and Wimmer, *Museen im Nationalsozialismus*, 115–28, here 123.

46. Alfred Rosenberg, 'Foreword', in Reichsstelle zur Förderung des deutschen Schrifttums u. Preußische Staatsbibliothek (ed.), *Ewiges Deutsch-*

land. Deutsches Schrifttum aus fünfzehn Jahrhunderten (Berlin, 1934). For an excellent discussion of the mega-exhibitions of the 'Third Reich', see Hans-Ulrich Thamer, 'Geschichte und Propaganda. Kulturhistorische Ausstellungen in der NS-Zeit', *Geschichte und Gesellschaft* 24 (1998), 349–81.

47. *Das deutsche Antlitz im Spiegel der Jahrhunderte. Große Ausstellung der Stadt Frankfurt am Main unter Mitwirkung des Rassenpolitischen Amtes der NSDAP* (Frankfurt/Main, 1937), vi.

48. Brigitte Zuber, 'Großmachttraum im Andachtsraum. Welche Ausstellungen Münchner Schülerinnen und Schüler 1933–1943 klassenweise besuchten', *Einsichten und Perspektiven. Bayerische Zeitschrift für Politik und Geschichte*, February 2009, http://www.blz.bayern.de/blz/eup/02_09/6.asp.

49. Hans Georg Otto (ed.), *Deutsche Größe*, foreword by Alfred Rosenberg, introduction by Karl Alexander von Müller (Munich, 1940), 12.

50. 'die Schauer der Ehrfurcht [. . .] vor dem, was unsterblich wirkt und waltet über die Jahrhunderte hinweg', in Anon., 'Deutsche Größe im Schritt von zwei Jahrtausenden. Heute Eröffnung der eindrucksvollen Ausstellung im Bibliotheksbau des Deutschen Museums', in *Münchner Neueste Nachrichten*, 8 November 1940, cited in Christof Kivelitz, *Die Propagandaausstellung in europäischen Diktaturen. Konfrontation und Vergleich. Nationalsozialismus in Deutschland, Faschismus in Italien und die UdSSR der Stalinzeit* (Bochum, 1999), 205.

51. Cited in Gianluca Falanga, *Berlin 1937. Die Ruhe vor dem Sturm* (Berlin, 2007), 122.

52. Kivelitz, *Propagandaausstellung*, 67.

53. Michael Tymkiw, 'Engaged Spectatorship. On the Relationship between Non-Museum Exhibitions and Museums in National Socialist Germany', in Baensch, Kratz-Kessemeier, and Wimmer, *Museen im Nationalsozialismus*, 161–76, here 164.

54. Reinhard Bollmus, 'Das "Amt Rosenberg", das "Ahnenerbe" und die Prähistoriker', in Achim Leube (ed.), *Prähistorie und Nationalsozialismus. Die mittel- und osteuropäische Ur- und Frühgeschichtsforschung in den Jahren 1933–1945* (Heidelberg, 2002), 21–48; see also Bollmus, *Das Amt Rosenberg und seine Gegner. Studien zum Machtkampf im Nationalsozialistischen Herrschaftssystem* (Stuttgart, 1970), 69–70, 161–62, 226–27.

55. See, for example, Max Wegner, 'Museen für die Volksgemeinschaft!', in *Völkischer Beobachter* (North German Edition), 13 April 1934; Beiblatt, *Volkstum, Kunst, Wissenschaft, Unterhaltung*, 1.

56. Wolfgang Pape, 'Zur Entwicklung des Faches Ur- und Frühgeschichte bis 1945', in Leube, *Prähistorie und Nationalsozialismus*, 163–226, esp. 167, 188, 206, 215–16; Uta Halle, Wichtige Ausgrabungen der NS-Zeit, in Focke-Museum, Bremen (ed.), *Graben für Germanien—Archäologie unterm Hakenkreuz* (Darmstadt, 2013), 65–73; Marion Bertram, 'Zur Situation der deutschen Ur- und Frühgeschichtsforschung während der Zeit der faschistischen Diktatur', *Staatliche Museen zu Berlin. Forschungen und Berichte* 31 (1991): 23–42.

57. Hanning Hassmann, 'Archäologie und Jugend im "Dritten Reich". Ur- und Frühgeschichte als Mittel der politisch-ideologischen Indokrination von Kindern und Jugendlichen', in Leube, *Prähistorie und Nationalsozialismus*, 107–46; on the upgrading of prehistory and its impact on museum exhibitions in the Rhineland, see Christina Kott, 'Museums on Display. Die Selbstinsze- nierung deutscher Museen auf der Pariser Weltausstellung', in Baensch, Kratz- Kessemeier, and Wimmer, *Museen im Nationalsozialismus*, 61–81.

58. Cited in Bettina Arnold, 'Archaeology in Nazi Germany', in Tim Murray and Christopher Evans (eds.), *Histories of Archaeology. A Reader in the History of Archaeology* (Oxford, 2008), 120–43, here 129–30; Goebbels shared this scep- ticism, see Helmut Heiber, *Walter Frank und sein Reichsinstitut für Geschichte des Neuen Deutschland* (Stuttgart, 1966), 256.

59. The classic study is Michael Kater, *Das "Ahnenerbe" der SS 1935–1945. Ein Beitrag zur Kulturpolitik des Dritten Reiches* (Munich, 1997).

60. Cited in Tschirner, 'Museumsgestalter mit eigener Position', 122.

61. Cited in Irene Ziehe, *Hans Hahne (1875 bis 1935), sein Leben und Wirken. Biographie eines völkischen Wissenschaftlers* (Halle/Saale, 1996), 28–29.

62. Dr Johannes Wiegelt, Eulogy for Hans Hahne in Walter Schulz, ed., *Hans Hahne zum Gedächtnis* (Halle, 1937), 7.

63. Gerhard Heberer, 'Hans Hahne und die rassenkundliche Forschung', in Schulz, *Hans Hahne zum Gedächtnis*, 11.

64. Hans Hahne to his mother, 23 May 1919, cited in Ziehe, *Hans Hahne*, 36.

65. Rothfels, *Bismarck und der Staat*, ix.

66. Eliade, *Myth of the Eternal Return*, 38. On the value of Eliade's diagnosis of 'archaic' temporalities for an understanding of fascism, see Carstocea, 'Break- ing the Teeth of Time', esp. 80–83.

67. Adolf Helbok, 'Volk und Staat der Germanen', *Historische Zeitschrift* 154 (1936), 229–40.

68. Hitler, *Mein Kampf*, 1:821, 835.

69. Ibid., 1:391.

70. Frank-Lother Kroll, 'Der Faktor "Zukunft" in Hitlers Geschchtsbild', in Kroll (ed.), *Neue Wege der Ideengeschichte. Festchrift für Kurt Kluxen zum 85. Geburtstag* (Paderborn, 1996), 391–410, here 394.

71. Hitler, *Mein Kampf*, 2:1289–90.

72. Adam Tooze, *The Wages of Destruction. The Making and Breaking of the Nazi Economy* (London, 2006), 3–12.

73. Gustav Stresemann, *Die Entwicklung des Berliner Flaschenbiergeschäfts* (Leipzig, 2010).

74. Hermann Wirth, *Vom Mythos und magischen Denken* (Jena, 1928), 22.

75. For some interesting reflections on the relationship between National Socialist spatiality and the regime's temporality, see Confino, 'Why Did the Nazis Burn the Hebrew Bible?', esp. 381–82.

76. Hitler, *Mein Kampf*, 1:705. Note that Hitler distinguished between two readings of this axiom: Bismarck (according to Hitler) had used it to mean

that every possible means was justified in the pursuit of a legitimate objective, a claim to which Hitler had no objection. But the majority of politicians, he claimed, had used it in a different sense, to mean that politics was an art of pragmatic compromise, a view Hitler vehemently rejected.

77. On prognosis and prophecy and the difference between their implicit temporalities, see, for example, Koselleck, 'Modernity and the Planes of Historicity', 9–25.

78. On the significance of this prophecy for Hitler's decision to embark on the extermination of European Jewry, see Tobias Jersak, 'Kriegsverlauf und Judenvernichtung. Ein Blick auf Hitlers Strategie im Spätsommer 1941', *Historische Zeitschrift* 268 (1999), 311–74, esp. 339, 340, 373; Jersak, 'Blitzkrieg Revisited: A New Look at Nazi War and Extermination Planning', *Historical Journal* 43 (2000), 565–82, esp. 574–75; cf. Hans Mommsen, 'Hitler's Reichstag Speech of 30 January 1939', *History and Memory* 9 (1997), 147–61.

79. Verhandlungen des Reichstages, 4. Wahlperiode 1939: Stenographische Berichte, 1939–42, 16.

80. The term was coined in Saul Friedländer, *The Years of Persecution. Nazi Germany and the Jews, 1933–1939* (New York, 1998); for a useful discussion, see A. Dirk Moses, 'Redemptive Antisemitism and the Imperialist Imaginary', in Christian Wiese and Paul Betts (eds.), *Years of Persecution, Years of Extermination. Saul Friedländer and the Future of Holocaust Studies* (London, 2010), 233–54. On anti-Semitism as the inversion of Pauline prophecy, see Christopher Clark, '"The Hope of Better Times": Pietism and the Jews', in Jonathan Strom, Hartmut Lehman, and James Van Horn Melton (eds.), *Pietism in Germany and North America, 1680–1820* (Farnham, 2009), 251–70, esp. 269–70; on 'salvation-historical' themes in theological anti-Semitism, see Anders Gerdmar, *Roots of Theological Anti-Semitism. German Biblical Interpretation and the Jews, from Herder and Semler to Kittel and Bultmann* (Leiden, 2009), esp. 189–317.

81. Jan Björn Potthast, *Das jüdische Zentralmuseum der SS in Prag. Gegnerforschung und Völkermord im Nationalsozialismus* (Frankfurt/Main, 2002); Dirk Rupnow, *Täter, Gedächtnis, Opfer. Das Jüdische Zentralmuseum in Prag 1942–1945* (Vienna, 2000).

82. Jochen Thies, 'Hitler's European Building Programme', *Journal of Contemporary History* 13 (1978), 413–31, 414.

83. Hitler, *Mein Kampf*, 1:693.

84. Ibid., 1:695.

85. Norman H. Baynes (ed.), *The Speeches of Adolf Hitler, April 1922–August 1939*, 2 vols. (London, 1942), 1:573.

86. Henry Picker, *Hitlers Tischgespräche im Fürherhauptquartier, 1941–42* (Stuttgart, 1963), 143–44, 190.

87. Eric Michaud, 'National Socialist Architecture as an Acceleration of Time', *Critical Inquiry* 19 (1993), 220–33, here 227.

88. It is an interesting feature of Reinhart Koselleck's writing on historical temporalities that he very rarely interrogated the work of historians, preferring

to draw on crown witnesses active in public intellectual, literary, and political life such as Friedrich Julius Stahl, Chateaubriand, Alexis de Tocqueville, Frederick II, Karl Marx, Germaine de Staël, and so on. He was less interested in historical writing as such than in the 'historical thinking' (in Ernst Troeltsch's sense) of contemporaries who were not professional historians.

89. Willi Oberkrome, *Volksgeschichte. Methodische Innovation und völkische Ideologisierung in der deutschen Geschichtswissenschaft 1918-1945* (Göttingen, 1993); Stefan Schweizer, *'Unserer Weltanschauung sichtbaren Ausdruck geben'. Nationalsozialistische Geschichtsbilder in historischen Festzügen* (Göttingen, 2007), 47; on the penetration of Volksgeschichte by biological and racist language and arguments, see Ingo Haar, 'Ostforschung im Nationalsozialismus. Die Genesis der Endlösung aus dem Geiste der Wissenschaften', in Rainer Mackensen (ed.), *Bevölkerungslehre und Bevölkerungspolitik im Dritten Reich* (Opladen, 2004), 219-40; on the emergent 'matrix' of racist 'population discourse', see Thomas Etzemüller, *Ein ewigwährender Untergang. Der apokalyptische Bevölkerungsdiskurs im 20. Jahrhundert* (Bielefeld, 2007), esp. 37-40; on the combination of 'tradition' and 'innovation' in one prominent practitioner, see Jan Eike Dunkhase, *Werner Conze. Ein deutscher Historiker im 20. Jahrhundert* (Göttingen, 2010).

90. That the historiography of the 'new' Germany should be focused on race and Volkstum was agreed at the 19. Historikertag in Erfurt in 1937; see Jürgen Elvert, 'Geschichtswissenschaft', in Franz-Rutger Hausmann (ed.), *Die Rolle der Geisteswissenschaften im Dritten Reich, 1933-1945* (Munich, 2002), 87-135, here 123.

91. Heiber, *Walter Frank und sein Reichsinstitut*, 636-937.

92. On the discipline of history under the dictatorship, see Michael Salewski, 'Geschichte als Waffe. Der natonalsozialistische Mißbrauch', *Jahrbuch des Instituts für deutsche Geschichte* 15 (1985), 289-310; Adam Wandruszka, 'Nationalsozialistische und "Gesamtdeutsche" Geschichtsauffassung', in Karl Dietrich Bracher and Leo Valiani (eds.), *Faschismus und Nationalsozialismus* (Berlin, 1991), 137-50; Winfried Schulze and Otto Gerhard Oexle (eds.), *Deutsche Historiker im Nationalsozialismus* (Frankfurt/Main, 1999); Ursula Wiggershaus-Müller, *Nationalsozialismus und Geschichtswissenschaft. Die Geschichte der Historischen Zeitschrift und des Historischen Jahrbuchs von 1933-1945* (Hamburg, 1998).

93. Joseph Goebbels, radio speech on the anti-Jewish boycott, 1 April 1933, transcribed in Wolfgang von Hippel (ed.), *Freiheit, Gleichheit, Brüderlichkeit? Die Französche Revolution im deutschen Urteil von 1789 bis 1945* (Munich, 1989), 344-45. Goebbels would make the same claim again on 2 September at the Nuremberg Party Rally; see K. D. Bracher, Wolfgang Sauer, and Gerhard Schulz, *Die nationalsozialistische Machtergreifung. Studien zur Errichtung des totalitären Herrschaftssystems in Deutschland 1933/34* (Cologne, 1960), 7.

94. Goebbels, 'Spiegel des Grauens'.

95. Fritzsche, *Stranded in the Present*, esp. 201, 212.

96. Paul Glennie and Nigel Thrift, 'Reworking E. P. Thompson's "Time, Work Discipline and Industrial Capitalism"', *Time & Society* 5 (1996), 275–99; Dieter Langewiesche, '"Postmoderne" als Ende der Moderne?', in Wolfram Pyta and Ludwig Richter (eds.), *Gestaltungskraft des Politischen. Festschrift für Eberhard Kolb* (Berlin, 1998), 331–47, here 336; Ernst Wolfgang Becker, *Zeit der Revolution!—Revolution der Zeit? Zeiterfahrungen in Deutschland in der Ära der Revolution 1789–1848/49* (Göttingen, 1999).

97. Frank-Lothar Kroll, *Utopie als Ideologie. Geschichtsdenken und politisches Handeln im Dritten Reich* (Paderborn, 1991), esp. 19.

98. On the diversity, diffuseness, and even incoherence of Nazi racial thought and its oblique relationship with regime practice, see Mark Roseman, 'Racial Discourse, Nazi Violence and the Limits of the Racial State Model' and Devin O. Pendas, 'Eugenics, Racial Science and Nazi Biopolitics. Was There a Genesis of the "Final Solution" from the Spirit of Science?', in Devin O. Pendas, Mark Roseman, and Richard F. Wetzell (eds.), *Beyond the Racial State. Rethinking Nazi Germany* (Cambridge, 2017), 31–57 and 147–75.

99. See Kroll, *Utopie als Ideologie*, 126, 223, 231, passim. On Darré, see also Klaus Bergmann, *Agrarromantik und Großstadtfeindschaft* (Meisenheim, 1970), esp. 297–360 and Mathias Eidenbenz, *'Blut und Boden'. Zu Funktion und Genese der Metaphern des Agrarismus und Biologismus in der nationalsozialistischen Bauernpropaganda R.W. Darrés* (Bern, 1993); on Himmler: Joseph Ackermann, *Heinrich Himmler als Ideologe* (Göttingen, 1970), esp. 171–77 and Peter Longerich, *Heinrich Himmler*, trans. Jeremy Noakes and Lesley Sharpe (Oxford, 2012), esp. 255–94. On the place of prophecy in the 'apocalyptic-chiliastic' thought of Joseph Goebbels, see Claus-Ekkehard Bärsch, 'Die Geschichtsprophetie des Joseph Goebbels', in Joachim H. Knoll and Julius H. Schoeps (eds.), *Von kommenden Zeiten. Geschichtsprophetien im 19. und 20. Jahrhundert* (Stuttgart, 1984), 169–79.

100. Maier, 'Politics of Time', 162; on the complex issue of the relationship between National Socialism and modernity, there is now a vast literature, but see Riccardo Bavaj, *Die Ambivalenz der Moderne im Nationalsozialismus. Eine Bilanz der Forschung* (Munich, 2004); see also the thought-provoking discussion by Paul Betts, 'The New Fascination with Fascism: The Case of Nazi Modernism', *Journal of Contemporary History* 37 (2002), 541–58.

101. Cf. the question posed by Alon Confino: 'What was the imagination of time and history that gave meaning and legitimacy to this radical spatial policy?' in Confino, 'Why Did the Nazis Burn the Hebrew Bible?', 381.

102. For a brilliant discussion of the place of Roman antiquity in fascist chronopolitics, see Joshua Arthurs, 'The Excavatory Intervention: Archaeology and the Chronopolitics of Roman Antiquity in Fascist Italy', *Journal of Modern European History* 13.2 (2015), 44–58.

103. Possible reasons include divergent attitudes to the era of nation building: whereas the Italian fascists seem to have been reluctant to jettison the historicist romance of the *Risorgimento*, the Nazis denigrated the nineteenth

century as a liberal 'epoch of decline'—on this contrast, see Esposito and Reichardt, 'Revolution and Eternity', 40. Defeat, the collapse of the state, and political unrest in 1918–19 Germany may have disturbed traditional historicist assumptions to an extent that was never matched in Italy, where the monarchy and the church remained powerful anchors of continuity. The special place of the Catholic Church in fascist Italy (and Rome in particular) may be another factor: for illuminating reflections on the rivalry between Catholic liturgical and fascist public representations in early 1930s Rome, see Richard J. B. Bosworth, 'L'Anno Santo (Holy Year) in Fascist Italy 1933–1934', *European History Quarterly* 40 (2010), 436–57. Fascist chronopolitics were not static, and the 'racial turn' of 1938 may have brought about a partial convergence with National Socialism, see Joshua Arthurs, *Excavating Modernity. The Roman Past in Fascist Italy* (Ithaca, NY, 2012), 125–50.

Conclusion and Epilogue

1. Hugo Lerchenfeld-Köfering, *Erinnerungen und Denkwürdigkeiten: 1843–1925*, 2nd ed. (Berlin: Mittler, 1935), 193–94.

2. Helmut Koenigsberger, 'Europäisches Ständewesen im 16. und 17. Jahrhundert', in Peter Baumgart and Jürgen Schmädeke (eds.), *Ständetum und Staatsbildung in Brandenbrug-Preussen. Ergebnisse einer internationalen Tagung* (Berlin, 1983), 18–31, here 21–24.

3. See Norman Saadi Nikro, 'Situating Postcolonial Trauma Studies', *Postcolonial Text* 9.2 (2014), 1–21, here 8; Ogaga Ifowodo, *History, Trauma and Healing in Postcolonial Narratives* (New York, 2013).

4. These reflections on Braudel draw on the important article by Olivia Harris, 'Braudel, Historical Time and the Horror of Discontinuity', *History Workshop Journal* 57 (2004), 161–74.

5. Fernand Braudel, 'Georges Gurvitch ou la discontinuité du social', *Annales. Economies, Sociétés, Civilisations* 9 (1953), 347–61; Harris, 'Braudel', 173.

6. Fernand Braudel, 'La Longue durée', *Annales. Economies, Sociétés, Civilisations* 13 (1958), 725–53, here 748.

7. M. K. Gandhi, *Hind Swaraj and Other Writings* (Cambridge, 1997), 89, 90, 56.

8. On Gandhi and Benjamin, see Aditya Nigam, 'Gandhi—the "Angel of History": Reading "Hind Swaraj" Today', *Economic and Political Weekly* 44.11 (14–20 March 2009), 41–47, here 47.

9. This policy is set out in an undated (early 1960s) German Foreign Ministry memo titled 'Die Bundesrepublik Deutschland ist der einzig rechtmaessige deutsche Staat'; see Kristina Spohr, *Germany and the Baltic Problem after the Cold War: The Development of a New Ostpolitik, 1989–2000* (London, 2004), 64 and 80 n. 56.

10. Heinrich August Winkler, *Germany. The Long Road West*, 2 vols. (Oxford, 2006), 2:143.

11. Walter Ulbricht, General Secretary of the Central Committee of the Socialist Unity Party, announced the long-postponed decision to begin the 'planned construction of socialism' in the GDR in 1952, after the West refused Stalin's controversial 'unification offer' in the spring of that year. Edgar Wolfrum, *Geschichte als Waffe. Vom Kaiserreich bis zur Wiedervereinigung* (Göttingen, 2001), 72.

12. On the importance of continuities with the pre-1933 past for leading communists in the GDR, see Catherine Epstein, *The Last Revolutionaries. The German Communists and Their Century* (Cambridge, MA, 2003).

13. Lucian Hölscher, *Die Entdeckung der Zukunft* (Frankfurt/Main, 1999), esp. 219–23.

14. Elke Seefried, *Zukünfte. Aufstieg und Krise der Zukunftsforschung, 1945–1980* (Berlin, 2015).

15. Alexander Schmidt-Gernig, 'Das Jahrzehnt der Zukunft: Leitbilder und Visionen der Zukunftsforschung in den 60er Jahren in Westeuropa und den USA', in Uta Gerhardt (ed.), *Zeitperspektiven. Studien zu Kultur und Gesellschaft* (Stuttgart, 2003), 305–45.

16. Peter Grieder, *The East German Leadership 1946–73. Conflict and Crisis* (New York, 1999), esp. 160–69.

17. Jenny Andersson, 'The Great Future Debate and the Struggle for the World', *American Historical Review* 117 (2012), 1411–30, here 1426.

18. On the future wave of the 1960s, with an overview of the literature, see Lucian Hölscher, 'Mysteries of Historical Order: Ruptures, Simultaneity and the Relationship of the Past, the Present and the Future', in Lorenz and Bevernage, *Breaking Up Time*, 134–51, here 149–50. At the Twenty-Sixth German Historians' Congress in 1964, Reinhart Koselleck and Reinhart Wittram introduced the idea of the submerged futures of past epochs as a hitherto neglected field of research; Koselleck elaborated his ideas further in his Heidelberg Inaugural Lecture in 1969; on this, see Lucian Hölscher, 'Von Leeren und gefüllten Zeiten. Zum Wandel historischer Zeitkonzepte seit dem 18. Jahrhundert', in Geppert and Kössler, *Obsession der Gegenwart*, 37–70, here 64–65. For the text of the Inaugural Lecture: Reinhart Koselleck, 'Vergangene Zukunft der frühen Neuzeit', in Koselleck, *Vergangene Zukunft*, 17–27.

19. Andersson, 'Great Future Debate', 1415.

20. Donella H. Meadows, Dennis L. Meadows, Jørgen Randers, and William W. Behrens III, *The Limits to Growth. A Report for the Club of Rome's Project on the Predicament of Mankind* (New York, 1972), 23.

21. See, for example, Osip K. Flechtheim, *Futurologie. Der Kampf um die Zukunft* (Cologne, 1970).

22. Marcus Colla, 'Time, Politics and Legitimacy in the German Democratic Republic' (conference presentation, German History Society Annual Conference, Newcastle, 8–10 September 2016).

23. Rainer Gries, 'Zum "Geburtstag der Republik"', *Universitas* 54 (1999), 307–11; on the problem of the future in the GDR more generally, see Martin

Sabrow, 'Zukunftspathos als Legitimationsressource. Zu Charakter und Wandel des Fortschrittsparadigmas in der DDR', in Heinz-Gerhard Haupt, Jörg Requate, and Maria Köhler-Baur (eds.), *Aufbruch in die Zukunft. Die 1960er Jahre zwischen Planungseuphorie und kulturellem Wandel. DDR, CSSR und Bundesrepublik Deutschland im Vergleich* (Weilerswist, 2004), 165–84; on the future as a problem in communist discourses, see Martin Sabrow, 'Chronos als Fortschrittsheld: Zeitvorstellungen und Zeitverständnis im kommunistischen Zukunftsdiskurs', in Igor Polianski and Matthias Schwartz (eds.), *Die Spur des Sputnik. Kulturhistorische Expeditionen ins kosmische Zeitalter* (Frankfurt/Main, 2009), 117–34.

24. André Keil, 'The *Preußenrenaissance* Revisited: German–German Entanglements, the Media and the Politics of History in the late German Democratic Republic', *German History* 34.2 (2016), 258–78; similar transitions took place in other Warsaw Pact states; see Roman Krakovsky, *Réinventer le monde. L'espace et le temps en Tchécoslovaquie communiste* (Paris, 2015) and the essays in Haupt, Requate, and Köhler-Baur (eds.), *Aufbruch in die Zukunft*. My understanding of this transition in the GDR is indebted to conversations with Marcus Colla at the University of Cambridge, whose dissertation on the GDR and the Prussian past explores these issues in depth.

25. Andersson, 'Great Future Debate', 1415.

26. Heinrich August Winkler, *Der Lange Weg nach Westen*, 2 vols. (Munich, 2000); see also Winkler, *Geschichte des Westens*, 4 vols. (Munich, 2009–).

27. Bruno Latour, *We Have Never Been Modern*, trans. Catherine Porter ([orig. French ed. 1991] Cambridge, MA, 1993).

28. On the end of the 'modern' regime of time, see Aleide Assmann, *Ist die Zeit aus den Fugen? Aufstieg und Fall des Zeitregimes der Moderne* (Munich, 2013).

29. Perry Anderson, 'Introduction', in Perry Anderson and Patrick Camiller (eds.), *Mapping the West European Left* (London, 1994), 1–22, here 11.

30. On 'deactivated politics', see Sergei Prozorov, 'Russian Postcommunism and the End of History', *Studies in East European Thought* 60.3, *Reviewing Perestrojka* (2008), 207–30, here 214, 218, 220, 224; on the 'plebiscitarian patrimonialism' of a regime that aligns itself with the 'national will' but obstructs the emergence of dissenting formations in the public sphere, see Stephen E. Hanson, 'Plebiscitarian patrimonialism in Putin's Russia: Legitimating Authoritarianism in a Postideological Era', *Annals of the American Academy of Political and Social Science* 636 (2011), 32–48.

31. Riszard Legutko, *The Demon in Democracy. Totalitarian Temptations in Free Societies* (New York, 2016), 5, 6, 11, 26.

32. President Bill Clinton referred to the 'right side of history' twenty-one times during his period in office; by December 2015, Barack Obama had used it fifteen times; Obama also used the converse phrase 'the wrong side of history' thirteen times, and it occurred on a further sixteen occasions in statements by his staffers; see David A. Graham, 'The Wrong Side of the "Right Side of

History"', *Atlantic*, 21 December 2015, https://www.theatlantic.com/politics /archive/2015/12/obama-right-side-of-history/420462/.

33. For a powerful recent description of this malaise, by a historian who had previously argued passionately for 'the West' as the goal and vanishing point of modern German history, see Heinrich August Winkler, *Zerbricht der Westen? Über die gegenwärtige Krise in Europe und Amerika* (Munich, 2017); also John Comaroff, 'The End of Neoliberalism? What Is left of the Left?', *Annals of the American Academy of Political and Social Science* 637 (2011), 141–47.

34. Thomas B. Edsall, 'The End of the Left and the Right as We Knew Them', *New York Times*, 22 June 2017, https://www.nytimes.com/2017/06/22 /opinion/nationalism-globalism-edsall.html; Damon Linker, 'The Stunning End of the Left and the Right', *The Week*, 5 January 2017, http://theweek.com/articles /670870/stunning-end-left-right; Christian Caryl, 'The End of Politics as We Know It', *Foreign Policy*, 3 May 2016, http://foreignpolicy.com/2016/05/03/the -end-of-politics-as-we-know-it-left-right-sanders-trump-corbyn/; John Comaroff, 'The End of Neoliberalism? What Is Left of the Left?', *Annals of the American Academy of Political and Social Sciences* 637.1 (1 September 2011), 141–47.

35. Wolfgang Streeck, 'How Will Capitalism End?', *New Left Review* 87 (May–June 2014), https://newleftreview.org/II/87/wolfgang-streeck-how-will -capitalism-end.

36. David Runciman, 'Is This How Democracy Ends?', *London Review of Books* 38.23 (1 December 2016). Runciman, *How Democracy Ends* (London, 2018), addresses this question in greater depth.

37. Francis Fukuyama, 'The End of History?', *National Interest*, Summer 1989, https://www.embl.de/aboutus/science_society/discussion/discussion_2006 /ref1-22june06.pdf.

38. Prozorov, 'Russian Postcommunism and the End of History', 229.

39. Amitav Ghosh, *The Great Derangement: Climate Change and the Unthinkable* (Chicago, 2016), 115.

40. Preamble, Treaty of Rome, 25 March 1957, https://ec.europa.eu/romania /sites/romania/files/tratatul_de_la_roma.pdf.

41. Emmanuel Macron, speech at the Sorbonne, 26 September 2017, http://international.blogs.ouest-france.fr/archive/2017/09/29/macron -sorbonne-verbatim-europe-18583.html.

42. For a discussion of temporal discourses as symptomatic of cultural and political change since the 1960s, see Fernando Esposito, 'Einführung', in Esposito (ed.), *Zeitenwandel. Transformationen geschichtlicher Zeitlichkeit nach dem Boom* (Göttingen, 2017), 7–62.

43. Cas Mudde, 'Can We Stop the Politics of Nostalgia That Have Dominated 2016?', *Newsweek*, 15 December 2016, http://www.newsweek.com/1950s-1930s -racism-us-europe-nostalgia-cas-mudde-531546; Zoe Williams, 'An Obsession with Nostalgia Offers Us Only Political Poison', *Guardian*, 20 November 2016, https://www.theguardian.com/commentisfree/2016/nov/20/nostalgia-political

-poison-strictly-bake-off; Diego Rubio, 'The Politics of Nostalgia', *Social Europe*, 21 April 2017, https://www.socialeurope.eu/the-politics-of-nostalgia; on Germany, see Dirk Schümer, 'Politische Nostalgie. Retrogrusel-Deutschland gehört auf den Müllhaufen', *Die Welt*, 24 March 2016, https://www.welt.de/politik/deutschland/article155639167/Retrogrusel-Deutschland-gehoert-auf-den-Muellhaufen.html; for examples of a politics of recursion, see the efforts of the Alternative für Deutschland to rehabilitate core concepts of National Socialism, such as the term 'völkisch' and the party's aspiration to reverse what it describes as the erasure of German *Volkstum*; see https://www.welt.de/politik/deutschland/article158348687/Die-Begrifflichkeit-voelkisch-ist-kontaminiert.html and http://www.tagesspiegel.de/politik/brandrede-in-dresden-der-totale-hoecke/19267154.html. On 'presentism' as a phenomenon in historical understanding and politics more generally, see the final part of François Hartog, *Régimes d'historicité* (Paris, 2003); also the essays by Alexandra Walsham, Robin Osborne, Peter Coss, Miri Rubin, Evelyn Welch, Catherine Hall, Rana Mitter, and S. A. Smith in *Past & Present* 234.1 (2017), 213–89 and Hans Ulrich Gumbrecht, *Unsere breite Gegenwart* (Berlin, 2010).

44. I am thinking here in particular of Amitav Ghosh, *Traveller in an Antique Land* (London, 1994); Arundhati Roy, *The Ministry of Utmost Happiness* (London, 2017); Don Delillo, *The Body Artist* (New York, 2001); David Mitchell, *Slade House* (London, 2015); Colson Whitehead, *Zone One* (London, 2011); Maja Lunde, *The History of Bees* (New York, 2017); but the list could be extended indefinitely.

45. See Matthew Biro, *Anselm Kiefer and the Philosophy of Martin Heidegger* (Cambridge, 1998), 137.

46. On Voigt's recent work, see Jorinde Voigt, *Now* (Munich, 2015); Voigt, *Pieces for Words and Views*, ed. John Yau (Berlin, 2012).

INDEX

Previous Lawrence Stone Lectures

A NOTE ON THE TYPE

THIS BOOK has been composed in Miller, a Scotch Roman typeface designed by Matthew Carter and first released by Font Bureau in 1997. It resembles Monticello, the typeface developed for The Papers of Thomas Jefferson in the 1940s by C. H. Griffith and P. J. Conkwright and reinterpreted in digital form by Carter in 2003.

Pleasant Jefferson ("P. J.") Conkwright (1905–1986) was Typographer at Princeton University Press from 1939 to 1970. He was an acclaimed book designer and AIGA Medalist.

The ornament used throughout this book was designed by Pierre Simon Fournier (1712–1768) and was a favorite of Conkwright's, used in his design of the *Princeton University Library Chronicle*.